UNCOMMON VALOR

Also by Dwight Jon Zimmerman
and John D. Gresham

Beyond Hell and Back:
How America's Special Operations Forces
Became the World's Greatest Fighting Unit

UNCOMMON VALOR

─────────★─────────

The Medal of Honor
and the Six Warriors
Who Earned It in
Afghanistan and Iraq

─────────★─────────

Dwight Jon Zimmerman
and John D. Gresham

ST. MARTIN'S PRESS 〰 NEW YORK

Dedicated with gratitude and friendship to
Charles "Chuck" Oldham
and Alexis "the Office Goddess" Vars,
who many times over many years have gone, and
continue to go, above and beyond the call of duty to
help wayward authors continue their craft.

Edited by Howard Zimmerman
Interior design by Gilda Hannah

A Z-FILE, INC. BOOK

Library of Congress Cataloging-in-Publication Data

Zimmerman, Dwight Jon.
  Uncommon valor : the medal of honor and the six warriors who
earned it in Afghanistan and Iraq / Dwight Jon Zimmerman and
John D. Gresham. — 1st ed.
    p. cm.
  Includes bibliographical references and index.
  ISBN 978-0-312-36385-7
  1. Medal of Honor—Biography. 2. Afghan War, 2001—Biography.
3. Iraq War, 2003—Biography. 4. Afghan War, 2001—Medals.
5. Iraq War, 2003—Medals. 6. United States—Armed Forces—
Biography. I. Gresham, John. II. Title.
  UB433.Z56 2010
  956.7044'34092273—dc22

                                                    2010021667

First Edition: September 2010

10 9 8 7 6 5 4 3 2 1

Contents

✮ ✮ ✮ ✮ ✮ ✮

ACKNOWLEDGMENTS

It is literally impossible for the authors to thank by name everyone who had a hand in assisting us in the creation of *Uncommon Valor.* Foremost on the list of those we can publicly thank is St. Martin's Press senior editor Marc Resnick and editor and project manager Howard Zimmerman (no relation to the author). This is our second book with the team of Resnick and Zimmerman and once again their support, guidance, advice, and patience made work on this project a true pleasure. Of the men and women in uniform, past and present, that we can publicly thank, we are grateful to Medal of Honor recipient Colonel Lee Mize, USA (Ret.), for graciously consenting to provide the foreword. Thanks also go to the Office of the Vice Chief of Staff, General Peter Chiarelli, USA, and his capable Public Affairs team led by Lieutenant Colonel Michelle L. Martin-Hing, USA.

As it has proved in so many other fields, the Internet has been an extraordinary boon for research. Thanks to it, the authors were able to obtain documents, photographs, and other images that would have taken months, if not years, to otherwise track down and copy. While the bibliography contains the full list of sources obtained through the Internet, we must single out one for particular praise: C. Douglas Sterner's remarkable website devoted to the Medal of Honor and its recipients, Home of Heroes, www.homeofheroes.com. Whether a visitor's purpose is casual curiosity or serious research, Sterner's website is a treasure.

Finally, to those whose names cannot be listed for reasons of discretion, our sincere and heartfelt gratitude for your key contributions in clarifying and augmenting the accounts of these six heroes.

Foreword

★ ★ ★ ★ ★ ★

By Colonel Lee Mize, USA (Ret.)

As a Korean War Medal of Honor awardee, I have on various occasions been asked the uncomfortable question, How does it feel to be a hero? Frankly, I really don't know, as I have never considered myself particularly heroic, or brave, compared to many of the fine soldiers I fought with in Korea and Vietnam. To me, my actions in combat always seemed driven by what needed to be done for my fellow soldiers, the units I served in, and the missions we were assigned. Perhaps it is the same for my fellow awardees, although it is not a subject we have talked much about, since our numbers begin to dwindle over time. I just know that terrible night in 1953 in Korea at Outpost Harry was one I would never want to repeat. Too many good young men, American, Greek, and Chinese, gave their lives to take or hold that miserable piece of high ground. And when our positions began to be overrun, I was fighting not to hold a position but to save the few surviving men around me, many who could no longer fight for themselves. That I was to be recognized with a Medal of Honor for my actions that night was more about their seeing me fighting back against the assaulting Chinese and surviving than anything else. I'm certain that other soldiers from Company K fought just as doggedly and hard as I did that night, perhaps even more so. Many did not survive to have their battles recognized by President Eisenhower, as I did. In my mind, they were the real heroes of the battle, giving what President Lincoln in the Gettysburg Address called "the last full measure of devotion" to hold onto that hill.

When my commanding officer informed me several months later that I was going to be awarded the Medal of Honor, I recall initially telling him I did not want it. I told him that I would prefer that my entire unit be recognized for their stubborn stand at Outpost Harry. Only later have I come to understand that my acceptance and wearing of the Medal of Honor honors not only the survivors I led down the hill the afternoon after the battle but also those who would never again walk anywhere on their own.

I fought many more battles in my army career, eventually retiring as a colonel in 1981. Along the way I joined the Special Forces, served in Vietnam, and saw many more young men fight and die in desperate combat. On those occasions when I get to wear the medal, I think of my comrades in arms, dead and alive. I do so with pride for them and the way we all fought America's battles during my career in the army. Thankfully, today we have the same kind of young men, fighting their own battles in distant places like Iraq and Afghanistan, and they too are slowly being given recognition. This includes a handful of soldiers, sailors, and

Marines who, since the attacks of 9/11, have been awarded the Medal of Honor for their actions. Sadly, all perished in the actions for which they were awarded the medal, so it is left to historians like Dwight Jon Zimmerman and John D. Gresham to make sure their stories are not forgotten. This book is a testament to those men and the men they fought with and for, and I hope that you find something of those men in the stories inside.

True heroism is remarkably sober, very undramatic. It is not the urge to surpass all others at whatever cost, but the urge to serve others at whatever cost.

—ARTHUR ASHE
American athlete and social activist

Introduction

★ ★ ★ ★ ★ ★

Most often, heroes are ordinary people in extraordinary situations who perform far above their own and others' expectations. Heroes come from all walks of life, from differing ethnic, educational, and economic backgrounds. The six Medal of Honor recipients profiled in this volume are all heroes by the very definition of the word (as you will see below). But there is no single template for making a hero, and this is a truly diverse group of men. One was born out of wedlock, all but abandoned by his natural mother, and died without knowing the identity of his biological father. Another grew up in a stable middle-class environment and graduated from an Ivy League university, then rejected a promising future as a lawyer to become a SEAL.

Arranged in chronological order according to the dates of their citations, *Uncommon Valor* relates the stories of these two men, plus four other ordinary young servicemen, all of whom fought in Iraq and/or Afghanistan. When the moment came, each acted boldly and selflessly, sacrificing his life in order to save his companions. For their actions, they each posthumously received their grateful country's highest award for military valor, the Medal of Honor.

These are America's twenty-first-century military heroes: Sergeant First Class Paul Ray Smith, U.S. Army; Corporal Jason Dunham, U.S. Marine Corps; SEAL Lieutenant Michael Patrick Murphy, U.S. Navy; SEAL Petty Officer Second Class Michael Anthony Monsoor, U.S. Navy; Specialist Ross A. McGinnis, U.S. Army; and Sergeant First Class Jared C. Monti, U.S. Army.

The 2005 edition of the *New Oxford American Dictionary* gives as its first definition of hero the following: "a person, typically a man, who is admired or idealized for courage, outstanding achievements, or noble qualities: *a war hero.*" This is followed by three other definitions, two of which elaborate on the first by including fictional and mythological characters; the third is a sandwich. That the definition retains a male bias is more a reflection of historic roles than modern reality, since women now serve in a variety of military career specialties that place them in harm's way.

Although *Uncommon Valor* focuses on the six servicemen listed above, it should be noted here that one does not have to wear a uniform to act heroically. On April 16, 2007, despite being shot five times and mortally wounded, the Holocaust survivor Professor Liviu Librescu held shut the door to his Norris Hall classroom long enough to allow all his students, save one, to escape from being killed in the Virginia Tech massacre. As a civilian, Professor Librescu could not qualify for the Medal of Honor, a military-only decoration, but he certainly was a hero.

Though there have been some exceptions, in general, there are eight criteria that provide the basis for awarding the Medal of Honor: setting a personal example under fire that has inspired other men; devotion to duty under fire; accepting danger; saving life; overcoming one's injuries; defeating great odds; taking command; and seizing an opportunity to strike a blow at the enemy.

As befitting the nation's highest military decoration for valor that is, according to the citation, "above and beyond the call of duty," the process for bestowing the Medal of Honor is lengthy and arduous. It begins with the recommendation made by either the individual's commanding officer or, on rare occasions, by a member of Congress. It is not unusual for the eight-stage review process to take more than eighteen months. At each stage the individual and the circumstances that prompted the recommendation undergo a rigorous scrutiny. And at every stage one of three decisions must be made about the recommendation: approval; disapproval based on Medal of Honor criteria; or downgrading. If approved, the recommendation is forwarded to the next level. If disapproved, the review process does allow for an appeal and for the disapproval to be overruled. If downgraded, the recommendation goes down what's known as the Pyramid of Valor—atop which the Medal of Honor sits—until it finds the level of decoration that is appropriate.

By the time the candidate's file reaches the desk of the president, every fact that can possibly be known about the individual and the action that prompted the recommendation has been studied and examined from every possible angle and with a care comparable to a background check on someone nominated for high government office. One reason for such an arduous review is the fairly sordid history of abuse in bestowing the decoration. There have been cheats. There have been liars. There have been scandals. And before the instituting of a rigorous review process, there was a time during the nineteenth century when one could receive a Medal of Honor just by asking for it, as Lieutenant Colonel Asa Gardiner did in 1872.

As of September 2009, there were just ninety-five living Medal of Honor recipients: men who fought in World War II, the Korean War, and the Vietnam War. Since the Vietnam War, only eight Medals of Honor have been awarded, two for combat action in Somalia (the "Black Hawk down" action) and six for the conflicts in Iraq and Afghanistan—all of them posthumous. This low number of post-Vietnam recipients, and the fact that *all* those who received it died during the action for which they were recommended, has not gone unnoticed by Congress. In early 2009, the California congressman Duncan Hunter, a former Marine who served combat tours in both Iraq and Afghanistan, sponsored legislation requiring the Secretary of Defense to assess the Medal of Honor review process to determine why there is such a low count. Congressman Hunter believes that more Medals of Honor should be awarded. It is, of course, entirely possible that more individuals, including women now that they can serve in combat, *have* been recommended and that their files are presently under review. All of the services observe a strict policy of silence regarding a candidate's Medal of Honor recommendation, and only after it has been approved is an official announcement released.

Along with the recipients' stories, the history of the medal, the need for it, and the efforts that have been made to keep the medal a unique and honored acknowledgment of service to this country are explored in this volume.

Heroes are the sinews of a strong nation and help inspire its people to greatness. As the six men herein are no longer with us, it imperfectly falls to others to tell their stories. It can only be hoped that in the future there will be more Medal of Honor recipients who survive their experiences to tell their accounts in their own words.

—DWIGHT JON ZIMMERMAN
Brooklyn, New York

—JOHN D. GRESHAM
Fairfax, Virginia

1

✮ ✮ ✮ ✮ ✮ ✮

Paul Ray Smith

───────────────✮───────────────

Sergeant First Class Paul R. Smith distinguished himself by acts of gallantry and intrepidity above and beyond the call of duty in action with an armed enemy near Baghdad International Airport, Baghdad, Iraq, on 4 April 2003. On that day, Sergeant First Class Smith was engaged in the construction of a prisoner of war holding area when his Task Force was violently attacked by a company-sized enemy force. Realizing the vulnerability of over 100 soldiers, Sergeant First Class Smith quickly organized a hasty defense consisting of two platoons of soldiers, one Bradley Fighting Vehicle and three armored personnel carriers. As the fight developed, Sergeant First Class Smith braved hostile enemy fire to personally engage the enemy with hand grenades and anti-tank weapons, and organized the evacuation of three wounded soldiers from an armored personnel carrier struck by a rocket propelled grenade and a 60 mm mortar round. Fearing the enemy would overrun their defenses, Sergeant First Class Smith moved under withering enemy fire to man a .50 caliber machine gun mounted on a damaged armored personnel carrier. In total disregard for his own life, he maintained his exposed position in order to engage the attacking enemy force. During this action, he was mortally wounded. His courageous actions helped defeat the enemy attack, and resulted in as many as 50 enemy soldiers killed, while allowing the safe withdrawal of numerous wounded soldiers. Sergeant First Class Smith's extraordinary heroism and uncommon valor are in keeping with the highest traditions of the military service and reflect great credit upon himself, the Third Infantry Division "Rock of the Marne," and the United States Army.

—Medal of Honor Citation, April 5, 2005

————————————————— ★ —————————————————

There are two ways to come home, stepping off the plane and being carried off the plane. It doesn't matter how I come home because I am prepared to give all that I am to ensure that all my boys make it home.

—Sergeant First Class Paul Ray Smith
(in a letter to his parents)[1]

A CAREER SOLDIER

Sergeant First Class Paul Ray Smith was a lanky, six-foot-tall veteran of Operation Desert Shield/Desert Storm with piercing green eyes, a well-trimmed mustache, and a tough, no-nonsense attitude toward training and preparedness that had made him the bane of his platoon. Whether or not he'd ever heard of General George S. Patton's dictum that "a pint of sweat saves a gallon of blood," Sergeant Smith drove his men like he believed it. That hadn't always been the case. Smith had become a tough-as-nails sergeant because of his experiences in the first Gulf War.

Paul Ray Smith was born on September 24, 1969, in El Paso, Texas, the third of four siblings. When he was nine years old, his family moved to South Tampa, Florida, where he grew up. His mother, Janice Pvirre, later recalled, "Paul was a very ordinary boy." He was a quiet kid who enjoyed football, bike riding, skateboarding, and collecting rocks. Another big hobby of his was fishing, though his sister Lisa DeVane later observed, "We'd have starved to death if we'd had to depend on his fishing skills."[2] In high school Paul displayed an interest in carpentry and got himself a part-time job as a carpenter's assistant. He also enjoyed taking things apart and putting them back together—anything from a radio to an old car was fair game to Paul. One year he restored a dune buggy with the help of a friend.

His mother remembered that, as a teenager, he became "very methodical. He seemed to be plotting . . . what he was going to do, and how he was going to do it." It was around this time, she remembered, that he told her, "I'm going to be a soldier. I'm going to join the military, be a soldier, get married, and have children."[3]

Smith graduated from Tampa Bay Vocational Technical High School in 1988. In October 1989, he fulfilled the first part of his dream by enlisting in the U.S. Army. He completed basic and combat engineering training in early 1990 at Fort Leonard Wood, Missouri. He was then assigned to the Eighty-second Engineer Battalion and sent to the army's primary maintenance center in Europe: the U.S. Army Garrison Bamberg, near the German city of Bamberg in the southern province of Bavaria. Once there, the twenty-one-year-old Smith soon discovered the off-post pleasures of German beer, cars, and women. Specialist Smith established a reputation for hard partying, occasionally getting so drunk that he had to be disciplined. This was a far cry from the quiet young man he had been . . . or the grim war veteran he was to become.

In June 1990, while at the Green Goose, a popular local bar for the soldiers, Smith met Birgit Bacher, a twenty-three-year-old German woman from the nearby city of Bayreuth (the birthplace of Richard Wagner and the home of the annual Wagner Opera Festival). It was something of a surprise for Birgit to be in the bar. In a story all too familiar to German girls, three years earlier an American soldier had gotten her pregnant with her daughter, Jessica, and then deserted them. The experience had naturally soured Birgit on Americans. But, upon the insistence of a girlfriend, there she was at the Green Goose, being entertained by Smith and two of his buddies.

The impromptu date continued with a nighttime walk to a nearby park after the bar closed. The evening was capped when, in the courtyard outside her hotel room, Smith (channeling his inner Tom Cruise) serenaded Birgit with a rendition of "You've Lost That Loving Feeling." Birgit responded by showering him with petals from the flower box on her window.

Birgit later said, "In the beginning he was not my type at all; he was not what I was looking for."[4] Yet she found something in him that attracted her. They dated regularly until November 1990. That's when Smith and his unit were deployed to Saudi Arabia as part of Operation Desert Shield, and they were there on January 17, 1991, as part of Operation Desert Storm.

From November 1990 until April 1991, when his unit returned to Bamberg, Birgit received no communication from Paul. Shortly after hearing that his unit had returned from Iraq, she went to the Green Goose hoping to meet him. She was sitting at the bar drinking a soda when Smith walked in, saw her . . . and walked right by without saying a word.

Stung, and baffled, she strode up to him and demanded to know why he was ignoring her. He replied gruffly, "I just don't want to talk."

Birgit realized that the Paul Ray Smith standing before her was far different from the one she had known six months earlier. Over the next several weeks, she discovered just how profoundly the experience of combat had changed him.

Because it dramatically ended in just one hundred hours and was a lopsided victory dominated by the use of airpower and armor, Operation Desert Storm has sometimes been incorrectly characterized as the "100-hour non-war."[5] Regardless of the campaign's brief duration, it retained all of war's terrible life-and-death intensity. Smith had "seen the elephant"—he had experienced combat. Afterward, in a rare moment of revelation to his relatives, he mentioned that a comrade had died in his arms. There was far more to the story than that. Command Sergeant Major Gary Coker, who fought with Smith in Operation Desert Storm and in Operation Iraqi Freedom, later said that at one point during the assault U.S. helicopter gunships had mistaken Smith's unit for an Iraqi force and had opened fire on the Americans. According to Coker, "He lost three friends right then and there." When the campaign ended, Coker said that Smith "knew what death was all about . . . what war was all about, and he was determined that it wouldn't happen to his guys."[6]

Gone was the "military goofball"[7] Birgit Bacher had known, replaced by someone with a new and sharply focused purpose in life. Having decided to make the army his career, Smith also made the decision that he was going to change his life—and spare nothing in preparing troops under his command for combat.

About nine months after his return to Germany, on January 24, 1992, Paul Ray Smith accomplished the next two goals in his life. He married Birgit in Denmark and became the adoptive father of Jessica. Two years later, they had a son, David. Smith was a devoted husband and father. In fact, he became such a homebody that occasionally Birgit grew concerned—and occasionally had to order him to go out and have a good time with his friends.

Smith applied an equally fierce dedication to his army career. He began hitting the books and taking courses to hone his skills and advance in rank. He took advantage of opportunities available to him while stationed in Europe. Already an expert marksman, Smith added to his shooting skills by earning the German Armed Forces Badge for Weapons Proficiency in Gold, which meant he was an expert with pistols, rifles, and machine guns. He also took the French commando course, earning the French Armed Forces Commando Badge.

Not long after his wedding, Paul Ray Smith was promoted to sergeant. For the next seven years, the Smiths led a typical nomadic army existence, traveling from one post to another and halfway around the world and back. In 1999, he was assigned to the Eleventh Engineer Battalion, part of the Third Infantry Division based at Fort Stewart, Georgia.

As he rose through the noncommissioned officer ranks, he strove to make himself what *The Army Noncommissioned Officer Guide* calls "the Backbone of the Army." He took to heart the admonition of retired Army Command Sergeant Major Gary L. Littrell, a Medal of Honor recipient, who wrote in the guide that the primary duty of a sergeant is "to train and take care of [a] soldier's every need." To accomplish that goal, Littrell said the sergeant has to identify the difference between being liked and being respected: "It is human nature to want to be liked, but we can never sacrifice respect for that. The respect you gain through properly training your soldiers to succeed and in ensuring they and their families are taken care of may not always make you popular, but it will earn their respect."[8]

A HARD-NOSED LEADER

Combat engineering is one of the most challenging of military professions. Combat engineers accompany frontline units and assist in such tasks as bridge building, mine laying and mine clearing, demolitions, the construction and repair of facilities, and logistics support. Many of these tasks are required to be conducted while under fire. The elite of the combat engineers are called "sappers" and are distinguished by a sapper tab worn on their left shoulder. The term *sapper* comes from the French word *sapeur*. The seventeenth-century French military was the first to use troops trained in engineering skills designed to "sap" the defensive strength of an enemy.

Smith was extraordinarily proud of being a sapper. In addition to the red and white sapper tab sewn on his dress uniform, he wore a subdued-colored sapper tab under his battle-dress-uniform pocket flap, and later in combat he wore a sapper tab just above his chest nameplate on his body armor. On the platoon wall behind his desk he hung a large painting of a sapper tab. And he chose for his call sign "Sapper 7"—the "7" signifying his role as the senior non-commissioned officer in the company. Sergeant Daniel Medrano, then a corporal in Smith's platoon, later said that Smith "was always trying to push you to go to sapper school. He knew what he was talking about, and he was always willing to share that knowledge."[9]

During the 1990s, Smith would go on to serve tours of duty with the First Engineer Battalion, based in Fort Riley, Kansas; the 317th Engineer Battalion in Fort Benning, Georgia; the Ninth Engineer Battalion in Schweinfurt, Germany; and, in 1999, the Eleventh Engineer Battalion, the "Jungle Cats" (a nickname acquired during a 1920s tour of duty in Panama), in Fort Stewart, Georgia. With each assignment, his men abruptly learned that their new noncom was holding them to a higher standard.

In 1995, he was part of the stabilization force following the NATO air campaign in Bosnia that lifted the siege of Sarajevo. And, in 1999, he returned to the Balkans as part of the operation that forced the withdrawal of Yugoslav troops from Kosovo.

But Smith's dedication and army-to-the-core attitude was not appreciated by everyone. Long before Paul Ray Smith

Sergeant First Class Paul Ray Smith at a base camp in an undisclosed location in Southwest Asia.
Photo: *Department of the Army*

reached the rank of first sergeant in 2002, he had, in truth, come to be hated by the men in his platoon because of how hard he worked them. Behind his back, they called him a number of names. One of the few printable ones was Superman. It was not then meant as a compliment.

Sergeant Medrano recalled that "teamwork was everything" to Smith, whose attitude was that if one member of the unit screwed up, the entire unit had screwed up. During inspection, the smallest infraction by a single soldier resulted in the entire platoon undergoing a meticulous reinspection. Smith became famous—or infamous—for pulling a cotton swab out of his breast pocket without warning and conducting a snap weapons inspection by swabbing the interior of a soldier's rifle or machine-gun barrel. If the swab had even a speck of dirt on it, everyone in the platoon had to stop what they were doing and clean their weapons.

Though he was tough and drove his men hard, Smith was not insensitive. In November 2001, shortly before Thanksgiving, the eighteen-month-old daughter of one of his men, Sergeant Harry DeLauter, had to be taken to a hospital in Savannah, Georgia, forty miles east of Fort Stewart. DeLauter was with his daughter when he heard a knock on the hospital room door. When he opened it, there was Sergeant Smith, holding a stuffed teddy bear for Sergeant DeLauter's daughter that was bigger than the little girl. Until Sergeant DeLauter's daughter was released, Smith made the one-hour drive every night from Fort Stewart to Savannah to support the family.

On another occasion, shortly before the Christmas holiday, the wife of another soldier in Smith's unit had to have surgery. As a result, the soldier was not able to provide a Christmas celebration for his family. Smith gathered food from the company Christmas party, Birgit purchased gifts for the kids, and then they drove to the soldier's home and presented the food and presents to the family.

It was also known among his men that if a private needed some money to tide him over until the next payday, Smith's wallet was always out. But this soft side of his character never got in the way of the serious business of soldiering.

When the Third Infantry Division (3-ID) arrived in Kuwait in early 2003 as part of what would become Operation Iraqi Freedom, First Sergeant Smith of Bravo Company took his dedication to training his men for combat to a new level. At the end of the day, while the soldiers in other units were allowed to rest, Smith could be found leading his men in running drills or cleaning weapons and vehicles. Occasionally sergeants from other units would approach Smith and recommend that he lighten up on his men a bit, but Smith refused.

Sergeant Smith was past wanting to be liked, and at this point he wasn't even looking for respect. He wanted his soldiers to have the skills and training necessary to successfully engage in—and survive—combat. In letters home he revealed that he knew his men's negative feelings about him; he accepted that as a price he had to pay because he repeatedly made clear that he was determined to bring them all home alive.

On the morning of April 4, 2003, Sergeant First Class Paul Ray Smith's men would discover the ground truth about weapons in combat: dirty weapons jam; clean weapons don't. Two weeks earlier in the southern Iraqi city of Nasiriyah, Private Jessica Lynch and the soldiers of the 507th Maintenance Company had learned this lesson the hard way. The 507th leaders and soldiers failed in their land navigation, took the wrong bridge, and ran into an ambush, and most of them died or were captured. An official investigation was formed to determine the cause. The investigation concluded that a contributing factor to the unit's defeat was that the unit was unable to defend itself because its

M16s had jammed. More important, the commanders of the unit had failed to uphold even the most basic U.S. Army standards for combat readiness.

Sergeant Smith's men *would* be ready for combat, and their weapons would be clean.

THE ENGAGEMENT

Operation Iraqi Freedom commenced on March 20, 2003. On April 1, the Third Infantry Division, nicknamed the Rock of the Marne for its heroic stand against the German army in World War I, roared through the Karbala Gap, the historic southern gateway to Baghdad. It was there, in a two-mile-wide corridor flanked by the Euphrates River on the east and the Bahr al Milh lake on the west, that General Tommy Franks, commander of the Coalition forces, and his staff expected Saddam Hussein to make a stand. But the only resistance they encountered was passive—untended mine-fields. What Coalition commanders and troops didn't know was that when it came to threat priorities, Saddam Hussein's concerns were elsewhere: preventing a palace coup and an attack by Iran. An offensive by the American-led Coalition came third—and a distant third at that—because even at this late date Saddam believed the Coalition units would stop before they reached Baghdad, just as they had a decade earlier in Operation Desert Storm.

Coalition command also didn't know that Iraq's military chain of command had devolved since 1991 into a balkanized agglomeration of fiefdoms dominated by members of Saddam Hussein's family or tribe. At the top of the heap were the Special Republican Guards, followed by the Republican Guards and the paramilitary Fedayeen Saddam. These formations had been supplied with vast amounts of light weapons, ammunition, and explosives, in the belief that a long-term insurgency would eventually defeat any occupation by foreign forces. At the bottom of the logistics chain was the regular Iraqi army.

A surreal sideshow to the unfolding military drama was provided by a character who seemed to have emerged from something written by Lewis Carroll or George Orwell: the Iraqi information minister Mohammed Saeed al-Sahhaf, more popularly known as Baghdad Bob. In his press briefings before groups of international journalists he bombastically and repeatedly proclaimed the doom, death, destruction, or outright nonexistence of approaching Coalition units. The contrast between his pronouncements and the reality on the ground baffled and bemused journalists and government leaders. But Baghdad Bob was only saying what Saddam Hussein wanted to hear. Understandable, since Saddam had a reputation for killing messengers who brought him or publicly acknowledged bad news. Thus it was that on April 4, 2003, he would proclaim in no uncertain terms, "We have retaken the airport! There are no Americans there! I will take you there and show you! In one hour!"[10]

The truth was somewhat more complex.

Located about eleven miles west of the city, Saddam International Airport (now Baghdad International Airport) was a dual-use civil-military facility possessing a 13,000-foot runway for civilian traffic and, west of it, an 8,800-foot military runway. The airport was surrounded by a concrete-block wall approximately ten feet high. Concrete observation towers, each about twenty feet high, were posted about every three hundred feet and were connected to Baghdad by Matar Saddam al-Duwali Road, a four-lane divided highway.

Like all major airports, Saddam International had an elaborate underground tunnel system for maintenance and servicing. What the Coalition senior command and the troops did not know was that the airport's tunnel system extended well beyond the airport grounds and was connected to a group of Saddam Hussein's nearby presidential palace complexes.

Three presidential palace complexes bordered the airport. The Radwaniyah Presidential Palace, which contained a large military command and control headquarters, was off the southwest corner, near the military airfield. The other two were on the east side, flanking Matar Saddam al-Duwali Road and part of the immense Abu Ghraib presidential-grounds complex. Stationed in those complexes was the Eighth Battalion (security), First Brigade, of the Special Republican Guard.

Distinguished by their red berets and red delta-shaped shoulder patches bordered in black, the Special Republican Guards (SRG) were Saddam Hussein's praetorian guard. In addition to providing for Saddam's personal security, the SRG were tasked with the security of all presidential palaces and the defense of Baghdad. In fact, the only military force allowed to operate in Baghdad and at the airport *was* the Special Republican Guard. Officers and ranks of the SRG were composed almost exclusively of men who were members of Saddam Hussein's al-Bu Nasir tribe. In addition to being the first in line for weapons, vehicles, and supplies, members of the SRG and their families were accorded special privileges that placed them first in line for goods, services, homes, and land. They were the pampered elite of the elite.

With its headquarters in the Abu Ghraib Presidential Palace, the First Brigade SRG, contained about 180 officers and almost seven thousand troops organized into five battalions, each containing 1,300 to 1,500 men. The First Brigade was composed of security battalions only, meaning it had fewer heavy tank and artillery units than the other brigades. But it was equipped and trained to be a highly mobile, quick-response unit. Morale was high and the men were well trained and intimately familiar with the local terrain and infrastructure, above and below ground.

The assault on Saddam International Airport was assigned to the Third Infantry Divison's First Brigade combat team, under the command of Colonel William Grimsley. Earlier in the morning of April 3, his unit had captured Objective Peach, a strategic bridge crossing the Euphrates River about twenty-five miles southwest of Baghdad. With his men tired, his units scattered, and their vehicles in need of maintenance, he thought he would have a couple of days to rest and regroup. But Major General Buford "Bluff" Blount III, the commanding officer of 3-ID, had other ideas. Blount had observed the operation that captured Objective Peach, and he wanted to exploit the initiative, continue the advance, and seize the airport before the Iraqis could organize resistance. But doing so aggravated some existing problems of his own. The Iraqis had succeeded in blowing up enough bridges to cause significant traffic congestion, and by accelerating the campaign's timetable, Blount risked making the congestion worse. But he felt the benefits outweighed the risk. Grimsley would just have to regroup on the fly as best he could. Shortly after 3 P.M., the first of Grimsley's units commenced the drive to Saddam International Airport.

Designed to conduct ad hoc operations independently during the course of a campaign, the First Brigade combat team was built around what is called an organic unit, so-named because all its subformations—combat, communications, medical, logistics, and so on—are integrally part of its table of organization. Administratively, the Brigade combat team is designed for maximum flexibility in order to appropriately respond to rapidly changing combat situations. Additional units, usually engineering, are assigned on a temporary basis by division headquarters. Once the particular mission is complete, the attached units are returned to the division.

To take the airport, Grimsley planned a three-prong combined armor and mechanized-infantry attack from the south, composed of the Third Battalion, Seventh Cavalry Regiment (3-7 CAV); Third Battalion, Sixty-ninth Armor Regiment (3-69 AR); and Second Battalion, Seventh Infantry Regiment (2-7 IN) and their attached units. His Brigade combat team was a unit heavy on armor, containing almost a hundred M1 Abrams main battle tanks, roughly an equal number of M2 Bradley fighting vehicles, assorted other tracked vehicles including Paladin 155mm self-propelled howitzers, bridging equipment, and approximately five thousand troops.

The troops were warned to expect everything from attacks with chemical weapons and pitched battles with Republican Guard units to ambushes by suicide squads and individual suicide bombers. Lieutenant Colonel Scott Rudder commanded the 2-7 IN, which included the attached

Eleventh Engineer Battalion and Sergeant Smith's Bravo Company.

The operation to occupy the airport called for engineers to breach the security wall around the airport. Then the assault force would rush through the openings and fan out to seize the facility and its eastern approaches. If there was little or no resistance, the bulk of the armor would then continue east along Matar Saddam al-Duwali Road and conduct probing attacks in the outskirts of Baghdad in order to set the stage for the western assault on the Iraqi capital. Lieutenant Colonel Rudder's task force was charged with establishing a blocking position about a mile east of the airport, at the junction where its periphery highway intersects with Matar Saddam al-Duwali Road.

Like everyone else in the brigade combat team, Rudder's men were hungry, tired, and grimy. They had literally been on the run with little sleep and less maintenance for their vehicles for three days. When they received their new orders, they were about thirty-one miles south of their jump-off point. To get there in time, in addition to battling military traffic, they had to travel over difficult urban and farmland terrain composed of interlocking irrigation canals and paved and unpaved roads and bridges that were not designed to support heavy vehicular traffic. The 2-7 IN, containing roughly fifteen hundred troops and approximately one hundred vehicles (including high-mobility multi-wheel-vehicles, often referred to as Humvees), more than fifty M2 Bradleys, and about a dozen M9 armored combat earthmovers, was still en route when the assault kicked off at about 6:00 P.M. on April 3.

Engineers supporting the other units smashed or blew

large holes in sections of the airport's south security wall and, as planned, elements of the First Brigade combat team promptly roared through the breaches and fanned out to clear their assigned areas. The combined mechanized-infantry and armor units encountered only sporadic artillery fire and almost no Iraqi infantry. Only a few wrecked or disassembled commercial aircraft were discovered in hangars; their engines and other parts hidden elsewhere. Defensive positions on the runways and near buildings and hangars were unmanned or abandoned, a fact that almost immediately raised concerns that the Iraqis planned a chemical-weapons counterattack.

Rudder's task force finally reached its assigned location at the junction of Matar Saddam al-Duwali Road and the airport's periphery highway about two hours before dawn. At the base of the junction, Matar Saddam Al-Duwali Road's two lanes split into four, one upper and three ground level, and formed graceful curves that connected to the airport's access highway, which paralleled the runway. An exceptional feature of the site was a ten-foot-high concrete-block wall and series of guard towers that extended east along both sides of the road, similar to what existed around the airport. The task force's tactical operations command, a mobile headquarters, was established at the junction's base, beneath an overpass. The rest of the unit continued east. After traveling about a half mile, they encountered a paved break in the meridian. In addition to allowing traffic to reverse directions, this intersection also connected on the south side to a service road that continued south. The location was promptly dubbed Four Corners. Here an advance base was established that included the unit's forward aid station and a parking lot for its vehicles, including Humvees, M113 armored personnel carriers, and M9 armored combat earthmovers—bulldozers designed for use in combat. As the site was being prepared, Sergeant Smith, in his personal command Humvee, led a motorized-heavy-construction team that continued east down the highway for another quarter mile, where it dragged and pushed concrete berms across the lanes as roadblocks.

Meanwhile, embedded journalists with the First Brigade

An M9 armored combat earthmover smashes down a cinder-block perimeter wall surrounding a suspected special weapons facility building in Rahsidiya, Iraq.
Photo: *Sergeant Rachel M. Ahner, U.S. Army*

combat team used their satellite feeds to beam around the world euphoric reports that American troops had captured Saddam International Airport. Strictly speaking that was an exaggeration; the airport had not been secured. Mopping-up operations to clear buildings of enemy troops were ongoing. Detection teams were conducting inspections for chemical, biological, and nuclear weapons. But, because the attack had gone so smoothly, most of the unit's armor was sent east to prepare for the next stage, the attack on Baghdad itself.

All deep-penetration assaults into enemy territory contain, for the offensive force, a combination of good and bad news. The American advance into Saddam International Airport succeeded in large part because it was done swiftly. That was the good news. But the bad news was that it was also done in haste. The organizational problems Colonel Grimsley experienced at Objective Peach were nothing compared with the situation he now had on his hands. In those early morning hours of April 4, reconnaissance satellite photos and images taken by a Global Hawk unmanned aerial vehicle flying sixty thousand feet above the area would show that the First Brigade combat team was anything but organized. Units stretched for miles, and the team's disposition somewhat resembled an elongated balloon squeezed in the middle, with the bulk of the American forces divided between the western "bulge" that was the airport and the eastern "bulge" in the outskirts of Baghdad. The narrow neck—Four Corners—contained the fewest troops. Bravo Company's heaviest weapons were the .50 caliber M2 machine guns mounted on the unit's M113 armored personnel carriers.

The troops of the First Brigade combat team had been told to expect an attack from the east—from Baghdad. But the truth was that there was no "front." What the Americans at Four Corners didn't know was that their position in particular was right in the middle of the Eighth Battalion Special Republican Guard's Abu Ghraib presidential grounds complex. They were surrounded by a well-organized, well-equipped, highly motivated, highly trained, hidden, and *rested* enemy.

The speed of the American attack had taken the commanders of the First Brigade Special Republican Guard by surprise. But they had quickly recovered. A response was organized. Orders were issued and troops deployed. A two-prong attack would begin in the south. After American attention was focused there, troops in the second prong would strike—from the north, through Four Corners.

The task force's executive officer, Major Kevin Cooney, was at the tactical operations center. The group had been in position almost four hours. During that time no one had seen any sign of enemy activity. Responding to the call of nature, he grabbed his entrenching tool and walked across a muddy, freshly plowed field to a patch of thick underbrush in a small grove of palm trees just south of their position. Shortly after he had dropped his pants, several bursts of AK-47 fire shattered the stillness. The gunfire was followed almost simultaneously by a salvo of airburst antipersonnel mortar fire. One mortar round exploded above the major. Miraculously, though the concussion knocked him to the ground, he was otherwise unhurt.

Quickly, about a half-dozen men began laying down cover fire. Holding up his pants with one hand, his gear in the other, and bent down to reduce his profile, Major Cooney burst out of the bushes and awkwardly waddled as fast as he could toward the vehicles. At one point in his "dash" over the wet field, the major tripped and belly-flopped into the mud, scattering entrenching tool, baby wipes, and other gear all about him. Almost immediately, Major Cooney was up again and managed to reach the safety of the armored vehicles. (It would have been a fabulously funny moment for the troops, had they not been under attack.)

On top of the nearby overpass, a Fox M93A1 vehicle, used for detecting nuclear, biological, and chemical weapons, and its crew came under fire from an Iraqi T-72 main battle tank. A number of forward positions started receiving sniper and rocket-powered-grenade (RPG) fire. Alerted by the firefight at the overpass, an American Abrams tank drove up from the airport. By this time, the American troops at the overpass discovered they were fighting not one tank, but a platoon of four T-72 tanks. Meanwhile, about an hour's drive south of the airport, an American supply convoy suddenly found itself having to fight its way through an ambush. At about the same time, unbeknownst to the Americans at Four Corners, Eighth Brigade SRG troops from the Abu Ghraib complex to the south were traveling through a tunnel beneath them in preparation for an assault from the north.

The Iraqi counterattack to retake the airport was on.

As the action from the south began heating up, Lieutenant Brian Borkowski, Bravo Company's commanding officer, received a call requesting an armored combat earthmover and additional support. Leaving Sergeant Smith in command of about eighteen men, Borkowski took most of the company's soldiers and headed south.

In the disconnect that is unique to combat, the troops at Four Corners were simultaneously a part of and apart from the battle. They could hear the staccato crackle of small-arms fire and the explosions of RPGs and tank shells. But since it was not directed at them, they were essentially just uniformed spectators—with the exception of the medical personnel caring and treating the wounded that had been and were still arriving. That was about to change.

Roughly a half an hour after Lieutenant Borkowski left, Smith received a message that a handful of prisoners had been captured and that a prisoner-of-war holding area was needed. "Hey, I've got a great place," Smith said. Earlier, Sergeant Smith had noticed a courtyard with a ten-foot-high wall and adjacent watchtower just north of where the forward aid station had been established. If it checked out, they could transform it into a large, temporary holding cell in what was regarded by the commanding officer as a boilerplate engineer mission.

After a little discussion, the decision was made to punch a hole in the southern wall with one of the platoon's bulldozers and then string up a security gate using concertina wire. Smith gathered with him a small group that included Staff Sergeant Lincoln Hollinsaid, Sergeant Derek Pelletier, Sergeant Joshua Henry, Private First Class Thomas Ketchum, and Private James Martens.

As the group headed to the southern wall of the courtyard, Sergeant Joshua Dean started up one of the armored combat earthmovers. With the basso profundo sound of the 295-horsepower Cummins diesel engine filling the air, the group watched Sergeant Dean drive the armored bulldozer into the wall, smashing through the masonry as if it were a sheet of cardboard. Sergeants Smith, Hollinsaid, and Pelletier followed, clambering over the rubble.

The courtyard was about half the size of a football field and shaped roughly like a right-angle triangle, with the wall they had entered through forming the base. The perpendicular side ran straight north to where it anchored a small aluminum gate. There was a watchtower to their left, where the base and perpendicular walls joined. The ground featured a number of small mounds and was covered with patches of thick brush. Once they had cleared the brush, run a concertina-wire barrier the length of the courtyard to separate officers from enlisted men, strung a concertina-wire gate across the breach in the south wall, and posted guards at the gates on both ends and in the watchtower, they'd have a serviceable temporary-holding compound for prisoners.

Tasks were assigned, and the soldiers began working.

The first order of business in the courtyard was the torching of the brush. Despite the recent rain, the brush burned quickly. After the fire had extinguished itself, Smith ordered Ketchum and Martens to take up sentry positions by the aluminum gate in the north. A few minutes later, Henry decided to walk over and check in on the two privates. When he got there, his eyes caught sight of some suspicious movement coming from a large compound about three hundred yards north of them. Seeing that Ketchum's rifle had a scope, Henry shouldered the weapon and peered through the lens. Within seconds, he identified a heavily armed Iraqi force of between fifteen and twenty soldiers. Henry immediately called out to Smith, who rushed up to see for himself. Looking through his own rifle scope in the direction Henry had pointed, Smith spotted an additional force of twenty-five to fifty men about two hundred yards away. Some were coming out of barracks, others were emerging from a tunnel opening. And more were coming.

OVERWHELMED BY THE ENEMY

Against what appeared to be a company-sized enemy unit of about one hundred soldiers equipped with AK-47s, mortars, and RPGs, Smith had just sixteen combat troops and three .50-caliber heavy machine guns mounted on the M113 armored personnel carriers parked at Four Corners. With a calmness that impressed his men, Smith said quietly, "We're in a world of hurt."[11]

As the Iraqi soldiers fanned out in their advance, Smith began issuing a rapid-fire string of orders. One man with a squad automatic weapon, another with an M240B light machine gun, and a third with an M203 40mm grenade launcher were told to get into defensive position just behind the aluminum gate. One of the sergeants was told to call for a Bradley fighting vehicle located at the roadblock about a quarter mile away to reinforce them ASAP. The rest of the men were ordered to stop work on the gate, grab their weapons, and prepare to form a skirmish line to repel an attack. Smith dashed over to a Humvee parked at Four Corners and grabbed some grenades and a single-shot AT-4 anti-tank rocket launcher.

By the time the Bradley arrived some fifteen minutes later, advance elements of the Iraqi force had reached the wall; they were running north to south and were continuing down to the watchtower. The Bradley entered the courtyard, followed by the rest of the combat troops. When it got close, the Bradley opened fire on the aluminum gate with its 25mm Bushmaster chain gun, dramatically ripping it free of its pole.

As this was happening, Sergeant Smith threw a couple of grenades over the wall to knock out any Iraqis waiting in ambush. After the grenades exploded, Smith led a small group of men—Private Gary Evans, Sergeant Matthew Keller, Private Martens, and Specialist Tony Garcia—past the gate and into the open ground north of the courtyard in support of the Bradley. As soon as the group emerged from the courtyard, they came under combined AK-47, RPG, and mortar fire.

Smith saw a number of Iraqi soldiers take up position in a ditch. "Cover me," Smith shouted as he shouldered his AT-4 and got into position in front of the stationary Bradley and, he thought, well away from his men. Taking aim at the Iraqis, Smith pulled the trigger. The AT-4's powerful back-blast knocked Keller, the soldier nearest him, off his feet and cleaned all the dust off the Bradley's chassis. They received no more enemy fire from the now-smoldering ditch. Another soldier with an AT-4 took aim at the watchtower from which some Iraqi troops were firing RPGs and AK-47s. His rocket exploded inside the tower, temporarily silencing the threat from that quarter.

But the enemy was too strong, and the troops killed by the AT-4 rocket were soon replaced. With a commanding view of the American positions, the Iraqi mortar fire became more concentrated and coordinated, indicating that an officer with a radio was probably directing the attack. In addition, flanking fire from Iraqi SRG troops who had climbed the north-south wall, along with snipers hidden in nearby trees, began raking the Americans in the courtyard and in the forward aid station.

Gunners in the three M113 armored personnel carriers at Four Corners trained their .50-caliber machine guns on the Iraqi-occupied tower and, together with nearby infantrymen, began returning fire. An Iraqi soldier in the tower with an RPG fired a point-blank shot at one of the M113s. The RPG round hit the vehicle's exterior rucksack rack and exploded. Clothing, personal items, and bedding erupted into the air; scattered cotton filler from sleeping bags fell like snow to the ground. Though the rucksacks and their contents had been annihilated and the M113 crippled, the personal effects had absorbed enough of the blast to save the crew inside, which was able to evacuate the vehicle unharmed.

Smith saw he needed more firepower at their forward position and ordered Sergeant Kevin Yetter to bring up one of the M113s. Yetter ran the length of the courtyard without getting hit, climbed into one of the two remaining M113s, and ordered it forward. With Sergeant Louis Berwald manning the vehicle's .50-caliber heavy machine gun, Yetter guided the M113, with its supply trailer still attached, through the courtyard and up behind the Bradley. The armored vehicles became the focus of intense RPG and mortar fire. The Bradley was repeatedly hit by RPG rounds, though it suffered little damage. Then, the first of three mortar rounds fired in a "walking" pattern landed near the M113. The third mortar shell struck the top hatch of the armored personnel carrier less than twelve inches from Sergeant Berwald and exploded

—blinding and wounding Berwald and wounding Yetter and the driver, Private Jimmy Hill. Amazingly, none were killed.

Smith dashed over to help pull the wounded out of the armored personnel carrier and apply first aid. Keller was behind the Bradley, firing his grenade launcher, when suddenly he saw that the armored fighting vehicle had shifted into reverse and was backing away from the fight. Keller watched, incredulous, as the Bradley retreated through the courtyard and retired from the battlefield. Sergeant Yetter, who was almost run over by the Bradley, couldn't figure out why it was leaving in the middle of a fight. Only much later did the men discover that the Bradley had to leave because it was almost out of ammunition.

The tactical situation was bad, bordering on disaster. Smith had three wounded men with him and scores more at Four Corners. They were receiving fire from the watchtower, from enemy troops in trees and on the courtyard wall, and from the main body approaching from the north.

His men needed time—time to get the wounded to the aid station, time to organize a better defense at Four Corners, and time for reinforcements to arrive. Smith made the decision to buy his men that time. He entered through the rear of the armored personnel carrier and tried to back it through the courtyard. But the attached supply trailer kept jackknifing on him.

Smith stuck his head out and shouted, "Get me a driver!" Private Michael Seaman ran up and jumped into the driver's seat. Smith ordered Seaman to back the armored personnel carrier into the courtyard and get into position in the eastern corner of the triangle, so that it had a clear view from the open gateway in the north down to the watchtower in the south. After they were in position, Smith told Seaman to keep him loaded as he was going up to man the .50-caliber machine gun. As Seaman threw the M113 into reverse, Smith climbed into the commander's hatch, swung the still-operational heavy machine gun around, took aim at the enemy, and pressed down on the "Cadillacs," the butterfly-shaped triggers.

The Browning M2 .50-caliber air-cooled heavy machine gun, nicknamed "Ma Deuce," is, because of its age, something of an anachronism, but arguably the finest automatic firearm ever made. Designed by John Browning, one of the world's great arms designers, it entered service in the U.S. military in 1921. The basic model has remained in service with surprisingly few modifications ever since. Its design is simple, and it's easy to shoot and maintain. And it is powerful. It can fire 450 rounds per minute under sustained use, but that rarely happens in combat situations—short bursts being most effective. This high volume combined with the bullet's size (2.31 inches long and .5 inches in diameter) and kinetic energy (minimum 2,800 feet per second) is devastating. Even a glancing wound can be fatal.

Smith had maneuvered the M113 into a position to make maximum use of his unit's most powerful weapon, which now became the target for every Iraqi SRG soldier from the watchtower to the gate.

To operate the machine gun, Smith had to stand up. Even though he was wearing his helmet and armored vest, he was exposed to enemy gunfire from the waist up because the machine gun was not equipped with a shield. Smith was repeatedly hit in the chest. (Afterward, thirteen bullet holes would be found in his armored vest.) Smith ignored the incoming bullets as he arced the machine gun back and forth, steadily squeezing off bursts in the manner that had earned him his machine-gun marksmanship awards, raking Iraqi positions from one end to the other. Even the courtyard wall opposite him was no protection for the enemy. Because it was within point-blank range, the .50-caliber bullets were able to easily smash through the masonry.

Smith's cover fire enabled his men to carry the wounded and retreat through the courtyard. At one point Keller shouted to Smith, calling him to leave. From across the courtyard, Smith locked eyes with Keller, shook his head slightly, and then made a short cutting motion across his throat with his right hand. He was staying.

A belt of .50-caliber bullets has a hundred rounds held together by links. Three times Private Seaman had to reload. Shortly before the third reload, Sergeant First Class Timothy Campbell took four soldiers with him in an effort to seize the watchtower. They had to pause during the third reload, since Smith's cover fire was vital for their attack. As soon as he heard the distinctive sound of the M2 firing resume, Campbell led the charge. They reached the tower and began shooting inside when Smith's machine gun again fell silent.

Inside the M113, Private Seaman wondered why his sergeant had stopped shooting; he had plenty of ammo. Then Sergeant Smith's body fell down the command hatch, blood flowing down the front of his vest. A bullet, probably fired from an Iraqi in the tower, had struck Smith in the head. Seaman, in shock, pulled himself out of the driver's hatch of the armored personnel carrier. As others arrived, Seaman muttered repeatedly, "I told him we should leave."

Private Gary Evans jumped inside and, calling encouragement to Smith, drove the M113 out of the courtyard, where it stalled. Others rushed up with a stretcher and carried the seriously wounded sergeant seventy-five yards to the aid station. Triage was performed. A medevac team was summoned and, minutes later, carried Sergeant Paul Ray Smith away in a helicopter.

Meanwhile, reinforcements, including Abrams tanks and Bradley fighting vehicles, had finally arrived. But by then the Iraqi attack had been broken up. Outnumbered and outgunned, Sergeant Smith and his men had successfully stopped the northern prong of the Iraqi attack, with Smith personally accounting for killing approximately fifty of the enemy's soldiers.

But the elation the men felt over their victory vanished quickly. News had come from the hospital about the hardcore sergeant they had hated in the States and in Germany, whose unending training had saved their lives in Iraq. Word was passed from soldier to soldier, "Superman is down." This time, Smith's nickname was spoken with respect and reverence.

An extraordinary soldier's life and career had come to an end, but a new chapter in the history of America's highest and most respected military decoration had begun. For the first time in the twenty-first century, an American warrior's actions in combat would result in the awarding of a Medal of Honor.

On the evening of April 4, at 11:30 P.M., the bell on the door rang at the Smith residence in Hinesville, Georgia, near Fort Stewart. Earlier that evening, Birgit Smith had finished writing a letter to her husband that she planned to mail the next day. In it she had penned the sentence, "Life without you here is just not the same."[12] Birgit was asleep when the doorbell rang. She later recalled, "I looked out through the peephole, and there were two soldiers. One was an E-7 [Sergeant First Class] like Paul's rank. The other was a chaplain." Birgit let them in, knowing immediately that something was wrong. After they sat down, she received the words all family members dread. She recalled, "The E-7 said, 'Paul is dead.' And I told him, 'Are you sure? Our last name is so common, maybe it was a mistake.' And, he said, 'Ma'am, I wouldn't be here if it's not a hundred percent.' "[13]

Two memorial services in the States for Sergeant Smith soon followed, the first at Fort Stewart, the second in Holiday, Florida, where Smith's mother and stepfather lived. Per the request in his will, Sergeant Smith was cremated and his remains scattered in the waters of the Tampa region, where he and his stepfather had fished. Birgit keeps a box with some of the ashes on her nightstand.

Sergeant Paul Ray Smith has received additional honors since the medal ceremony. In Holiday, the post office and a recently built middle school now bear his name, as does an army simulation and training technology center in Orlando, and a fitness center at Fort Benning.

On April 15 at 8:00 A.M. Baghdad time, the soldiers of Bravo Company assembled in formation at Four Corners. They stood at parade rest before a pair of empty boots, flanking an upended M16, its bayonet embedded in the desert soil and a helmet resting on its stock, the symbol of a comrade fallen in battle, and prepared for Sergeant Smith's final roll call—a memorial service eloquent in its Spartan simplicity.

On April 6, 2009, a special memorial service honoring Sergeant First Class Paul Ray Smith was held at Four Corners. First Sergeant David Roman, A Company, Forty-sixth Engineer Combat Battalion (Heavy), is recounting the battle scene that occurred six years earlier. In the background is the concrete observation tower, still pockmarked with bullet holes from that battle.
Photo: *Sergeant Rebekah Malone, U.S. Army*

Sergeant First Class Timothy Campbell faced the company and called the roll of the company's platoon sergeants.

"Sgt. Bergman."
"Here, first sergeant."

"Sgt. Roush."
"Here, first sergeant."

"Sgt. Brown."
"Here, first sergeant."

"Sgt. Smith."
Silence.

"Sgt. 1st Class Paul Smith."
Silence.

"Sgt. 1st Class Paul R. Smith."
Silence.[14]

The company then stood at attention. A twenty-one-gun salute was fired. As the echo of the last round faded, the company heard the martial skirl of bagpipes over the loud-speakers and the air of Four Corners resounded with the sounds of "Amazing Grace."

NOTES

1. Myers, Steven Lee, "The Struggle for Iraq: Casualties; Medals for His Valor, Ashes for His Wife," *New York Times*, September 23, 2003, http://www.nytimes.com (accessed May 24, 2009).
2. "Paul Ray Smith," Arlington National Cemetery, http://www.arlingtoncemetery.net/prsmith-03.htm (accessed July 3, 2009).
3. Janice Pvirre interview, "Sergeant First Class Paul R. Smith," Medal of Honor, http://www.army.mil/medalofhonor/smith/video/pvirre.html (accessed June 28, 2009).
4. Birgit Smith interview, "Sergeant First Class Paul R. Smith," Medal of Honor,

http://www.army.mil/medalofhonor/smith/video/birgit.html
(accessed June 28, 2009).

5. Gresham, John D., H. Ross Perot Interview, *The Year in Special Operations 2009* (Tampa, FL: Faircount Media Group), 2009, 95.

6. Freedberg, Sydney J. Jr., "Paul Ray Smith," *National Journal*, http://www.nationaljournal.com/njmagazine/print_friendly.php?I=nj_20070113_5, January 13, 2007 (accessed June 17, 2009).

7. Leary, Alex, "The Last Full Measure of Devotion: Part 3; Beer, Women, Fast Cars," *St. Petersburg Times* (FL), January 25, 2004, http://www.sptimes.com/2004/webspecials04/medalofhonor/story3/shtml (accessed May 13, 2009).

8. U.S. Army, *The Army Noncommissioned Officer Guide* Field Manual 7-22.7 (Washington, D.C., 2002), page ix.

9. Seymour, Shatara, "Comrades Tell of Smith's Leadership," TRADOC News Service, April 8, 2005, http://www.tradoc.army.mil/pao/TNSarchives/April05/040805.htm (accessed July 3, 2009).

10. Fontenot, Gregory, E. J. Degen, and David Tohn, *On Point: The United States Army in Operation Iraqi Freedom Through 1 May 2003*, (Fort Leavenworth, KS: Combat Studies Inst. Press, 2004), 299.

11. Leary, "The Last Full Measure of Devotion: Part 2: The Tactical Situation." *St. Petersburg Times* (FL), January 25, 2004, http://www.sptimes.com/2004/webspecials04/medalofhonor/story2/shtml (accessed May 13, 2009).

12. Myers, "Struggle for Iraq."

13. Birgit Smith interview.

14. Leary, "The Last Full Measure of Devotion: Part 4; April 4 10:30 A.M."

BIBLIOGRAPHY

BOOKS

U.S. Army. *The Army Noncommissioned Officer Guide*. Washington, D.C., 2002.

Gordon, Michael R., and Bernard E. Trainor. *Cobra II: The Inside Story of the Invasion and Occupation of Iraq*. New York: Pantheon Books, 2006.

Murray, Williamson, and Robert H. Scales Jr. *The Iraq War: A Military History.* Cambridge, MA: Belknap Press, 2005.

ARTICLES

Finn, Chris. "Air Aspects of Operation Iraqi Freedom." *Royal Air Force Air Power Review* 6. 4 (2003): 1-22.

MONOGRAPHS

Grant, Rebecca. *The War of 9/11: How the World Conflict Transformed America's Air and Space Weapon.* Arlington, VA: Air Force Assn., 2005.

INTERNET

Anderson, Jon R. "Pentagon Pays Tribute to Fallen Warrior." *Stars and Stripes,* http://www.stripes.com/articleprint.asp?section=104&article=28254 (accessed May 13, 2009).

Bennett, Ralph Kinney. "Common Name, Uncommon Valor: The Story of Paul Smith, the Iraq War's Only Medal of Honor Recipient So Far." *OpinionJournal Federation.* http://www.opinionjournal.co/federation/feature/?id=110008153 (accessed June 17, 2009).

Bonasia, J. "Paul Smith Sacrificed His Life and Won the Medal of Honor." *IBDeditorials.com,* February 1, 2007. http://www.ibdeditorials.com/IBDArticles.aspx?id=255222149233313&type=wh (accessed June 17, 2009).

Corkery, Michael. "Everything Up There Is the Enemy." *Providence Journal* (RI), April 2, 2003. http://www.projo.com/news/michaelcorkery/projo_20030402_battle1.b162c.html (accessed May 13, 2009).

———. "Iraqi Guerillas Are No Match for U.S. Soldiers." *Providence Journal* (RI), April 4, 2003. http://www.projo.com/news/michaelcorkery/projo_20030404_mussayib4.d1d39.html (accessed May 13, 2009).

———. "U.S. Forces Push to Edge of Baghdad." *Providence Journal* (RI), April 4, 2003. http://www.projo.com/news/michaelcorkery/projo_20030404_mc4.a135e.html (accessed May 13, 2009).

———. "U.S. Troops Repel Iraqi Ambush at Airport."
Providence Journal (RI), April 4, 2003.
www.projo.com/news/michaelcorkery/projo_20030405_
http://airport5.c1955.html (accessed May 13, 2009).
———. "Unit Had a Feeling Airport was Too Quiet."
Providence Journal (RI), April 6, 2003.
http://www.projo.com/news/michaelcorkery/
projo_20030406_end6.6187.html (accessed May 13, 2009).
———. "When Engineers Crashed Gate, Iraqi Troops Charged."
Providence Journal (RI), April 7, 2003.
http://www.projo.com/news/michaelcorkery/projo_
20030204_smight7.96bd2.html (accessed May 13, 2009).
———. "Infantry Battalion Takes Fight into Capital." *Providence
Journal* (RI), April 8, 2003.
http://www.projo.com/news/michaelcorkery/
projo_20030408_cork8.2fed5.html (accessed May 13, 2009).
"Camp al-Tahreer." *Patriot Files*.
http://www.patriotfiles.com/index.php?name = Section&req
=viewarticle&artid=8134&page=1 (accessed June 17, 2009).
Cramer, Eric W. "First Medal of Honor Flag to Be Presented."
Arnews: Army News Service, March 29, 2005.
http://www4.army.mil/ocpa/read.php?story_id_key=7085
(accessed July 15, 2007).
———. "First Medal of Honor to Be Awarded in Operation Iraqi
Freedom." *Arnews: Army News Service*, March 29, 2005.
http://www4.army.mil/ocpa/read.php?story_id_key=7091
(accessed July 15, 2007).
———. "Soldiers Relate Smith's Courage Under Fire, Care in
Garrison." *Arnews: Army News Service*, March 29, 2005.
http://www4.army.mil/ocpa/read.php?story_id_key=7087
(accessed July 15, 2007).
———. "A Soldier's Wife Remembers." *Arnews: Army News
Service*, March 29, 2005.
http://www4.army.mil/ocpa/read.php?stoyr_id_key=7084
(accessed July 15, 2007).
———. "Special Forces Veteran's Idea Leads to New Medal of
Honor Flag." *Arnews: Army News Service*, April 28, 2005.
http://www4.army.mil/ocpa/read.php?story_id_key=7244

(accessed July 15, 2007).

Fontenot, Gregory, U.S. Army (Ret.), E. J. Degen, and David Tohn. *On Point: The United States Army in Operation Iraqi Freedom Through 01 May 2003*. Fort Leavenworth, KS: Combat Studies Institute Press, 2004. http://www-cgsc.army.mil/carl/download/csipubs/ OnPointI.pdf (accessed May 20, 2009).

"1st Brigade—Special Republican Guard (SRG)." *GlobalSecurity.org*. http://www.globalsecurity.org/intell/world/iraq/1srg.htm (accessed June 17, 2009).

Freedberg, Sydney J. Jr. "Paul Ray Smith." *National Journal* January 13, 2007. http://www.nationaljournal.com/njmagazine/print_ friendly.php?I=nj_20070113_5 (accessed June 17, 2009).

"Hundreds Die in Airport Battle." *The Age*, April 4, 2003. http://www.theage.com.au/cgi-bin/common/popupPrint ARticle.pl?path=articles/2003/04/04/0148962907484.html (accessed May 20, 2009).

"Iraqi Special Republican Guard." *AbsoluteAstronomy.com*. http://www.absoluteastronomy.co/topics/Iraqi_Special_ Republican_Guard (accessed June 17, 2009).

Kaplan, Robert D. "No Greater Honor." *Atlantic Online*, June 2008. http://www.theatlantic.com/doc/print/200806u/medal-of- honor (accessed May 13, 2009).

"Leadership: Medal of Honor Awarded for Iraq Action." *Free Republic*. http://www.freerepublic.com/focus/news/1006552/posts (accessed June 17, 2009).

"The Iraq War Report for 2003-04-06." http://www.serendipity.li/iraqwar/report20030406.htm (accessed May 20, 2009).

Leary, Alex. "The Last Full Measure of Devotion: Part 5; Epilogue." *St. Petersburg Times* (FL), January 25, 2004. http://www.stimes.com/2004/webspecials04/medalofhonor/ story5.shtml (accessed May 13, 2009).

———. "The Last Full Measure of Devotion: Part 4; April 4,

10:30 A.M." *St. Petersburg Times* (FL), January 25, 2004.
http://www.sptimes.com/2004/webspecials04/
medalofhonor/story4.shtml (accessed May 13, 2009).
———. "The Last Full Measure of Devotion: Part 1."
St. Petersburg Times (FL), January 25, 2004.
http://www.sptimes.com/2004/webspecials04/
medalofhonor/story.shtml (accessed May 13, 2009).
———. "The Last Full Measure of Devotion: Part 3: Beer,
Women, Fast Cars." *St. Petersburg Times* (FL), January 25,
2004.
http://www.sptimes.com/2004/webspecials04/
medalofhonor/story3.shtml (accessed May 13, 2009).
———. "The Last Full Measure of Devotion: Part 2; The Tactical
Situation." *St. Petersburg* (FL) *Times*, January 25, 2004.
http://www.sptimes.com/2004/webspecials04/
medal of honor/story2.shtml (accessed May 13, 2009).
———. "Selfless Final Act Saved His Troops." *St. Petersburg
Times* (FL), April 17, 2003.
http://www.sptimes.com/2003/04/17/Worldandnation/
Selfless_final_act_sa.shtml (accessed May 13, 2009).
Myers, Steven Lee. "The Struggle for Iraq: Casualties; Medals
for His Valor, Ashes for His Wife." *New York Times*,
September 23, 2003.
http://www.nytimes.com/2003/09/23/world/the-struggle-for-
iraq-casualties-medals-for-his-valor-ashes-for-his-
wife.html?pagewanted=print (accessed May 24, 2009).
"Paul Ray Smith." Arlington National Cemetery. April 7, 2005.
http://www.arlingtoncemetery.net/prsmith-03htm
(accessed July 3, 2009)
Sapperd. "My War in Iraq." http://blog.360.yahoo.com/blog-
rnXb-wAieraAy12UbwFpa_aOyw—?cq=1&I=6&u=10&mx
=36&Imt=5 (accessed June 17, 2009).
Seymour, Shatara. "Comrades Tell of Smith's Leadership." United
States Army Training and Doctrine Command (TRADOC)
Office of the Chief of Public Affairs, April 8, 2005.
http://www.tradoc.army.mil/pao/TNSarchives/April05/
040805.htm (accessed July 3, 2009).
U.S. Army. "Medal of Honor—Sergeant First Class Paul R.

Smith." *Biography*.
http://www.army.mil/medalofhonor/smith/profile/index.html
(accessed July 15, 2007).
"War in Iraq: Forces: Iraq/Army, Special Republican Guard,
Republican Guard." *CNN.com*.
http://www.cnn.com/SPECIALS/2003/iraq/forces/iraq/army/
(accessed June 17, 2009).
Wright, Donald P., Timothy R. Reese. *On Point II: Transition to
the New Campaign: The United States Army in Operation
Iraqi Freedom May 2003–January 2005*. Fort Leavenworth, KS:
Combat Studies Institute Press, 2008.
http://www.cgsc.army.mil/carl/download/csipubs/on_pointII/
On%20Point%20II.pdf (accessed May 20, 2009).

2

Building a Pyramid
of Honor

The utility of medals has ever been impressed strongly
upon my mind. Pride, ambition and indeed what a
philosopher would call vanity, is the strongest passion
in human nature, and next to religion, the enthusiasm
most operative ... to great actions.

— May 9, 1777 letter from John Adams
to Nathanael Greene.[1]

AMERICA'S FIRST MILITARY DECORATIONS

The formal recognition of heroic feats during combat is one
of the oldest traditions in the profession of arms. The
ancient Greeks presented crowns to their heroes. Roman
military heroes wore gold or silver torques and decorative
disks. In 2009, the United States military, inclusive of all
branches, had seventy-two medals recognizing individual
and unit valor in combat and meritorious service. The

awards are organized into what is referred to as the Pyramid of Honor because of the awards' escalating criteria, which has at its base a variety of decorations of equal merit (whose order is arranged by date of citation) and at its pinnacle just one: the Medal of Honor. This is a far cry from the honor accorded our nation's heroes during the early days of our country, when there were no such decorations or awards.

It's not that the Continental Congress didn't care. As the colonial and Revolutionary War historian Philander D. Chase has noted, "What most of the Founding Fathers objected to was *hereditary* honors and titles. They did not object to individual honors and distinctions. In fact, officers and soldiers, especially the officers, were expected to seek those things within context of service to society and in particular, to the American cause."[2]

In recognition of service to the country during the revolution, the Continental Congress authorized a total of fourteen gold and silver medals (eight were awarded during the war) for specific individuals. General George Washington received the first gold medal for his victory at Dorchester Heights in March 1776, which resulted in the British evacuation of Boston. General Horatio Gates received one for his victory at Saratoga in October 1778. As John Adams noted, for some people the possibility of receiving one was a powerful incentive. Washington's aide, "Light Horse Harry" Lee, could not rest until Washington gave him a chance to earn one by leading an attack against British troops during a battle at Paulus Hook, New Jersey, in August 1779. Lee's desire was fulfilled when Congress later awarded him a gold medal.

But even with these gestures of recognition, the Continental Congress was following historical tradition by presenting its awards only to officers. It was Washington himself who broke new ground. On August 7, 1782, he signed an order from his headquarters in Newburgh, New York, directing that "whenever any singularly meritorious action is performed, the author of it shall be permitted to wear on his facings, over his left breast, the figure of a heart in purple cloth or silk, edged with narrow lace or binding."[3]

This Medal of Military Merit (or Badge of Military Merit), as it came to be known, was America's first decoration. As the historian Colonel Robert E. Wyllie noted, "it was the first in history which had a general application to enlisted men."[4] Few records referring to the Medal of Military Merit exist beyond the August 7 order. As far as is known, only three were awarded, all to enlisted men from Connecticut. About ten months after Washington created the decoration, on May 3, 1783, he presented the Medal of Military Merit to Sergeants Elijah Churchill and William Brown. A little over a month later, on June 10, Sergeant Daniel Bissell Jr. received one. The Medal of Military Merit then apparently fell into disuse. In fact, by the time the War of 1812 erupted, it was forgotten. It's impossible now to know exactly why, but one reason may be that the award was authorized by Washington rather than Congress, effectively making it a personal rather than a national medal. Also, what can't be discounted was the popular sentiment against wearing *any* badge or medal, a feeling that carried on well into the nineteenth century. In fact, for a number of years after its authorization, it was not unusual for a Medal of Honor recipient to be mocked for wearing his award because such an action was viewed as a pretentious European affectation. It's also worth mentioning that Congress never officially discontinued the Medal of Military Merit, perhaps out of respect to the first president, allowing it to "die" from neglect.

But the presentation of commemorative awards survived. Congress, state and city governments, and sometimes even private organizations or companies created individual awards, usually in the forms of gold or silver medals or plates that could rest on a mantel or hang from a wall, or elaborately engraved swords or firearms that were given in recognition of exemplary service in a particular battle.

Two other types of honors were also popular: official praise and brevets. Official praise came in two forms: mentions in dispatches and the thanks of Congress. The former occurred when a commanding officer wrote an official letter to a superior or the President of the United States or even Congress specifically commending a subordinate and including a summary of that subordinate's action. As the term suggests, the "thanks of Congress" was a proclamation by the legislative body expressing its gratitude for the officer's role in a particular victory.

Brevets were temporary promotions that allowed the officer to wear and be addressed by the new rank, but they did not confer the authority or the pay. Officers could receive numerous brevets during a campaign or war. For instance, in the Mexican-American War, Captain Robert E. Lee received three brevets, raising him to the temporary rank of colonel (but at a captain's pay).

In 1847, during the Mexican-American War, Congress authorized an award for enlisted and noncommissioned officers only, called the Certificate of Merit. Though not a decoration, the document was at least a formal recognition of distinguished service. Probably more important to the recipient was that it came with a raise of $2 a month. Privates then received either $7 (infantry) or $8 (cavalry) per month,[5] so it was a considerable boost in pay. Valued in today's dollars, it was equivalent to about $460 per month.

THE MEDAL OF HONOR

Until 1947, when they were incorporated into the Department of Defense, the army and navy were administered by two separate cabinet-level positions, the Department of War (established 1789) and the Department of the Navy (established 1798). President Abraham Lincoln's secretary of war was Simon Cameron (replaced in January 1862 by Edwin Stanton), and his secretary of the navy was Gideon Welles.

Though the navy was the first branch to have the Medal of Honor, the concept for it originated in the army—an ironic situation given the state of interservice rivalry back then. The individual who came up with the idea was Assistant Adjutant General Lieutenant Colonel Edward Davis Townsend (founder of the military prison at Fort Leavenworth). In March 1861, in addition to his assistant adjutant general duties, he was named chief of staff to General Winfield Scott, the secretary of war's most senior officer. It was at one point during that tenure, probably after the First Battle of Bull Run (Manassas) in July, that he made his suggestion to General Scott. But the general didn't like it. The country's greatest soldier in the first half of the nineteenth century, Scott began his illustrious military career fighting the British in the War of 1812, during which he rose to the rank of brigadier general. To him, this sort of medal smacked of British frippery and was wholly inappropriate to the republican principles laid down by the founding fathers. He rejected it.

But Townsend's idea found an advocate when it reached the ear of Gideon Welles. In the first year of the war, Welles was in a particularly desperate situation. When the Southern states seceded, almost all U.S. Army and Navy officers from those states submitted their resignations and became officers for the Confederacy. The mass defection hit the U.S. Navy hard, dramatically depleting its ranks and causing the morale of those who stayed to hit rock bottom. Compounding Secretary Welles's problem was the fact that General Scott was proposing a blockade of Southern ports—the Anaconda Plan—and Welles had only 7,600 sailors and just seventy-six ships of all types.

A skilled organizer, Welles created a crash program to expand and make the navy more efficient. In his report to Congress, he requested the creation of a medal of honor designed to promote efficiency in the navy, which would be awarded to enlisted personnel. On December 9, 1861, Senator James W. Grimes of Iowa, chairman of the Senate Naval Committee, introduced the bill calling for two hundred Medals of Honor to be made for the navy. When President Abraham Lincoln signed the bill into law on December 21, 1861, the criteria had been expanded to include acts of gallantry and heroism in times of war and peace. This medal was only to be a temporary one, set to expire upon the conclusion of the Civil War. By this time, the seventy-five-year-old Scott was no longer head of the army, having retired on November 1, 1861. The way was now clear for the army to have its own Medal of Honor.

On February 17, 1862, Senator Henry Wilson of Massachusetts, chairman of the Senate Committee on Military Affairs, introduced a bill for the Army's Medal of Honor, which was signed by President Lincoln on July 12, 1862. It authorized that two thousand army Medals of Honor be made and that they would be "presented, in the name of Congress, to such non-commissioned officers and privates as shall most distinguish themselves by their gallantry in action, and other soldier-like qualities, during the present insurrection."[6] On March 3, 1863, a bill was passed regarding the army Medal of Honor that made officers eligible to receive it. The navy didn't expand its eligibility criteria until March 3, 1915.

The artist, Christian Schuller, under the guidance of Director of the United States Mint James Pollock, was tasked with designing the navy's Medal of Honor. The medal itself was a five-pointed star, displayed point down. It had thirty-four stars, symbolizing the number of states at the time, and in its middle it showed Minerva, the Roman goddess of warriors, medicine, and wisdom, fighting the goddess of discord. The medal was linked to the suspension ribbon by an anchor. The ribbon had alternating vertical red and white stripes and was capped with a metal clasp. The army's version essentially copied the navy's, substituting the naval accents with an eagle, crossed cannons, and cannonballs.

Finally, after eighty-five years as a nation, we had a medal designed to be awarded in acknowledgment of valorous service in the military. Unfortunately, it was the nation's *only* official military decoration. More important, the army's vaguely worded criteria—"gallantry in action, and other soldier-like qualities, during the present insurrection"—left the Medal of Honor open to abuse as a catchall decoration that could be awarded for *any* reason. That's what happened with the Twenty-seventh Maine Volunteer Infantry Regiment.

THE "SAGA" OF THE TWENTY-SEVENTH MAINE

A total of 2,445 Medals of Honor were originally presented to individuals who served during the Civil War. The key word here is *originally*. Following the 2010 awarding of a posthumous Medal of Honor to Lt. Alonzo Cushing, the official number is 1,528. A number went to individuals who performed actions that now would scarcely receive mention, let alone a recommendation for a Medal of Honor. For instance, a common reason was the capture of the colors (flag) of a Confederate unit, a highly esteemed action of the period. But many were awarded for truly valorous acts on the battlefield at great risk of life.

Of that original total, 864 went to the men of the Twenty-seventh Maine Volunteer Infantry Regiment—which was the entire unit. By way of comparison, only sixty-four *total* Medals of Honor were awarded to Union soldiers who fought at Gettysburg. The Twenty-seventh Maine received their medals as a result of their defense of Washington, D.C., in late June to early July 1863, when General Robert E. Lee led his Army of Northern Virginia into Pennsylvania. During that period, the nation's capital was never directly threatened, and no shots were ever fired.

So . . . what did the men of the Twenty-seventh Maine do that outshone the heroic efforts of the 88,000 soldiers of the Army of the Potomac? Quite simply, they reenlisted.

For four days. Actually, only about a third reenlisted—but they *all* received the Medal of Honor.

During the Civil War, the armies on both sides were composed of two types of units: regular and volunteer—volunteer units being comparable to today's National Guard. The Twenty-

The original design for the U.S. Navy Medal of Honor.
Photo: *National Archives*

seventh Maine was a volunteer unit composed of men primarily from York County in the southwest corner of the state, whose members agreed to an enlistment of nine months beginning on September 30, 1862, and ending on June 30, 1863. At that point the men would be free to return home.

On June 21, 1863, General Robert E. Lee and his Army of Northern Virginia crossed the Potomac River and commenced their second invasion of the North. This created a panic in Washington, D.C., because almost all the troops that had previously guarded the capital had been transferred to the Army of the Potomac, which was out searching for Lee's army. Two units that had not been reassigned, because their enlistments were imminently due to expire, were the Twenty-seventh Maine and another volunteer regiment from the state, the Twenty-fifth Maine.

On June 26, Secretary of War Edwin Stanton made a desperate appeal to the commanders of both regiments, asking them to convince their troops to agree to a short-term extension of their enlistments, one that would expire when the present crisis had passed. The men of the Twenty-fifth Maine refused, and on July 1 returned to their home state. Colonel Mark Wentworth, commander of the Twenty-seventh Maine, was able to convince about a third of his troops to reenlist, and he and 311 men remained at their post, guarding the capital, while about sixty miles to the north, two mighty armies slugged it out for three days at Gettysburg. On July 5, with the crisis over and without ever having fired a shot in anger during the period, this rump group of the Twenty-seventh Maine returned to York County.

Secretary of War Stanton, who had a powerful temper and a reputation for carrying grudges, was furious over the

Twenty-fifth Maine's refusal to stay. Wanting to extend a gesture of gratitude, and possibly to exact some revenge against the Twenty-fifth Maine, on June 29 he ordered that the 311 men of the Twenty-seventh Maine who had stayed to defend the capital would receive the Medal of Honor. Unfortunately, Stanton's order was worded in such a way that the entire unit—all 864 members—was awarded the medals. These Medals of Honor were ready in January 1865 and sent to Governor Samuel Cony of Maine for distribution. Cony forwarded the medals to Mark Wentworth for final presentation.

Upon the expiration of his term as commander of the Twenty-seventh Maine, Wentworth had chosen to remain in service and commanded another volunteer unit, the Thirty-second Maine, before being mustered out in October 1864 with the brevet rank of Brigadier General, U.S. Volunteers. This time around, Wentworth saw a lot of action, participating in engagements that included the Battles of the Wilderness, Spotsylvania, Cold Harbor, Petersburg, and the Battle of the Crater.

To Wentworth's credit, even though he was one of the beneficiaries who received the Medal of Honor for "volunteering to remain at Arlington Heights, Va., until the result of the battle of Gettysburg, Pa., was known, the term of the regiment having expired before that time,"[7] he felt uncomfortable about passing them out to troops who had simply performed garrison duty. In an effort to follow the spirit and not the letter of his orders, he did all he could to at least make sure that only those who had actually reenlisted received their medals. That task was made difficult by the fact that no reliable roster had been made of the Twenty-seventh Maine volunteers who stayed behind to guard Washington. But eventually he managed to deliver the Medals of Honor to the 311 who had fulfilled their obligation. The rest he stored in his barn. At one point, thieves broke into the barn and stole a number of them. The rest disappeared shortly after his death in 1897.

Though it was the largest, the Twenty-seventh Maine was not the only unit to receive Medals of Honor for reasons other than exemplary valor in combat. Another group was the four officers and twenty-five senior noncommissioned officers who served as President Abraham Lincoln's funeral honor guard.

Then there was the handful of downright frivolous awardings. Unlike some individuals who inflated their claims, Lieutenant Colonel Asa Gardiner was forthright. At that time, an individual could personally file for a medal. Gardiner, in his application submitted in 1872 and referring to his service in the Civil War, wrote, "I request I be allowed one as a souvenir of memorable times past."[8] His candor must have been disarming. He got it.

Individuals who received their Medals of Honor as a result of gallant and life-risking actions on the battlefield didn't like this situation. But for years, so long as the criteria was worded the way it was, and given that it was the nation's only military decoration, the only thing these veterans could do was ignore those whom they believed had inappropriately received their medals.

CLOSING THE LOOPHOLES BEGINS

In the first couple of decades following the Civil War, incremental changes were made to refine the Medal of Honor's criteria. The most important change during this period occurred in 1878 when a board of review was convened to consider the high number of recommendations for Medals of Honor for soldiers of the Seventh Cavalry—those who had fought at the Battle of the Little Big Horn in 1876. What made this board's task particularly notable was that one of the men who died in the battle was Captain Tom Custer, the younger brother of Lieutenant Colonel George Armstrong Custer. Tom was a double Medal of Honor recipient, having received both during the Civil War. It's not known today if his name was on the list, but if it were and if the board approved the recommendation, he would then have posthumously received an unprecedented *third* Medal of Honor.

The board ultimately determined that only twenty-four Medals of Honor should be awarded (neither Custer was in that group), and that the guiding policy should be "the conduct which deserves such recognition should not be the simple discharge of duty, but such acts beyond this that if omitted or refused to be done should not justly subject the person to censure for shortcoming or failure."[9] For the first time, the medal was seen as honoring actions that are above and beyond what is expected of a soldier during wartime engagements.

The board's report, then, was a significant step in establishing the criteria for future recipients. But it allowed two controversies to fester. The first centered on whether or not some recipients, and here the finger was pointed at the men of the Twenty-seventh Maine, had truly qualified for the Medal of Honor. The second was the hijacking of the Medal of Honor's design by veterans' organizations, particularly the Grand Army of the Republic.

Founded in 1866 in Decatur, Illinois, by Dr. Benjamin F. Stephenson, the Grand Army of the Republic (GAR) was the largest and most influential of the veterans' groups organized after the war. At its peak in 1890, it had more than 490,000 members. The GAR was active in veterans' welfare legislation, relief work, and the founding of Old Soldiers' Homes to care for wounded, aged, infirm, and indigent veterans. Its political influence was enormous. GAR endorsement, or lack thereof, could make or break the careers of high-ranking politicians, even presidents—as Grover Cleveland discovered when he vetoed a pension bill for veterans. The GAR was instrumental in his failure to be reelected in 1888.

The GAR incorporated into its charter a variety of military structures and traditions, including the wearing of uniforms and the issuing of medals. When placed side by side, the GAR medal is almost indistinguishable from the original army Medal of Honor. This knockoff caused resentment among many Medal of Honor recipients, especially those who were *not* GAR members.

Finally, in 1890, a group of Medal of Honor recipients formed the Medal of Honor Legion, whose purpose was to ensure the integrity of the Medal of Honor. This included a redesign of the medal, with copyright and patent protection. In an action that demonstrated just how much the American attitude had changed from revolutionary times regarding military decorations, the legion lobbied for legislation that would "give the Medal of Honor the same position among military orders of the world which similar medals occupy."[10] Their efforts took time—twenty-nine years, in fact. But by 1919, every aspect of the Medal of Honor had been overhauled.

In 1896, Congress authorized the first design changes, a revision of the suspension ribbon of the army's version (the navy's was unaffected), and the creation of a rosette and a small ribbon that could be worn in lieu of the medal itself. A greater breakthrough occurred the following year. With no statute of limitations regarding the submission of claims, and with individuals allowed to personally file applications, by 1897 more than seven hundred Civil War Medal of Honor claims had been filed. President William McKinley, himself a Civil War veteran, directed the War Department to establish new and clear policies regarding applications and awards.

On June 26, 1897, the War Department issued an executive order that codified policy regarding the awarding of the Medal of Honor. The executive order stated:

In order that the Congressional Medal of Honor may be deserved, service must have been performed in action of such a conspicuous character as to clearly distinguish the man for gallantry and intrepidity above his comrades—service that involves extreme jeopardy of life or the performance of extraordinarily hazardous duty. Recommendations for the decoration will be judged by this standard of extraordinary merit, and incontestable proof of performance of the service will be exacted.

Soldiers of the Union have ever displayed bravery in battle, else victories could not have been gained; but as courage and self-sacrifice are the characteristics of every true soldier, such a badge of distinction as the Congressional medal is not to be expected as the reward of conduct that does not clearly distinguish the soldier above other men whose bravery and gallantry have been proved in battle.[11]

In addition, the War Department established that, beginning on June 26, 1897, a statute of limitations would exist. From that point on, any Medal of Honor application had to be made within twelve months of the action. And all submissions for the Medal of Honor now had to be made by someone else (usually, but not restricted to, the commanding officer) and not the individual who had performed the heroic deed; the submission had to include the sworn testimony of at least one eyewitness.

Unintentionally, the precisely worded high standard made recognition of acts of valor an all-or-nothing choice. Something else was needed to acknowledge lesser acts of heroism. With earlier recognitions—the commemorative medals, mentions in dispatches, and the thanks of Congress—having either fallen out of favor or become impractical, and with the antimedal bias now a thing of the past, the way was open to expand the number of medals for courageous action in combat.

In 1905, Congress revived the Certificate of Merit, this time making it a medal with a red, white, and blue ribbon. Like the original Certificate of Merit of the Mexican-American War, it was only awarded to noncommissioned officers and enlisted men, and it ranked below the Medal of Honor. So, in the beginning of the twentieth century, aside from the two grades of Lifesaving Medals (which could be awarded to both the military and civilians), enlisted men had two medals for valor and officers had only one.

This Grand Army of the Republic poster has at its center the veterans organization's membership medal. Though different in detail, the GAR medal design was similar enough to the Medal of Honor to cause confusion and resentment amongst many Medal of Honor recipients.
Photo: *Library of Congress*

In the meantime, Congress took a further step in changing the Medal of Honor's design. On April 23, 1904, it authorized for the army what came to be known as the Gillespie Medal, named after the Medal of Honor recipient Brigadier General George Gillespie Jr., who drafted it. The design is quite similar to today's army version, the main difference being that the Gillespie Medal was designed to be pinned on the chest, not suspended from a neck ribbon. To protect it from imitations, its design was copyrighted and patented. In 1913, the navy adopted a modified version of the Gillespie medal. This design was also patented and copyrighted.

Then, on April 27, 1916, Congress passed a bill sponsored by Congressman Isaac R. Sherwood of Ohio that authorized a monthly stipend for life of $10 to "holders of the Medal of Honor who had reached the age of 65 and who had been awarded the medal for action involving actual conflict with the enemy, distinguishable by conspicuous gallantry or intrepidity at the risk of life, above and beyond the call of duty."[12] It also authorized a Medal of Honor roll, an official list of every recipient, because at the time no such listing existed. The roll, the monthly stipend, the wording "for action involving actual conflict with the enemy," and external events along the United States–Mexico border and in Europe set the stage for the watershed moment in Medal of Honor history.

THE PURGE OF 1917
The case of the Twenty-seventh Maine was regarded by the Medal of Honor Legion as a major impediment to maintaining the integrity of the decoration. Not surprisingly, the

Twenty-seventh Maine veterans objected to any retroactive action to "clean up" the list of recipients. They felt they had just as much right to their award as any other recipient—perhaps even more so than some. After all, unlike some other recipients, *they* had never stooped to petitioning for it; it was recommended by the secretary of war and signed by President Abraham Lincoln himself! They were also smart enough to buttress their position with the support of powerful political and military allies. The most important of these were Army Adjutant General Fred C. Ainsworth, Army Judge Advocate General Major General George B. Davis, and Secretary of War William Taft. With Ainsworth and Davis on the side of the Twenty-seventh Maine, any attempt for change through the army's legal system was dead. Taft's support of the Twenty-seventh Maine veterans may have been influenced by the experience of his boss, President Theodore Roosevelt. Roosevelt had lobbied to receive the Medal of Honor himself for his role in the Battle of San Juan Hill during the Spanish-American War (1898), and his application had been rejected.

But the situation began to turn in the Medal of Honor Legion's favor during the twentieth century's second decade. In 1911, Davis retired. In 1912, Ainsworth, a prickly individual jealous of his military prerogatives and resentful of what he regarded as civilian meddling in military affairs, crossed swords one too many times with Taft's successor, Secretary of War Henry Stimson (Taft having been elected president). When Ainsworth chose to take a public stand on the wrong side of an army reform bill then working its way through Congress, Stimson gave Ainsworth a choice: retire or face court-martial for insubordination. Ainsworth retired. In 1912,

Taft's bid for a second term failed and Woodrow Wilson was elected president. Also in that year, Europe plunged into the conflict that would later be known as World War I.

In March 1916, the Mexican revolutionary Pancho Villa led five hundred soldiers across the U.S. border in a spectacular attack on Columbus, New Mexico, an action that terrified Americans living along the border and that outraged the rest of the nation. In April, Congressman Sherwood submitted his Medal of Honor bill. In May and June, Villa staged two more major raids, this time in Texas. Meanwhile, the war in Europe had entered its third year. Public opinion now made national defense a priority. Congress was quick to act. On June 3, it passed the National Defense Act of 1916, the most sweeping piece of legislation to affect the military since the Civil War. Its primary focus was a dramatic increase in the army and National Guard, and the expansion of presidential authority regarding military matters. But buried on page 44 of the sixty-seven-page document was one paragraph devoted solely to the Medal of Honor:

Sec. 122. Investigation concerning medals of honor.— A board to consist of five general officers on the retired list of the Army shall be convened by the Secretary of War, within sixty days after the approval of this Act, for the purpose of investigating and reporting upon past awards or issues of the so-called congressional medal of honor by or through the War Department; this with a view to ascertain what medals of honor, if any, have been awarded or issued for any cause other than distinguished conduct by an officer or enlisted man in action involving actual conflict with an enemy by such officer or enlisted man or by troops with which he was serving at the time of such action. And in any case in which said board shall find and report that said medal was issued for any cause other than that hereinbefore specified the name of the recipient of the medal so issued shall be stricken permanently from the official medal of honor list. It shall be a misdemeanor for him to wear or publicly display said medal, and, if he shall still be in the Army, he shall be required to return said medal to the War Department for cancellation. Said board shall have full and free access to and use of all records pertaining to the award or issue of medals of honor by or through the War Department. The actual and necessary expenses of said board and its members shall be paid out of any appropriations available for contingent expenses of the Army of the War Department.[13]

On October 16, 1916, the first army Medal of Honor review commission convened. This blue-ribbon group of retired generals was led by Lieutenant General Nelson A. Miles, and included Lieutenant General Samuel B. M. Young, Major General Joseph P. Sanger, and Brigadier Generals Butler D. Price and Oswald H. Ernst. Miles, who had married the niece of General William Tecumseh Sherman, was a former commanding general of the army, a Civil War Medal of Honor recipient, and a past commander of the Medal of Honor Legion.

The board's task was daunting. It had to review and pass judgment on 2,625 army Medals of Honor that had been awarded to that date. To counter any allegations that they

Lieutenant General Nelson A. Miles was the leader of the army's Medal of Honor review commission. As this 1902 photo shows, his Medal of Honor had the new ribbon design, instituted in 1896.
Photo: *Library of Congress*

were conducting a witch hunt and to avoid any appearance of being influenced by an individual's name (after all, Miles was one of the recipients whose citation was being reviewed), each recipient's file was identified only by a number. The review lasted three months and concluded on January 17, 1917. On February 5, 1917, the board presented its findings. Of the 2,625 medals awarded, it had determined that 911 did not fit the guidelines and that these individuals should be stricken from the Medal of Honor roll and the medals returned. The group included the veterans of the Twenty-seventh Maine, the honor guard for Lincoln's funeral, the handful of individuals who had submitted frivolous applications (Gardiner lost his "souvenir"), a foreign national, and six civilians. It was now clear that to receive the Medal of Honor, one had to display valor in combat above and beyond the call of duty, be a member of the military, and be an American citizen. (Lost in the brouhaha in the wake of the army review board's decision is the fact that the navy conducted one as well. Shortly after World War I, the navy convened a Medal of Honor review and eliminated seventeen sailors from the list.)

Known as the Purge of 1917, the army board's action went a long way in eliminating the issues that had tainted the Medal of Honor since its inception. But the board's decision inevitably wrought controversy of its own. This mostly focused on the issue of the six civilians who had received the Medal of Honor—five scouts who had served in the Indian wars, and one doctor. The most famous of the scouts was William F. "Buffalo Bill" Cody. The doctor was Mary Edwards Walker.

To date the only woman to be awarded the Medal of Honor, Dr. Walker's career as a civilian surgeon working for the army began in 1861 at the First Battle of Bull Run (Manassas). Following her experience at the Battle of Fredericksburg, she went west, where she served as an assistant surgeon in the Army of the Cumberland. She repeatedly traveled back and forth between enemy lines, treating civilians. During one such trip she was captured, accused of being a spy, and held as a prisoner of war. She was freed in a prisoner exchange and later was with Sherman's army at the Battle of Atlanta.

Her Medal of Honor recommendation was made by both Sherman and Major General George Thomas, and the citation was signed by President Andrew Johnson. Walker met the Medal of Honor conditions of courage above and beyond the call of duty on the battlefield. The only reason her medal was revoked was because she was a civilian. And because Congress had, for the first time, made the unauthorized possession and display of the Medal of Honor a misdemeanor (though the penalty was not specified), she now risked arrest.

Dr. Walker, who after the war had become an activist for a variety of social causes including women's suffrage, refused to surrender her medal. She died in 1919, and during the two years before her death she wore it every day, even defiantly in the presence of Congress, whom she relentlessly petitioned to reverse the board's decision.

Eventually, a number of the decorations were restored. In 1977, President Jimmy Carter reinstated Dr. Walker's award, and in 1990, President George Bush did the same for Buffalo Bill and the four other civilian scouts.

THE PYRAMID OF HONOR

On April 6, 1917, the United States declared war on Germany and joined the Allies, led by Great Britain and France, in World War I. Now the unredressed other side of the

Medal of Honor coin, a dearth of other awards, came to a head. General John J. Pershing, commander of the American Expeditionary Forces in Europe, later recalled in his memoirs:

The problem of decorations in our army had long been a knotty one, and except for the Medal of Honor and Certificate of Merit we had only campaign badges and those given for marksmanship. The Allies desired to confer their decorations on our men who served with distinction under them, but we were not permitted to accept foreign decorations without permission from Congress. . . . As it was a matter of importance to our officers and men, the whole question of decorations was taken up by the War Department on my suggestion with the result that Congressional action established certain medals of our own and authorized our soldiers to receive those of foreign governments.[14]

The War Department responded with two service awards for members of the army and the new army air corps (forerunner of the air force) that ranked second only to the Medal of Honor. In so doing, it created for the first time a decoration that specifically recognized exemplary staff and other noncombat service. Congress authorized the Distinguished Service Cross (combat) and the Distinguished Service Medal (noncombat) on January 2, 1918. That same year, in July, it discontinued the Certificate of Merit. Earlier, on the same day America entered the war, the Navy Department issued the Navy Cross (combat—U.S. Navy, Marine Corps, U.S. Coast Guard). The navy's noncombat Distinguished Service

Medal was authorized on February 4, 1919. On July 9, 1918, the Certificate of Merit was replaced with the Citation Star, ranking below the Distinguished Service Cross and Navy Cross and issued to all branches. Instead of a medal, it was a silver star designed to be affixed to the ribbon of the campaign medal for which the citation was given and was meant to signify gallantry in action. The Citation Star was replaced in 1932 by the Silver Star.

Additional legislation regarding the Medal of Honor was also passed on July 9, 1918. As the example of Tom Custer shows, it was possible for individuals to receive more than one Medal of Honor. Over the years, nineteen men had become double recipients. That was changed. Henceforth, only one Medal of Honor could be awarded to a single person. The time period in which a recommendation could be made was expanded to two years, with the presentation having to occur within three. The Medal of Honor retained its distinction of being the only decoration presented by the president "in the name of the Congress." All other awards are given only by the president.

Additional medals were to come. Interest in reviving Washington's Badge of Military Merit occurred in 1927. This interest waned, only to be renewed in 1931 by Army Chief of Staff General Douglas MacArthur. He commissioned a new design of the medal, intending to have it issued on the bicentennial of Washington's birth. On February 22, 1932, the War Department revived it under the name Purple Heart and initially authorized it to be presented to soldiers for meritorious service or to those who received wounds in battle. It was retroactively issued to soldiers wounded during World War I. Initially, the Navy Department chose to regard it as strictly an army decoration. In 1942, President Franklin Roosevelt signed an executive order extending it to all services. That same year, the Legion of Merit was created, and it inherited the Purple Heart's meritorious service criteria. In 1944, the Bronze Star, a decoration for both combat and noncombat actions that ranked below the Silver Star, was created and made retroactive to December 7, 1941.

On February 26, 1942, President Roosevelt signed an executive order that eliminated a final, confusing loophole created by the Twenty-seventh Maine: whether or not a recipient's decoration was awarded for his exemplary service as an *individual* or as part of a *unit*. The Distinguished Unit Citation (now known as the Presidential Unit Citation and made retroactive to December 7, 1941) is equal in merit to the Distinguished Service Cross; the Navy Cross; and, when the air force became a separate branch, the Air Force Cross. As its name suggests, it is a decoration that recognizes the exemplary efforts of an entire unit during a battle or campaign.

Problems, including charges of racism in the denial of awarding the Medal of Honor and fraudulent sales and possession, would continue to occur. But with the creation of these new medals, codified escalating sets of criteria, and clear standards for what constituted Medal of Honor–worthy acts, the goal of the Medal of Honor Legion was finally realized, and the medal achieved the status with which it is regarded today. For the first time, the U.S. military had a standardized set of decorations for both officers and enlisted personnel, providing a means for a grateful nation to recognize the exceptional acts of those fighting in its defense.

NOTES

1. "Letters of Delegates to Congress," *A Century of Lawmaking for a New Nation: U.S. Congressional Documents and Debates, 1774-1875*, Vol. 7, May 1, 1777–September 18, 1777. John Adams to Nathanael Greene. May 9, 1777, http://memory.loc.gov/ammem/hlawquery.html (accessed September 6, 2007).
2. Philander D. Chase to Dwight Jon Zimmerman, August 22, 2007.
3. Wyllie, Robert E., *Orders, Decorations, and Insignia: Military and Civil*, (New York: Putnam, 1921), 6.
4. Ibid, 8.
5. U.S. Army Pay/Pensions/Bounties, U.S. Army Military History Institute. Ibiblio.org, http://www.ibiblio.org/pub/academic/history/marshall/military/mil_hist_inst/p/pay.asc (accessed July 25, 2009).
6. "Senate Resolution 82," Library of Congress, http://memory.loc.gov/cgi-bin/ampage?collId=llsr&filename=037/llsr037.db&recNum=67 (accessed September 6, 2007).
7. Boatner, Mark M. III, *The Civil War Dictionary*, (New York: Vintage, 1987), 901.
8. Home of Heroes, "The Purge of 1917," *HomeofHeroes.com*, http://www.homeofheroes.com/moh/corrections/purge_army.html (accessed July 20, 2009).
9. Wyllie, *Orders, Decorations, and Insignia*, 42.
10. Home of Heroes, "The Purge of 1917."
11. Wyllie, *Orders, Decorations, and Insignia*, 42.
12. Home of Heroes, "The Purge of 1917."
13. *The National Defense Act Approved June 3, 1916*, Government Printing Office, Washington, D.C., 1921.
14. Pershing, John J., *My Experiences in the World War*, (New York: Frederick A. Stokes Co., 1931), 1: 341–342.

BIBLIOGRAPHY

BOOKS

Beschloss, Michael, ed. *American Heritage Illustrated History of the Presidents*. New York: Crown, 2000.

Boatner, Mark Mayo III. *Cassell's Biographical Dictionary of the American War of Independence 1763–1783*. London: Cassel & Co., 1966.

———. *The Civil War Dictionary*. New York: Vintage, 1991.

Chambers, John Whiteclay II. *The Oxford Companion to American Military History*. New York: Oxford University Press, 1999.

Johnson, Thomas H., ed. *The Oxford Companion to American History*. New York: Oxford University Press, 1966.

Dupuy, Trevor N., Curt Johnson, and David L. Bongard. *The Harper Encyclopedia of Military Biography*. New York: Castle Books, 1992.

Goodwin, Doris Kearns. *Team of Rivals: The Political Genius of Abraham Lincoln*. New York: Simon & Schuster, 2005.

The National Defense Act Approved June 3, 1916. Washington, D.C.: Government Printing Office, 1921.

Pershing, John J. *My Experiences in the World War*. Vol. 1. New York: Frederick A. Stokes Co., 1931.

Pullen, John J. *A Shower of Stars: The Medal of Honor and the 27th Maine*. Mechanicsburg, PA: Stackpole Books, 1997.

Symonds, Craig L. *American Heritage History of the Battle of Gettysburg*. New York: HarperCollins, 2001.

Wyllie, Robert E. *Orders, Decorations, and Insignia: Military and Civil*. New York: Putnam, 1921.

Zimmerman, Dwight Jon. *First Command: Paths to Leadership*. St. Petersburg, FL: Vandamere Press, 2005.

INTERNET

Congressional Medal of Honor Society. "History of the Society." http://www.cmohs.org/society-history.php.

"History of the Navy Medal of Honor." *Jacklummus.com*. http://www.jacklummus.com/Files/Files_H/history_of_the_navy_medal_of_honor.htm.

Home of Heroes. "The Medal of Honor . . . Blessing or Burden." *HomeofHeroes.com*. http://www.homeofheroes.com/moh/history/editorial.html (accessed July 20, 2009).

———. "Navy Medals Rescinded." *HomeofHeroes.com*. http://www.homeofheroes.com/moh/corrections/purge_navy.

html (accessed July 20, 2009).
———."The Purge of 1917." *HomeofHeroes.com.*
http://www.homeofheroes.com/moh/corrections/purge_
army/html (accessed July 20, 2009).
———."Restoration of 6 Awards Previously Purged from the Roll
of Honor." *HomeofHeroes.com.*
http://www.homeofheroes.com/moh/corrections/
restorations.html (accessed July 20, 2009).
———. "Time Line of Medal of Honor History."
HomeofHeroes.com. http://www.homeofheroes.com/moh/
history/history_timeline.html (accessed July 20, 2009).
"Senate Resolution 82." Library of Congress.
http://Memory.loc.gov/cgi=bin/ampage?collld=
llsr&filename=037/llsr037.db&recNum=67.
Military Order of the Loyal Legion of the United States.
http://www.suvcw.org/mollus/mollus.htm.
Union Army Uniforms and Insignia of the Civil War.
"Medals and Decorations: Army Medal of Honor."
http://www.howardlandham.tripod.com/linkgr4/link185.html.
United States Department of Defense. "A Brief History—The
Medal of Honor."
http://www.defenselink.mil/faq/pis/med_of_honor.html.
"U.S. Army Pay/Pensions/Bounties." U.S. Army Military
History Institute. Ibiblio.org.
http://www.ibiblio.org/pub/academic/history/marshall/
military/mil_hist_inst/p/pay.asc.

3

★ ★ ★ ★ ★ ★

Jason Dunham

─────────────────────── ☆ ───────────────────────

For conspicuous gallantry and intrepidity at the risk of his life above and beyond the call of duty while serving as a Rifle Squad Leader, 4th Platoon, Company K, Third Battalion, Seventh Marines (Reinforced), Regimental Combat Team 7, First Marine Division (Reinforced), on 14 April 2004. Corporal Dunham's squad was conducting a reconnaissance mission in the town of Karabilah, Iraq, when they heard rocket-propelled grenade and small arms fire erupt approximately two kilometers to the west.

Corporal Dunham led his Combined Anti-Armor Team towards the engagement to provide fire support to their Battalion Commander's convoy, which had been ambushed as it was traveling to Camp Husaybah. As Corporal Dunham and his Marines advanced, they quickly began to receive enemy fire. Corporal Dunham ordered his squad to dismount their vehicles and led one of his fire teams on foot several blocks south of the ambush convoy. Discovering seven Iraqi vehicles in a column attempting to depart, Corporal Dunham and his team stopped the vehicles to search them for weapons. As they approached the vehicles, an insurgent leaped out and attacked Corporal Dunham. Corporal Dunham wrestled the insurgent to the ground and in the ensuing struggle saw the insurgent release a grenade. Corporal Dunham immediately alerted his fellow Marines to the threat. Aware of the imminent danger and without hesitation, Corporal Dunham covered the grenade with his helmet and body, bearing the brunt of the explosion and shielding his Marines from the blast. In an ultimate and selfless act of bravery in which he was mortally wounded, he saved the lives of at least two fellow Marines. By his undaunted courage, intrepid fighting spirit, and unwavering devotion to duty, Corporal Dunham gallantly gave his life for his country, thereby reflecting great credit upon himself and upholding the highest traditions of the Marine Corps and the United States Naval Service.

—Medal of Honor Citation, January 11, 2007

★

I'm going to do my best to do the right thing and get us back home.

—Corporal Jason Dunham, 2004

A TOWN NAMED SCIO

Jason Dunham was born on November 10, 1981, the 206th anniversary of the founding of the Marine Corps, in the one-stoplight town of Scio, New York, located in Allegany County, about eighty miles southeast of Buffalo. At the time of the 2000 census, it had a population of 1,914.

The town that became known as Scio ("sigh-oh") was settled around 1805 by Joseph Knight, who had served as a minuteman during the American Revolution. Scio took its name from the Greek island of Chios, located off the coast of Turkey. The reason for this is wrapped up in the passions of revolution and the empassioned speech of one of America's most famous orators.

In 1822, during the Greek war for independence, a revolt by Greek peasants on Chios against their Turkish rulers was brutally crushed by the Turkish army. When the suppression ended, of the approximately 120,000 Greek inhabitants of the island, roughly 100,000 had been killed, enslaved, or forced into exile.

The atrocity was brought to the attention of the American public by the freshman congressman of Boston, Daniel Webster. Though new to national politics, at the age of forty, Webster was already a famous jurist. He had successfully argued the landmark case of *Dartmouth College v. Woodworth* before the U.S. Supreme Court, upholding the constitutional protection of contracts. He was popular on the lecture circuit at a time when it was both an important form of entertainment and a primary means of gaining national prominence. Webster delivered a fiery condemnation of the 1822 slaughter on Chios to the House of Representatives. It was later published in newspapers throughout the country. Referring to the island as "Scio," the Italian version of its name, Webster detailed the island's rich culture and heritage. Then he swept into the main point of his speech: the horrors of the attack. He said in part, "[Turkish troops] entered the city and began an indiscriminate massacre. The city was fired; and in four days the fire and sword of the

Turk rendered the beautiful Scio a clotted mass of blood and ashes."[1]

Webster's speech against the "unparalleled excesses of Turkish barbarity" and his extolling of the heroic efforts of the Greeks attempting to throw off the yoke of Turkish rule seized the imagination of a young nation less than thirty years removed from having gained its own independence from a foreign power. The Turkish action was condemned by the Western nations, which provided support and assistance from such individuals as the poet Lord Byron. In a gesture of solidarity, in 1823, the pioneers living in that Allegany County community voted to change the name of their town to Scio. Such gestures of civic solidarity are not unique. In 1942, the Stern Park neighborhood of Crest Hill, Illinois, voted to rename itself Lidice to honor the Czechoslovakian town massacred and razed by Nazi troops.

A booming lumber industry and railroad access to major markets enabled Scio to reach its peak in population (3,184) and prosperity by the mid-1800s. The town's decline came as a result of devastating forest fires and an inability to replace the economic loss with other industries. Long before Jason Dunham was born, Scio had become a backwater whose citizens mostly earned their living by commuting to jobs in neighboring towns.

A BOYHOOD BROKEN—AND REPAIRED

Like Jason himself, his mother, Natalie Walker, of the nearby town of Wellsville, was the product of a broken home. Her father deserted the family when she was five years old; Natalie became pregnant with Jason at the age of sixteen. The boyfriend who got her pregnant refused to acknowledge his responsibility or help with the baby's expenses. Though many in town, including the couple that would raise Jason, were aware of the man's identity, Jason never learned the name of his biological father.

Natalie dropped out of high school, went on welfare, and found herself an apartment across from a mini-mall. Jason was five months old when Natalie met a local twenty-one-year-old, beer-drinking hell-raiser named Dan Dunham. Though Dan had a talent for getting in trouble in general and with the law in particular from time to time, he was also a good worker who had been employed for years at a local dairy farm near Scio. Instead of being scared off by the prospect of becoming an instant father, three months after they started dating Dan and Natalie got married. By the end of their first year of marriage, Natalie had given birth to a second son, Justin. But, about a year later, the marriage had begun falling apart. Soon the rift between them became too great to repair, though on one subject both Natalie and Dan were in total agreement—Dan should have custody of the boys. Dan filed for adoption of Jason, and the divorce was scheduled to occur after the adoption was finalized. The divorce judge acceded to the couple's wishes, and Dan received custody of the kids. Though Natalie had visitation rights, over the years she exercised them so rarely and maintained such little contact with her sons, even during a period when she lived only two houses away from them, that eventually she became a virtual stranger to them.

Even in the best of times, a farmhand's life is anything but easy or financially rewarding. Despite having an employer who generously augmented Dan's wages of $600 a month by allowing him and the boys to live rent free in an old farmhouse on the property, Dan literally had his hands full. But life on a farm also has its rewards, especially for two active, healthy, preschool-aged boys. While their counterparts in town were watched over by grandmothers, aunts, or paid day-care workers, Jason and Justin had cattle, horses, and other farm animals as their friends and babysitters. Fishing, camping, and endless war games filled their preschool days.

In 1986, Dan met Debra Kinkead, a home economics teacher at Scio Central School, a two-story stone Gothic-revival schoolhouse that contained the town's lower, middle, and upper schools. The occasion was anything but a date; both were chaperones for a school soccer game. Winter comes early in that part of the state, and there was snow on the ground during the match. The players at least had the advantage of physical activity to help keep them warm. Not so those standing on the sidelines, and Debra was so bundled up that the only thing Dan could see of her face was her pale blue eyes. On top of that, she was educated, had lived a prim and proper life, and was respectable—hardly a woman who would be expected to accept the affections of someone of Dan's reputation. Even so, as he was going home after the game, Dan decided he had found the woman he was going to marry.

Their courtship lasted about two years. Because her doctor had told Debra that she couldn't have children, Debra was prepared to marry into a ready-made family. Dan's drinking was another matter. It took four proposals to convince her, the final one when he was stone-cold sober in Debra's kitchen. They got married in 1988. Soon after that, they joyfully discovered that the doctor's diagnosis about

Debra was wrong. She gave birth to a son, Kyle, in 1989, and three years later to a daughter, Katie.

Jason was seven years old and in elementary school when Dan and Debra got married. Academically, Jason proved to be an indifferent student—at best, average. Where he excelled was at sports, first demonstrated with his love for basketball. Up at the crack of dawn, Jason was soon out the door. Within minutes, the rest of the family was up as well, awakened by the rat-a-tat dribbling of Jason's basketball and the clanging of it against a homemade backboard. Cannily, Debra used Jason's love of the game to teach him spelling. Playing the shooting games of HORSE and PIG with him, she substituted words from his teacher's spelling lists. And, if he wanted to watch television, she allowed it only after he read to her the program's entry in *TV Guide*.

Like many small towns, Scio took immense pride in its school athletic teams. The school's colors are blue and gold and the logo is a tiger leaping over a large *S*. Though class sizes were small—Jason's graduating class in 2000 had just thirty-seven students—the Scio Central Tigers lived up to their competitive motto, "Don't mess with the Tigers."

Jason became a three-sport athlete, playing baseball, soccer, and basketball. He was confident enough in his own abilities to compete with athletes that were better skilled and more talented. He studied opponents to learn from them and raise his own level of performance. Jason was also a natural leader, and he honed those skills on the field, encouraging teammates and practicing with them to help them develop their own skills. Over the years, Jason's athletic accomplishments were reflected in the increasing number of team championships and individual achievement trophies and plaques that adorned the walls and trophy cases of Scio Central School. Jason Dunham had become a respected team leader.

During his junior year, in a burst of school spirit, Jason decided to dye his hair blue for an important basketball game. Needless to say, when he mentioned his plan to Debra, she promptly nixed that idea. Jason seemed to acquiesce, but he decided her objection was over his using a *permanent* dye. She wouldn't forbid him using a temporary dye of food coloring—especially if she didn't know about it. Just before the game, Jason worked blue food coloring into his sandy blond hair and then joined the team on the court, where his cerulean locks promptly became the talk of the stadium. All went well until the moment when he began working up a sweat. Suddenly his face and neck became streaked with lines of blue food coloring, and Jason's "skin remained stained for days."[2] It was something for the neighbors to laugh about and for his friends and teammates to remember him by.

As distinctive as that night was, Jason's most distinguishing athletic accomplishment occurred during his senior year, in the spring of 2000. The Scio Tigers baseball team was at home playing the Bulldogs from the nearby town of Belfast. Jason, by now at his full height of six feet one, played multiple positions for the team, including pitcher, catcher, second base, shortstop, and center field. That evening he was the Tigers' catcher, but it was his offense that got all the attention. In his first at bat, Jason smashed a triple. With his second visit to the plate, he hit a double. The hot streak continued with his third at bat when he launched a long-distance fly ball that, because the outfield was fenceless, resulted in an inside-the-park home run. In his fourth time at the plate, the Bulldogs' outfielders prepared for another moon shot by retreating to about the same distance where his previous hit had landed. This time, Jason crushed the ball even deeper. It rocketed into left field, landing in front of a distant clump of trees: a second home run.

In his fifth and final at bat, the bases were loaded. As Jason stepped up to the plate, the Bulldogs' outfielders again backed up, this time even farther. Given what had happened in the previous four at bats, the smart move would have been for the manager to signal the pitcher to intentionally walk Jason, driving in only one run. Instead, the Bulldogs pitched to him. Jason launched the ball into dead center field, and the ball landed ten feet *behind* the center fielder—a grand slam inside-the-park home run. The game ended in a 22–12 victory for the Tigers. Jason concluded his high school baseball career with a .414 batting average, a Tigers record.

BECOMING A MARINE
It was in the summer of 1999, between his junior and senior years in high school, that Jason met a Marine Corps recruiter. Small towns have a tradition of sending their sons, and more recently daughters, into the military, and Scio is no different. One wall of Scio Central School contained names and photos of graduates who had answered the call of duty. Dan Dunham was an air force veteran, and he credited his time in the service with giving him the discipline he needed to make it in the adult world. Jason had another reason for looking at the military. Though not poor, the Dunhams were far from rich, and the cost of college was beyond

their means. If Jason was going to further his education, the GI Bill, which paid for college, was not just an attractive option, it was the only option. The real question then was, Which branch?

The Marine Corps has made recruiting both a science and an art, and only the best marines are selected and trained to be recruiters. It did not take the local ambassador of the corps long to convince Jason that if he wanted to be among the toughest of the tough, his one and only choice was the Marine Corps. Jason agreed to a deferred enlistment, to take place after he graduated from high school. Because he was only seventeen, he had to get written permission from his legal parents, Dan and Natalie. Though Jason and Justin had long since thought of and treated Debra as their mother, she had never formally adopted them. Dan was happy to sign the forms, and then it was up to Natalie. When Jason and the marine recruiter approached her at the hardware store in nearby Wellsville where she worked, she pointedly questioned whether or not he was certain this was what he wanted to do. It was an extremely uncomfortable moment for him because he resented her attitude and the unspoken implication that he was not qualified to make this decision about his own life. Not wanting to lose his temper in front of the recruiter, Jason replied simply, "Yep—this is what I'm going to do."[3] Natalie signed the permission form.

On July 31, 2000, Jason Dunham reported to the military entrance processing station in Buffalo, New York. The following day he found himself one of a busload of recruits traveling over the 2.3-mile causeway that straddled the tidal swamps of Archer Creek and delivered them at night—always at night—to the place that for the next eleven weeks would be their home, the Marine Corps recruit depot, Parris Island, South Carolina.

As part of a platoon of sixty-three and as one of approximately 4,300 recruits during that training period, Jason went through the challenging mental and physical regimen designed to transform civilians into marines. Not all can or do complete the training. The attrition rate averages about 14 percent, with the majority of recruits dropping out in the first week and many of those opting out during the initial twenty-four hours. The climax of the training is a fifty-four-hour endurance test known as The Crucible, or The Crucible Event, described on the Parris Island Web site as "A Rite of Passage for all Marines."[4]

General Charles Krulak, the thirty-first commandant of the Marine Corps (1995–1999), called The Crucible: "a final gut check, a challenge, to see how badly [recruits] want to become Marines."[5] It "is a physically and mentally challenging event that involves food and sleep deprivation and the completion of various obstacles for the potential Marine to negotiate."[6] Allowed a maximum of four hours of sleep a night and only a total of three MREs (meals, ready to eat), recruits travel at a frenetic pace to complete the forty-eight-mile course over rugged terrain, on foot and regardless of weather conditions. Along the way, they must successfully complete twenty-nine problem-solving exercises and overcome the additional physical and mental challenges presented in thirty-six different "warrior stations." The course includes natural terrain obstacles such as flooded streams and swamps, pugil-stick fighting arenas, and battlefield defenses such as simulated minefields and barbed-wire entanglements, among other features. It is a grueling test that can only be successfully completed by recruits working together. Each of the thirty-six warrior stations is named after a marine Medal of Honor recipient. And at each station, a drill instructor is there, loudly declaiming that recipient's deeds and challenging the recruits to perform up to expectations that would make them worthy to wear the same uniform as the marine whose name graces that station.

In November 2000, Jason Dunham was among the group of survivors who proudly stood at attention on the main parade deck in the graduation area at Parris Island, and he officially became a private in the United States Marine Corps.

Following leave, Jason was stationed at the U.S. Naval Submarine Base Kings Bay in Camden County, in the southeast corner of Georgia, where he served as a guard in the Marine Security Force Battalion. During Operation Iraqi Freedom, in the spring of 2003, he transferred to the infantry and was sent to Twentynine Palms, California, the Marine Corps's largest base in the world and premier training facility. There he underwent additional training as a machine gunner. When the Third Battalion, Seventh Marines, returned from its tour of duty in Iraq to its home base of Twentynine Palms in September of that year, Jason was assigned to its Kilo Company. Two months later, the battalion was informed that it would be returning for a second tour of duty in Iraq, commencing in March 2004.

OPERATION IRAQI FREEDOM II

In November 2003, Major General James Mattis, commander of the First Marine Division, informed his troops that the division was returning to Iraq as part of Operation

Iraqi Freedom II, the second year of operations in the country. During what is now known as Operation Iraqi Freedom I, the division had been part of a two-prong advance from the south to Baghdad. Now, instead of operating in an area dominated by Shiite Muslims, the majority of the Iraqi population, they would be stationed in the populous region northwest of Baghdad primarily inhabited by Sunni Muslims and known as the Sunni Triangle. The marines would be relieving the Army's Eighty-second Airborne Division operating in al Anbar province. Iraq's largest province by territory, al Anbar begins just west of Baghdad and abuts the borders of Saudi Arabia, Jordan, and Syria. Its largest cities are Fallujah and Ramadi, located in the eastern section of the province on the Euphrates River.

In mid-December 2003, Mattis called a staff conference to discuss the transition with the Eighty-second Airborne and how the marines would act in the area of operations. Senior commanders in the corps had been close observers of events in Iraq after the fall of Baghdad. They were concerned about the chaotic and heavy-handed methods of reconstruction and pacification used by the Coalition Provisional Authority chief, L. Paul Bremer III, and the overall military commander, Army Lieutenant General Ricardo Sanchez. Particularly troubling was the rise of insurgent activity everywhere except in the north, the home of the ethnic Kurds. As much as possible, Mattis wanted to avoid repeating mistakes that were adding to the tension.

Mattis and his staff noted that the Eighty-second Airborne was using what was described as a "get tough"[7] policy in the Sunni Triangle. This included the sealing off of entire suspect villages with barbed wire, random searches of houses and

Corporal Jason Dunham's official Marine Corps
photograph together with several mementoes from
his service in the Corps.
Photo: *Staff Sgt. Scott Dunn*

businesses, destruction of neighborhoods believed to be havens for insurgents with bombs and artillery, and the burning of orchards.

Mattis was determined to take a different, more culturally sensitive approach, one patterned after the Marine Corps's Combined Action Platoon (CAP) program of the Vietnam War, one of the few American success stories during that conflict. Under CAP, small units of up to twelve marines were imbedded in a village, freely interacting with the populace and working side by side with the local police or militia to assist and train them. The program was designed to build trust, protect the local residents so that they could rebuild their village and go on with their lives, and train the local security forces to the point where they were self-sufficient.

As in Vietnam, the key to its success would be winning over the local civilians. Mattis told his staff, "Both the insurgency and the military force are competing for the same thing: the support of the people." And with regard to the insurgents themselves, Mattis was firm: "There is only one 'retirement plan' for terrorists."[8] Mattis's staff prepared a list of what the marines of the First Division needed to know and instructions for responding to likely situations. The list was wide-ranging, covering things big and small. Particular emphasis was paid to the Iraqi sense of honor, a complex subject easily misunderstood. For instance, there are times when a lie is less a denial of a truth, especially when the truth is clearly known by all parties, than it is a statement that enables a family to preserve its honor even as it is surrendering to authority.[9]

New protocols were created that respected this sense of honor while allowing the men to perform their duties.

Instead of surprise raids that began with the sudden kicking down of a door, the forcible rounding up and cuffing of all male members, and furniture-busting ransack searches that had been the norm, the marines would act with respect and deference to the head of a family. Even when incriminating items were discovered, the leader of the household would be given an opportunity to speak with his family before being escorted out of the house in cuffs. Under prior protocols, he would have been summarily thrown to the floor, a gun to his head, cuffed, and then forcibly removed—all in full view of the family and neighborhood.

Mattis sent three mass e-mails to his officers before the division's deployment, totaling more than one thousand pages, that culled commentaries and news articles about insurgencies. This was on top of having them reread the Marine Corps's classic work on the subject, the *Small Wars Manual*. One important work he included was "27 Articles" by the British officer T. E. Lawrence, commonly known as Lawrence of Arabia. This list of observations and instructions was the condensation of Lawrence's experience leading and fighting with Arabs during World War I. Perhaps the most important of them was article 15, which states: "Do not try to do too much with your own hands. Better the Arabs do it tolerably than you do it perfectly. It is their war, and you are to help them, not to win it for them. Actually, also, under the very odd conditions of Arabia, your practical work will not be as good, perhaps, as you think it is."[10]

Finally, Mattis visited each battalion in the division at least three times. His speeches were designed to brief his troops on what they could expect in their new area of operations—all the situations, the drudgery, and the terror. They would have to contend with being attacked by ambush and seeing buddies killed or maimed one day, and then have to interact with Iraqi civilians with respect, and without hostility, the next. His overarching message to his troops was: "Iraqis aren't your enemy, don't let the insurgents make you think that. *The people are the prize.*"[11]

Defense Intelligence Agency analysts gave Mattis's plan high marks, as did army military police officers with recent experience in Iraq, and advisors to Bremer's Coalition Provisional Authority who felt that the existing approach was counterproductive. At the same time, some expressed skepticism that an Iraqi version of the CAP would work in the Sunni Triangle. Their doubts were based on two realities: a hostile local population and undependable local security forces. With roughly 40 percent of the population, the Sunnis constituted the largest minority in the country. Under Saddam Hussein, they had controlled all political power in Iraq. After Saddam's overthrow, the tables had turned. Now the Shiites and the Kurds held the political reins, and the Sunnis resented being on the receiving end of the slights and abuses of power they had once meted out. Marines would have their hands full.

The First Marine Division arrived in Iraq in February 2004, part of the wholesale troop rotation that initiated Operation Iraqi Freedom II. This countrywide rotation of troops in Iraq went ahead with few disruptions. In fact, insurgent activity all but halted. This lulled the senior commanders into believing that the pacification program was working. But the insurgents hadn't given up. Ahmed Hashim, a professor of strategic studies at the U.S. Naval War College observes that, according to the harsh Darwinian world of combat, "American forces had killed most of the incompetent ones; the tactics, techniques, and procedures of the surviving insurgents became more lethal as a result of experience."[12] The survivors were simply biding their time, waiting for the right moment to strike.

WEST TO AL QA'IM AND HUSAYBAH

The Third Battalion's task was to reduce or stop the flow of insurgents across the porous Iraq-Syria border. Battalion

A night patrol in Iraq as seen through night vision goggles.
Photo: *Department of Defense*

commander Lieutenant Colonel Matt Lopez established the main base for his nine hundred marines beside the rail yards in Al Qa'im. Located on the Euphrates River, about twenty miles from the Syrian border, Al Qa'im had a population of about 250,000 and was an important transit station for insurgents coming from Syria.

For most of March, Corporal Jason Dunham found himself part of a forward operating force assigned to the border town of Husaybah, a key entry point for the insurgents. His new home away from home that his platoon shared with another company was Camp Husaybah, a fortified compound located between the city and the border, just south of the main highway going into Syria. Husaybah had a population of about 100,000 and, like Al Qa'im, was located on the Euphrates River.

Corporal Dunham joined 3-7's Kilo Company in September 2003, after the battalion had rotated back to the States, making this his first deployment. In the unstated pecking order that is an extension of the formal hierarchy of rank, this put him at the bottom among his fellow noncommissioned officers, for whom it was their second deployment, and made him a target for some of the petty harassment "head games" that typically come with the territory. But unlike others in the same situation—particularly the new privates sarcastically referred to as Boots—he encountered little of it, and what he did he accepted with good grace. Dunham's attitude was that things were tough enough at Camp Husaybah, there was no need to make life worse.

The Marine Corps gives a lot of authority to its corporals, but only after they've been properly trained. The success of the Corps's method was observed by the journalist Thomas

E. Ricks. In December 1992, Ricks, then a reporter for *The Wall Street Journal*, was with a squad of marines on night patrol in Mogadishu, where eleven months later the dramatic incident recounted in Mark Bowden's book (and the subsequent movie) *Black Hawk Down*, would occur. Ricks wrote that, as they were walking through the dark and dangerous streets, "I realized that I had placed my life in the hands of the young corporal leading the patrol, a twenty-two-year-old Marine. In my office back in Washington, we wouldn't let a twenty-two-year-old run the copying machine without adult supervision. Here, after just two days on the ground in Africa, the corporal was leading his squad into unknown territory, with a confidence that was contagious."[13]

Despite his inexperience and youth, the twenty-two-year-old Jason Dunham had already displayed the qualities the Marine Corps most values. His quiet, confident leadership had made a strong impression among his peers. And the care he showed for the welfare of his squad of marines, particularly his protection of them from the occasional hazing, and his willingness to participate in the sweaty drudgery of securing the camp gained him the respect and admiration of his men. Shortly after they arrived at Camp Husaybah, Dunham's squad was tasked with helping fortify it against mortar and car-bomb attack. This meant filling sandbags and blast walls called HESCO barriers, so named after the manufacturer, Hercules Engineering Solutions Consortium. These were collapsible, welded-mesh, interlocking steel containers ranging in height from three to six feet and up to thirty-three feet long. Once in place, engineers used front-end loaders and backhoes to fill them with sand. Typically they were stacked two high and topped with concertina wire. Instead of just overseeing the work, Corporal Dunham pitched in during the week it took to set up the blast walls. His willingness to do the grunt work to get the job done was not lost on his men.

He was not trying to earn points with people—Jason Dunham just wanted to be a good marine. In a freshman composition class he took while attending Copper Mountain College, a community college in Twentynine Palms, he wrote that a good marine leads by example and "understands that people make mistakes, and that there are some things that really seem not to make much sense therefore he doesn't pressure his Marines to completely abide by them." Even though his superior position required him to keep some distance from the marines in his command, at the same time he observed, "How are your Marines supposed to trust you if they know nothing about you aside [from] work?"[14] At one point, shortly after they had taken over Camp Husaybah, Dunham gathered his men around him and said, "For you guys who were here last year, good on you. But I'm going to do my best to do the right thing and get us back home. If you see me slipping, let me know."[15]

Lieutenant Brian Robinson had become the commander of Dunham's platoon just two days before its deployment to Iraq and was still in the process of getting to know his men. Shortly after they arrived at Camp Husaybah, he found himself "talking shop" with Corporal Dunham in the warehouse that served as their barracks. The discussion was lively and at times included comments from nearby marines adding their own two cents' worth. The tone was serious but casual, in the same way one would talk about the performance specs and virtues of one car over those of another. The topic was the best response in dealing with an incoming hand grenade. This is something of a chestnut among marines, if for no other reason than it is one of the few things for which the Marine Corps has *not* published a manual.

Dunham told Robinson he believed that if one managed to cover the grenade with his "Fritz" helmet (so named for its resemblance to the World War II German helmet) the bullet-resistant Kevlar material inside would contain the blast. Recalling one of his courses shortly after his commissioning, in which he saw photos of Fritz helmets perforated by bullets fired from an AK-47 at close range, the lieutenant shook his head. He said that the ceramic plates of their SAPI (small-arms protective insert) body-armor vests offered better protection. The discussion went back and forth, with Dunham finally asking, "What about the helmet *and* the SAPI plate?"

Thirty-year-old Staff Sergeant John Ferguson, the senior noncom in the platoon and a veteran of operations in Somalia and Kuwait, replied, "It would increase your chance of surviving, but I don't think it would work."

Dunham replied, "I think it would work."[16] Dunham was perhaps correct in theory. But the reality of combat rarely leaves a soldier with the time or in a circumstance to best apply a theory.

The month of March became a routine of patrols. Some, particularly when improvised explosive devices (IEDs) were discovered or set off, were eventful. The IEDs, placed along a roadside and remotely detonated, were a serious threat to vehicles and marines on foot. Even those days in which nothing happened were tense. Camp Husaybah was a refuge of only relative safety. Periodically, insurgents would fire mortars or rocket-propelled grenades (RPGs) at the base.

Typically, these attacks were isolated and involved the launching of a single mortar or RPG round, with the shooter leaving before the source of the attack could be determined. But the marines had not forgotten the lesson of Beruit. In 1983, during the Lebanese civil war, a suicide truck bomber had succeeded in entering the lightly guarded military compound housing American and French forces. Two hundred and twenty marines were killed when the truck bomb exploded. Since then, marines make sure that any base they establish will be as well protected as possible. Thanks to the HESCO blast walls, the harassing fire caused little damage. Inevitably some marines were wounded, but none were killed.

LOSING THE "OTHER WAR" OF HEARTS AND MINDS

For the marines, the situation in al Anbar Province was dangerous and frustrating as the days and weeks went by and no real headway was made. One aspect of the CAP program was to have platoon-sized units assigned to the local police station to work with members of the Iraqi police force and civil-defense corps and help them on patrols—a combined show of force designed to demonstrate that the marines were not going to abandon the civilian population to the insurgents. All the members of the security forces were carryovers from the Saddam Hussein regime and had undergone a reeducation and reorientation program before returning to their old jobs. Despite this, the marines were never sure whom they could trust and who was an informant for the insurgents. The civilian population was equally difficult to read. Sometimes they were friendly, other times reticent—but one was never sure if the reticence was caused by fear or hatred. The actual reason pointed out the depth of failure in the postinvasion program of reconstruction.

David Dunford, a retired foreign service officer who assisted in the creation of a new Iraqi foreign affairs ministry later said, "Iraqis became disappointed. Each Iraqi owed it to himself and his family to decide whether it made more sense to cooperate with us or to cooperate with somebody else, the insurgents." Dunford ruefully added that "because of our incompetence"[17] more and more Iraqis during this period decided to throw their lot in with the insurgents. Because of circumstances outside his control, Major General James Mattis's nation-building program never had a chance.

The first major sign that things were about to go violently wrong occurred in the east. Fallujah, with an estimated twenty thousand insurgents, had become a major center of anti-Coalition activity. On March 27, 2004, marines found themselves locked in a series of firefights throughout the city that lasted thirty-six hours, leaving an estimated fifteen Iraqis dead. The death blow to Mattis's CAP program occurred on March 31. For reasons that continue to remain unclear, two SUVs containing four contractors from the private Blackwater security company drove into a well-prepared ambush. Their SUVs were destroyed by AK-47 and RPG fire; they were dragged from their vehicles, killed, and dismembered. Two torsos were hung from a bridge before being tossed onto a pile of burning tires. One of the bloodiest months of the conflict was about to begin.

Initially, the explosive situation in the east did not significantly impact the 3-7's area of operations in the west. Though the environment remained dangerous, there was no sudden rise in attacks. At the end of March, Lieutenant Robinson's platoon returned to Al Qa'im, and for about ten days, Dunham and his squad of nine men found themselves on a "vacation"—guard duty of a restricted corner of the base occupied by the CIA and the Army Special Forces. With no officers or senior noncoms looking over their shoulders, Dunham and his marines enjoyed eating a higher grade of chow and rubbing shoulders with the spooks and special operations troops.

Meanwhile, Mattis was being pushed hard by Washington to organize a major campaign to wipe out the insurgents in Fallujah. In the words of the deputy director of operations, U.S. Army Brigadier General Mark Kimmitt, the response needed to be "overwhelming."[18] Mattis preferred a lower-level effort better designed for the asymmetric war he and his marines had been experiencing. But, acceding to the prodding, he issued attack orders that said, in part, that the marines were to "capture/kill the murderers of the coalition contractors while conducting offensive operations . . . to restore law and order and build long-term stability."[19] Launched on April 5, Operation Vigilant Justice was a conventional warfare-style combined air, armor, and infantry attack. Though more famously known as the First Battle of Fallujah because the main effort was in that city, it included operations throughout al Anbar province. The Iraqi army units in the area refused to assist the coalition troops, stating, "We did not sign up to fight Iraqis."[20] It was a sign of bad days ahead.

The marines established a cordon around Fallujah and then moved into the city, determined to find and destroy the estimated twenty thousand insurgents based there. The insurgents proved better prepared and trained than the troops expected, and fighting was heavy. On April 8, after just three days, Mattis suddenly received orders from Washington to suspend operations and implement a cease-fire. Washington had misread international response, and the Iraqi Governing Council demanded the campaign cease. The consequences of the stop order were enormous. Prestige of the insurgents, who were viewed in the Arab world as the victors of the battle, skyrocketed. Its impact in western Iraq was felt that same day.

ACTIVITY IN THE WEST

On April 8, marine squads and platoons on foot patrol in Husaybah found themselves encountering coordinated ambushes in which IEDs placed along a route would be triggered at the moment when marines or their vehicles passed near it; an indication that the triggerman was in visual contact with the patrol. In one of those patrols, on Market Street, the commercial center of town, a platoon led by Lieutenant Brad Watson had been ambushed by IEDs while it was handing out toys and soccer balls to kids and announcing over a loudspeaker a message in Arabic about a new curfew. The platoon suffered one dead and six wounded, two so severely they later had to be medically discharged from the Marine Corps. The next day, Marine Corps M1 tank reinforcements arrived in the area for the first time.

Dunham's guard duty ended on April 10. Upon his return to the company's warehouse barracks, he saw that his squad was assigned a mission for the morning of April 14 around the newly renovated police station in the nearby village of Karabilah.

Karabilah is a narrow strip of buildings and farmland located on the eastern edge of Husaybah. April 14 was going to be a busy day for marines in and around the village. Lieutenant Watson, who had been lightly wounded in the April 8 IED explosion, was concerned about the routine the marine patrols had settled into: regardless of the time of day, they all started and ended at Camp Husaybah. He wanted to shake things up by running marine patrols from a different location. While recovering in the field hospital, he formed a plan that would take his thirty-eight marines to a place they called the Crackhouse. An abandoned three-story building on the other side of the city adjoining Karabilah, it had been used at various times by the insurgents. After securing it, Watson would use it as a daytime forward operating base for his patrols, with an observation post on the roof. His company commander, Captain Richard Gannon II, approved the plan and added to it two two-man sniper teams that would establish observation posts in neighboring buildings for additional support. Watson's plan would go into effect on April 14.

But the big event of that day was a visit by Lieutenant Colonel Lopez, the battalion commander. Lopez, leading a convoy of six Humvees and twenty-five marines, was to meet a local contractor hired to renovate the Karabilah police station to see if it had been completed to his specifications. If it was, Lopez planned to give the contractor the agreed-upon price of $70,000 cash. There he would also meet Dunham and his squad, who would inspect the station's suitability as a base of operations for Kilo Company and do a short patrol. Lopez would continue on with the Iraqi police chief to the new Husaybah police station for a

An example of the type of weapons caches found by marines during their patrols. RPG rounds are visible on the ground, wrapped in plastic, and in a pouch leaning against the wall.
Photo: *Department of Defense*

spot inspection to see if the Iraqi police were actually doing what they were supposed to.

As the April 14 date approached, Sergeant Tom Hendricks, a member of Dunham's platoon, became more and more concerned about the convoy mission. Too many people—too many Iraqis—knew about Lopez's convoy and the route it would be taking. Hendricks was convinced that at least one of the locals was an informant and that at some point they'd be ambushed. On the evening of April 13, he opened his journal and wrote, "Almost guaranteed action. Well, if this is my last entry because we get hit . . . it's been fun. Goodnight."[21]

HUSAYBAH, WEDNESDAY, APRIL 14, 2004

Watson and his platoon, together with the sniper teams, drove up to the Crackhouse in their Humvees at about 8:00 A.M. The marines then split up for their assigned duties that day. Some squads began their patrols. Two fire teams of four men each left with the sniper teams, a necessary precaution in a hostile urban environment where passing unnoticed was impossible. Watson led the rest of the marines into the Crackhouse to begin the process of searching and securing it. A little after 9:00 A.M., Watson; Corporal Daniel Lightfoot, the squad leader; and Lance Corporal Kevin Roshak, the platoon's radio operator, emerged onto the roof of the building. As Roshak began taking photos of the roof and surrounding streets for the company's intelligence files, Watson saw a large pile of scrap lumber, about three feet high, off to one side. Watson had been in Iraq long enough to know that such piles were common sights; the roofs of Iraqi homes are generally flat and make handy storage places. Leftover pieces of lumber were typically used as firewood and stored on rooftops. Paying no attention to it, he began mentally reviewing the day's operation. Then seeing that Roshak had completed his picture taking and had taken off his radio backpack, he strode over to establish radio contact with company headquarters at Camp Husaybah.

Hidden beneath the pile of wood was a 155mm artillery shell wired with a remote-controlled electronic detonator. At 9:33 A.M., the IED exploded. The noise ruptured Watson's eardrums, and the concussion almost knocked him off the roof. Shrapnel tore into Corporal Lightfoot's left foot. Lance Corporal Roshak felt something hit him in the shoulder. But it was the second wound that got everybody's attention—a wedge-shaped, nail-studded length of two-by-four, about nine inches long, had penetrated his neck and lodged itself below his left ear. One of the platoon's medics, Hospitalman Third Class Tivey Mathews, was inside the building when the explosion occurred. Worried that the two-by-four might have pierced an artery or vein, Mathews decided the best thing was to secure it in place, which he did with a wrapping of gauze bandages.

As this was going on, a firefight erupted. The detonation of the woodpile appeared to be a signal, and suddenly the marines in the area began taking heavy fire from insurgents. The Battle of Karabilah had begun.

Meanwhile, Lieutenant Colonel Lopez and his convoy, together with most of Kilo Company, including Corporal Dunham and his squad, arrived at the Karabilah police station. They were inevitably met by a cluster of young boys who typically gathered for handouts. For some reason, the contractor failed to show up, so Lopez met with the local Iraqi police chief. Dunham and his men checked out the building and its suitability for combined marine and Iraqi security-force patrols. Everything seemed in order. At one point during their stay at the station, Lopez began receiving radio reports of the firefight at the Crackhouse, news of which quickly spread to the rest of the marines. The fate of Watson's platoon was much on Lopez's mind when he emerged from the building and prepared to lead his convoy into Husaybah. Lopez and the convoy's commander, Major Ezra Carbins, suspected that the Husaybah police chief was an ally of the insurgents. Just before they were about to drive off, the major told the police chief to take a different route to the Husaybah police station, one that had not been discussed. With the police chief's vehicle in the lead, the convoy got onto the main highway into Husaybah, code-named Jade.

The route change didn't make any difference. Shortly after the convoy entered Route Jade, a group of green and red Roman-candle bursts rose into the sky. At 12:15 P.M., the convoy reached a traffic circle and was hit by a barrage of RPG and AK-47 fire. The convoy had entered a well-laid ambush. The police chief's vehicle had vanished.

GRENADE

Earlier, Dunham and the other marines at the Karabilah police station had become concerned. The small crowd of kids seeking handouts had abruptly vanished, a sure warning sign of danger. In addition to the sounds of RPGs and AK-47s, they also began hearing mortar-round explosions coming from the Crackhouse area southwest of them. Shortly after Lopez and the convoy had left, Captain Trent Gibson ordered his men to split into teams; spread out; take different, parallel streets; and begin working their way south and west in a step pattern that would eventually take them to the Crackhouse. This expanded the area of their patrol but kept them close enough to provide support in the event they encountered insurgents. But the maneuver required a high degree of coordination and excellent radio contact. Radio transmissions kept breaking up, and there were periods when the teams were out of touch with one another for up to ten minutes.

Corporal Dunham and Sergeant Ferguson were part of a team that was leapfrogging its way south down a dusty, unpaved road bordered by half-finished cinderblock homes and empty lots surrounded by yellow-tan stone walls. Alert to danger, for several blocks they encountered nothing more threatening than a stalled bus that some Iraqi men were trying to get started. Just before 12:20 P.M., they reached a T-junction in the road, where they encountered a row of eight vehicles, including a small bus, a van, a white Toyota Land Cruiser, another SUV of a different make, a red tractor, a black BMW sedan, a white truck that had stopped in the middle in an attempt to do a U-turn, and a white sedan with all four doors open.

The team's point man, Private First Class Kelly Miller, paused at the sight as soon as he emerged at the junction. He was soon met by Dunham and Sergeant Ferguson. A short discussion ensued. Dunham wanted to continue their patrol. But earlier, at the Karabilah police station, another sergeant had told Ferguson that he had seen a white SUV suspiciously speed off down the road. It was a well-known fact that white SUVs, particularly white Toyota Land Cruisers, were so common in Iraq that they were practically the national vehicle. But there was something about this group of vehicles, perhaps the size of the group, perhaps the presence of the BMW in this run-down neighborhood, that aroused Ferguson's suspicions. "We're going to search these cars," he said.

The marines spread out and quickly advanced toward the group. Miller and Dunham teamed up to search the third vehicle in the line, the Toyota Land Cruiser. Sitting behind the wheel was a young Iraqi male wearing a black track suit. While Dunham covered the driver side, Miller advanced along the passenger side. When he got close, he saw poking out from beneath a floor mat the muzzle and wood front grip of an AK-47. Just then the driver threw open the door and attacked Dunham. The two fell to the ground, fighting.

As soon as Miller saw the Iraqi lunge toward the corporal, he started running around to help. As he did so, he reached for a collapsible police baton that his brother—a deputy sheriff back in the States—had sent him. Snapping it to full extension, he arrived to see the two still struggling, with Dunham on top of the Iraqi. Bracing himself with his left hand on the corporal's back, Miller hit the Iraqi's forehead as hard as he could with the butt of the baton. Amazingly, the Iraqi continued fighting, and Miller tried to jam the baton against the Iraqi's neck in an attempt to pinch off blood flow through the carotid artery.

As this was going on, Lance Corporal Bill Hampton rushed up. He raised his M16, hoping to get in a shot, but the three were moving around so much Hampton was afraid he'd shoot Dunham or Miller.

Suddenly the marines heard Dunham shout, "No, no,

no—watch his hand!"[22] The next thing Hampton knew, Dunham's helmet was off, and Dunham appeared to be shoving it onto something. It was a grenade, and the firing pin had been pulled.

The British-made Mills bomb exploded an instant later. Shrapnel from the pineapple-design hand grenade hit Hampton in the face, leg, and arm. Miller was knocked onto his back, with shrapnel wounds on his face and other parts of his body. Dunham was lying facedown on the ground, a pool of blood expanding around his head. The Iraqi, wounded in the left arm, staggered up and tried to dash down the street. Lance Corporal Jason Sanders, the team's radio operator, thinking that all four were dead, was momentarily stunned to see a "dead" man suddenly leap up and start running away. But the Iraqi had taken no more than three steps when Sanders snapped out of it and fired his M16 at the Iraqi's legs. The Iraqi fell to the ground. In pain, he continued to crawl away. Sanders then let loose a long burst that "walked" up the Iraqi's body, killing him.

The area was a whirlwind of activity as some marines tended to the wounded and others set up a perimeter to defend against any further attack. Sanders got on the radio and called for "any corpsman," stating his location and that they had three wounded, "one that's pretty bad."[23]

By this time, the firefight at the Crackhouse had ended, and one of the medics there, Hospitalman Third Class Joseph Lynott, answered the call in a Humvee gun truck, a heavy-duty Humvee equipped with .50-caliber machine guns. Lynott saw that Dunham had a serious head wound and no other apparent injuries. By the time he got Dunham stabilized, two additional Humvee gun trucks arrived. Dunham was quickly loaded into one of the Humvees, and with the other two gun trucks as escort, they made a two-mile high-speed dash to the helicopter pad at Camp Husaybah.

For the next four days, medical teams fought to save Jason Dunham's life. First at Camp Husaybah; then at the battalion hospital at Al Qa'im; then at the large Coalition medical facility at Al Asad, about 110 miles west of Baghdad; then in Baghdad itself; then at the army's Landstuhl Regional Medical Center in Germany; and finally, on April 18, at the National Naval Medical Center in Bethesda, Maryland.

Dan and Deb Dunham were notified within hours of their son's injuries. When word got out to the community, collections were taken to help pay for travel expenses. Dan and Deb arrived in Washington, D.C., on April 21 and took up rooms at the Fisher House, a colonial-style brick home set aside for families whose loved ones are being treated. The next day they had a meeting with the doctors who had been treating their son. The prognosis was the most wrenching that a parent can receive. Jason's brain had been so damaged that there was virtually no chance for recovery. The only thing keeping him alive was life support. The two were then left alone.

The Dunhams had with them a copy of Jason's living will, in which Jason requested that he be taken off life support should he be in the situation that he was now in. They knew what they had to do, but before they gave the doctors their permission, they spent a few hours alone with their thoughts, then spoke with Navy Command Master Chief Jim Piner and his wife, Sarah, who lived beside the Fisher House and had taken the couple under their wing. Finally, having composed themselves, they returned to Bethesda and told the doctors to take Jason off life support. One of the doctors, Lieutenant Colonel Jim Byrne, then asked if they wanted Jason to immediately receive the Purple Heart. Deb promptly said that they did.

Every time a marine was wounded or killed during this period, Marine Corps Commandant General Michael Hagee received a report of it. When notified that Jason's parents were taking him off life support and that they had requested he receive the Purple Heart before that happened, he decided to skip his scheduled meeting with the Joint Chiefs of Staff. Instead, he appeared at Jason Dunham's hospital room where he met with Dan and Deb and, in a brief and solemn ceremony, pinned the Purple Heart, the nation's medal for soldiers wounded in combat, onto Jason's pillow.

At 4:43 P.M., on April 22, 2004, Corporal Jason Dunham breathed his last breath.

HONORS

More than fifteen hundred people, almost the entire town of Scio, filled the gymnasium of Scio Central School for Jason Dunham's memorial service on a rain-swept May 1. When the funeral procession reached Fairlawn Cemetery, the clouds parted. A seven-man U.S. Marine honor guard gave a twenty-one-gun salute, and a bugler played "Taps." The flag that covered Jason's coffin was folded into a triangle and given to Dan. Tucked in each corner was the brass casing of a shell that had been fired in salute.

Other honors followed. On March 14, 2006, the Scio post

In May 2009, Secretary of Defense Robert M. Gates (middle, white shirt) posed with some members of the crew of the guided-missile destroyer *Jason Dunham* (DDG-109) under construction at the Bath Iron Works in Maine.
Photo: *Department of Defense, Master Sergeant Jerry Morrison, U.S. Air Force*

office was officially renamed the Corporal Jason Dunham Post Office. Then, in March 2007, the Navy announced that one of its new *Arleigh Burke*-class guided-missile destroyers would be christened the USS *Jason Dunham*. In April, the Marine Corps security force barracks at the U.S. Naval Submarine Base Kings Bay, Georgia, where Jason had been stationed early in his career, announced it would now bear his name.

On August 17, 2007, a thirty-seventh ground-fighting-technique warrior station was added to The Crucible event at Parris Island. It is named Dunham's Defense.

The act of throwing one's body on a live grenade to save those nearby is almost a marine cliché. At least seven such acts during the battle for Iwo Jima in 1945 earned posthumous awards of the Medal of Honor.[24] But no marine had been awarded the medal since 1970, when it was given for actions above and beyond the call of duty in Vietnam. Now Jason Dunham's act of uncommon valor in Iraq has been similarly recognized.

Two weeks after his death, Dunham was remembered at Camp Al Qa'im in Iraq by Corporal Mark E. Dean of Kilo Company, Third Battalion, Seventh Marine Regiment—a brother in arms. Corporal Dean said, "God made something special when he made Jason. It was a privilege and honor to know him. It's sad he is gone, but he is living it up in heaven, and I'm happy for that."[25]

NOTES

1. Whipple, Edwin P., *The Great Speeches and Orations of Daniel Webster with an Essay on Daniel Webster as a Master of English Style,* (Boston: Little, Brown, 1889), 73.

2. Phillips, Michael M., *The Gift of Valor: A War Story,* (New York: Broadway Books, 2005), 41.
3. Ibid, 45.
4. Marine Corps Recruit Depot, Parris Island, "The Crucible," http://www.mcrdpi.usmc.mil/training/crucible/index.asp (accessed July 15, 2009).
5. Perry, Tony, "Putting Marines through a 'Crucible,'" *Los Angeles Times,* March 7, 1998, http://www.articles.latimes.com/1998/mar/07/news/mn-26377?pg=3 (accessed July 15, 2009).
6. Marine Corps Recruit Depot, "The Crucible."
7. Ricks, Thomas E., *Fiasco: The American Military Adventure in Iraq,* (New York: Penguin, 2006), 312.
8. Ibid, 315.
9. Ibid, 314.
10. Ibid, 318.
11. Ibid, 318.
12. Ibid, 322.
13. Ricks, Thomas E., *Making the Corps,* (New York: Scribner, 1997),
14. Phillips, *The Gift of Valor,* 15-16.
15. Ibid, 13.
16. Ibid, 4-5.
17. Ricks, *Fiasco,* 325–326.
18. *CNN.com,* "U.S. Army: 'We Will Respond' to Contractor Killings," April 1, 2004, http://www.cnn.com/2004/WORLD/meast/04/01/iraq.main/ (accessed July 31, 2009).
19. Ricks, *Fiasco,* 343.
20. Ibid, 339.
21. Phillips, *The Gift of Valor,* 76.
22. Ibid, 108.
23. Ibid, 114.
24. A complete list of Iwo Jima Medal of Honor recipients can be found on Wikipedia, http://en.wikipedia.org/wiki/List_of_Medal_of_Honor_recipients_for_the_Battle_of_Iwo_Jima.
25. *USA Patriotism!,* "Marine Corporal Jason Dunham," http://www.usa-patriotism.com/heroes/fallen/Jason_dunham1.htm (accessed July 27, 2009).

BIBLIOGRAPHY

BOOKS

Phillips, Michael M. *The Gift of Valor: A War Story*. New York: Broadway Books, 2005.

Ricks, Thomas E. *Fiasco: The American Military Adventure in Iraq*. New York: Penguin, 2006.

——. *Making the Corps*. New York: Scribner. 1997.

MONOGRAPHS

Hoffman, Frank G. "Changing Tires on the Fly: The Marines and Postconflict Stability Ops." Philadelphia: Foreign Policy Research Institute, 2006. http://www.fpri.org/books/Hoffman.ChangingTiresonthe Fly.pdf (accessed July 31, 2009).

United States Army National Ground Intelligence Center. "Complex Environments: Battle of Fallujah I, April 2004." http://www.comw.org/warreport/fulltext/0801fallujah.pdf (accessed July 31, 2009).

INTERNET

"Honor the Fallen: Operation Iraqi Freedom and Operation Enduring Freedom Casualties." *Military Times*. http://www.militarycity.com/valor/honor_april_2004.html (accessed July 26, 2009).

Lima/37. "Chapter 7: Training and Deployment for Husaybah." *From Desert Mech to Ramadi SWAT*. http://lima37.com/blog/chapter-7-training-and-deployment-for-husaybah/ (accessed July 26, 2009).

——. "Chapter 8: 8 April 2004, Market Street Patrol, Husaybah." *From Desert Mech to Ramadi SWAT*. http://lima37.com/blog/chapter-8-8-april-2004-market-street-patrol-husaybah/ (accessed July 26, 2009).

——. "Chapter 9: 14 April 2004, Crackhouse OP." *From Desert Mech to Ramadi SWAT*. http://lima37.com/blog/chapter-9-14-april-2004-crackhouse-op/ (accessed July 26, 2009).

——. "Chapter 10: Battle of Husaybah." *From Desert Mech to*

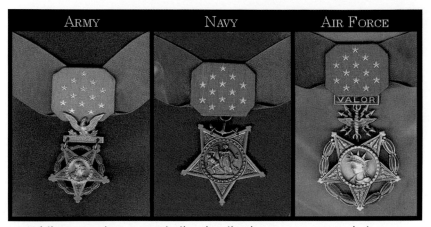

ARMY   NAVY   AIR FORCE

While possessing many similar details, the army, navy, and air force Medals of Honor also incorporate design features reflecting their individual services. The inverted five-pointed stars in each medal are tipped with trefoils, symbolizing perpetuity (the leaves of the trefoil represent past, present, and future). The laurel leaves represent victory. The thirteen stars on the neck ribbon symbolize the thirteen states. Both the army and navy Medals of Honor feature Minerva, the Roman goddess of wisdom and war.
Source: *Wikipedia*

The Medal of Honor is the only military decoration that is suspended from a neck ribbon.
Photo: *U.S. Army*

Above: Sergeant First Class Paul Ray Smith on duty in Iraq, probably taken during the pause in the advance toward Baghdad when a severe sandstorm swept the region for two days, beginning in March 24, 2003.
Photo: *U.S. Army*

Right: The unveiling of the "Sgt. Paul R. Smith Fitness Center" in Fort Benning, Georgia, in June 2007, just one of a number of honors posthumously bestowed on Sergeant Smith.
Photo: *U.S. Army*

Above: Lieutenant Michael P. Murphy and members of his SEAL Delivery Vehicle Team 1. From left to right: Sonar Technician–Surface 2nd Class Matthew G. Axelson; Information Systems Technician Senior Chief Daniel R. Healy; Quartermaster 2nd Class James Suh; Hospital Corpsman Second Class Marcus Luttrell; Machinist Mate 2nd Class Shane Patton; and Lieutenant Michael P. Murphy. Luttrell was the only member to survive. Both he and Axelson would later receive the Navy Cross, second only to the Medal of Honor.
Photo: *U.S. Navy*

Below: Michael Murphy (left) and Matthew Axelson (right) taking a break somewhere in Afghanistan.
Photo: *U.S. Navy*

Staff Sergeant Jared Monti (center) poses
with some local tribesmen in Afghanistan.
Photo: *U.S. Army*

Staff Sergeant Monti together with some fellow soldiers of the
10th Mountain Division on June 23, 2005. Monti is in the middle,
squatting below two snipers draped in camouflage cover.
Photo: *U.S. Army*

Above: Petty Officer Second Class Michael A. Monsoor pauses during cold weather training in Kodiak, Alaska in 2004.
Photo: *U.S. Navy*

Left: Official U.S. Navy photomontage of Petty Officer Second Class Michael A. Monsoor includes his Medal of Honor (lower), Silver Star (middle), and Bronze Star (top). On the right is his SEAL badge, nicknamed "the Budweiser" (because it resembles the Anheuser-Busch logo).
Photo: *U.S. Navy*

Marines from the Seventh Marine Regiment on a patrol in March 2007, searching for weapons and insurgent activity in Zaidon, a town south of Fallujah in Al Anbar Province. Corporal Jason Dunham was on a similar patrol on April 14, 2004 in Karabilah.
Photo: *Corporal Samuel D. Corum, USMC*

USS JASON DUNHAM (DDG 109)

Semper Fidelis Semper Fortis

Official photomontage shows Corporal Jason Dunham in his dress uniform and beside the guided-missile destroyer that bears his name.
Photo: *Department of Defense*

Private First Class Ross McGinnis and his sister, Katie, in 2005.
Photo: *U.S. Army*

The official U.S. Army photograph of Ross McGinnis that appears on the army's website created to honor him.
Photo: *U.S. Army*

George and Sally Monsoor, the parents of Petty Officer Second Class Michael A. Monsoor, talk with President George W. Bush following the White House East Wing ceremony in which he presented them with their son's Medal of Honor. It is at events such as this that the impact of command responsibility can almost overwhelm a president. On April 8, 2008, President Bush broke down during the Medal of Honor ceremony for Petty Officer Monsoor and was unable to complete his speech.

Photo: *Mass Communication Specialist 1st Class Brian Aho, U.S. Navy*

Ramadi SWAT.
http://lima37.com/blog/chapter-10-battle-of-husaybah/
(accessed July 26, 2009).
Garcia, Jose L. "Marines Honor Corporal's Heroic Sacrifice."
April 29, 2004.
http://www.usa-patriotism.com/heroes/
fallen/Jason_dunham1.htm (accessed July 15, 2009).
"Operation Vigilant Resolve." *GlobalSecurity.org*.
http://www.globalsecurity.org/military/ops/oif-vigilant-
resolve.htm (accessed July 26, 2009).

4

★ ★ ★ ★ ★ ★

Michael P. Murphy

─────────────────── ☆ ───────────────────

For conspicuous gallantry and intrepidity at the risk of his life above and beyond the call of duty as the leader of a special reconnaissance element with Naval Special Warfare Task Unit Afghanistan on 27 and 28 June 2005. While leading a mission to locate a high-level anti-coalition militia leader, Lieutenant Murphy demonstrated extraordinary heroism in the face of grave danger in the vicinity of Asadabad, Konar Province, Afghanistan. On 28 June 2005, operating in an extremely rugged enemy-controlled area, Lieutenant Murphy's team was discovered by anti-coalition militia sympathizers who revealed their position to Taliban fighters. As a result, between 30 and 40 enemy fighters besieged his four-member team. Demonstrating exceptional resolve, Lieutenant Murphy valiantly led his men in engaging the large enemy force. The ensuing fierce firefight resulted in numerous enemy casualties as well as the wounding of all four members of the team. Ignoring his own wounds and demonstrating exceptional composure, Lieutenant Murphy continued to lead and encourage his men. When the primary communicator fell mortally wounded, Lieutenant Murphy repeatedly attempted to call for assistance for his beleaguered teammates. Realizing the impossibility of communicating in the extreme terrain, and in the face of almost certain death, he fought his way into open terrain to gain a better position to transmit a call. This deliberate, heroic act deprived him of cover, exposing him to direct enemy fire. Finally achieving contact with his headquarters, Lieutenant Murphy maintained his exposed position while he provided his location and requested immediate support for his team. In his final act of bravery, he continued to engage the enemy until he was mortally wounded, gallantly giving his life for his country and for the cause of freedom. By his selfless leadership, courageous actions, and extraordinary devotion to duty, Lieutenant Murphy reflected great credit upon himself and upheld the highest traditions of the United States Naval service.

—Medal of Honor Citation, October 22, 2007

————————————————— ☆ —————————————————

Brave men have fought and died building the proud tradition and feared reputation that I am bound to uphold. In the worst of conditions, the legacy of my teammates steadies my resolve and silently guides my every deed. I will not fail.

—U.S. Navy SEAL Creed[1]

A LONG ISLAND CHILDHOOD

Lieutenant Michael Patrick Murphy was born in Smithtown, New York, on May 7, 1976, but grew up on Patchogue, Long Island, in New York's Suffolk County, where his father, Daniel Murphy, was the assistant district attorney. It was a working- and middle-class community mostly composed of third- and fourth-generation Irish, Italian, and German immigrants.

Shortly after the family moved into their new home, the blue-eyed, brown-haired Michael began displaying his daredevil streak—one of two traits that would define his childhood and adolescence. The Murphys' next-door neighbors had a swimming pool in their backyard. One summer day as his parents chatted with their neighbors, two-year-old Michael quietly headed for the pool. A pleasant day turned frantic as the adults suddenly heard the sound of someone jumping off the diving board and into the pool. When the frightened group arrived in the backyard, they saw the tot emerging from the far end, grinning mischievously from ear to ear. Michael knew how to swim and apparently knew how to jump off a diving board as well.

In high school, Mike Murphy and his friends earned money as lifeguards at public pools in nearby towns—Holtsville, Corey Beach, Lake Ronkonkoma, and Oyster Bay. Mike's best friend, Jim Emmerich, recalled that Murph, as his friends called him, liked to climb to the top of the flagpole at Corey Beach and to perform daredevil dives into the Dive Tank at Holtsville. He remembered that Mike "adjusted the spring on the diving board to project him over next to the wall . . . he'd do back flips, gainers, he'd go as close to the wall as possible."[2] John Perri, who was a lifeguard with Mike, Jim Emmerich, and the others over in Oyster Bay, remembered one prank they enjoyed most. Mike would climb up the steel "hurricane pole" beside the pool and then use his arms to lift himself up *perpendicular* to it, until he was "completely sideways in the air," making it look as if he were holding onto the pole for dear life because of the "high winds."[3]

Mike's other obvious trait was that of *protector*. It became his nickname at Saxton Middle School, in Patchogue, after he jumped into a fight to help a classmate who had been cornered by bullies. His father recalled that Michael "never liked seeing people getting taken advantage of or getting picked on."[4] His mother remembered that he once actually got "in trouble" at Saxton because of it. She said, "His middle school principal called me . . . Mike had been in a fight. Three bullies had pushed a special-ed kid into a locker, and Mike got into [a] fight to protect the kid."[5] And, years later, he came to the rescue again. Serge Korepin was lifeguarding in Oyster Bay with Mike one summer. Not a close friend, more of a casual acquaintance, Serge was nevertheless Mike's co-worker and therefore under his protection. One evening, Serge recalled, "I was going to get beat up by a big guy looking for trouble. Even though Mike was half the size of the guy, [Mike] really scared him and got me out of that situation."[6]

A straight-A student, Mike was a member of the National Honor Society in the Patchogue-Medford High School. His favorite subject was history, although he loved sports, too. With his father as his coach, Mike played youth soccer, peewee football, and Little League baseball for the North

Patchogue Medford Youth Athletic Club. Later, at Patchogue-Medford High School, Mike played defensive back for the Raiders—the school's football team.

After graduation in 1994, Mike enrolled at Pennsylvania State University. There he took a double major in political science and psychology, played hockey, and fell in love with another Long Island native attending Penn State, Heather Duggan. The feeling was to become mutual, although it took Heather a while to take to Mike.

Mike had a close relationship with his father that continued through his college years. Even though it was 295 miles between the Penn State campus and Patchogue, Long Island, Mike would come home as often as possible. When it was time for Mike to return to college, he and his father would get into Daniel Murphy's green Buick at about 10:00 or 11:00 P.M. on a Sunday evening and head west on a five-hour road trip to Pennsylvania. During the drive to Penn State, Dan and his "buddy boy"[7] would engage in far-ranging discussions, with Dan letting Mike choose the subject. Mike was a good student, and among the many topics they discussed was what he would do after graduation. Dan pushed for him to become a teacher; but a career in law, following in the footsteps of his father, was also discussed, as was the military.

Five hours later, after he had dropped off his son, Dan would gas up, turn the car around, and drive back through the night—arriving at his office in time for work on Monday morning.

THE DECISION TO BECOME A SEAL

Dan Murphy tried to steer Mike away from a military career. Daniel had served in the army with the Twenty-fifth Infantry

Division during the Vietnam War, was severely wounded in action, and had received the Purple Heart. He was medically discharged from the army with a 40 percent disability. The entire experience left "a bad taste"[8] in his mouth, for he felt that the troops had been used as cannon fodder.

By his senior year at Penn State, Mike had narrowed his choices down to two careers: law or the military. When a third law school accepted his application, it appeared that career path had won out. Then, during one of their night-into-morning road trips back to Penn State, Mike told his father what he knew Daniel Murphy didn't want to hear. He said that wanted to be a SEAL warrior. His father was stunned. He replied, "Michael, you know my disenchantment with the military after being in Vietnam. I thought you wanted to go to law school?"[9] As it turned out, as much as Mike respected his father, he was drawn to follow the path of an older generation.

Mike's friend Jim Emmerich later said, "I think his 'Pop' [Mike's paternal grandfather] had a lot to do with his decision to join." The older Murphy had served in the New York Army National Guard's Sixty-ninth Infantry Regiment, the "Fighting Sixty-ninth," and saw action in the Pacific theater during World War II. Mike loved his grandfather as deeply as he did his father.

Dan Murphy was struck by the fact that his son didn't just want to enter the military, he wanted to become a member of one of the elite special operations units, the basic training for which is so rigorous that it averages an 80 percent washout rate. But Daniel had always encouraged his son to think for himself. If Mike wanted to shoot for the moon, Dan was not going to stand in the way of his dream.

Mike had done his homework and knew that being athletic wasn't enough, especially with his slight build and moderate height of five feet ten. He wanted to be as prepared as possible *before* he entered the navy's BUD/S (basic underwater demolition/SEAL school) boot camp. Fortu-

The official 2002 graduation photograph of Basic Underwater Demolition/SEAL (BUD/S) class 236. Lieutenant Michael P. Murphy is in the last row, last man on the right.
Photo: *U.S. Navy*

nately, help was around the corner, or more accurately, nearby on the north shore of Long Island, at the U.S. Merchant Marine Academy at Kings Point. It was a special volunteer organization, dedicated to helping individuals pass the grueling BUD/S program, called the SEAL Recruiting District Assistance Council, or, in the acronym-filled world of the military: SEAL RDAC.

Founded in 1996 by the retired SEAL captain Andrew E. Bisset, SEAL RDAC was created in response to concerns of the navy's high command that the BUD/S program would have to lower its standards a bit to meet SEAL-team manpower requirements. Believing that the high attrition rate was simply a cost of doing business, Bisset thought that instead of lowering the standards, the pool of candidates should be expanded. Up to that time, all SEAL candidates came from within the military (special operations draws its members from all branches). Bisset decided to create a "SEAL prep school" to take in civilians and put them through a program *tougher* than BUD/S. Successful graduates would stand a greater chance of passing BUD/S and, with a larger group to draw from, SEAL manpower needs would be met without a degradation in the physical and mental fitness of the candidates.

The candidates in his program would be evaluated, mentored, and trained by former SEALs. As Bisset said, "Who knows better about what SEALs do than SEALs themselves?"[10]

Though the physical requirements are strict, the overall program timetable is flexible, and it is not unknown for candidates to remain in the program for up to a year. Mike met with Captain Bisset, who was impressed with what he saw.

"Mike was definitely above and beyond just the normal guy," he said. "He was very determined; he had a very strong inner focus." Bisset was also impressed with Mike's attitude, which he described as being "humble and patriotic."

Bisset gave Mike copies of the exacting physical fitness requirements for Navy SEAL qualification and SEAL RDAC requirements.

Navy SEAL basic entry requirements:
- 500-yard swim in 12.5 minutes
- 42 push-ups within two minutes
- 50 sit-ups within two minutes
- 6 pull-ups with no time limit
- 1.5 mile run (in combat boots)
  in under 11.5 minutes

SEAL RDAC minimum requirements:
- 500-yard swim in 9 minutes (side or breast stroke)
- 80 push-ups within two minutes
- 80 sit-ups within two minutes
- 15 pull-ups with no time limit
- 1.5 mile run (in combat boots)
  in under 10 minutes[11]

Mike had his work cut out for him if he was going to achieve the requirements in the monthly strength tests. During the summer, while working as a lifeguard at Lake Ronkonkoma, Mike began building up his strength—and getting his fellow lifeguards to join him. Longtime friends Jim Emmerich and Owen O'Callaghan were among those he challenged. Jim recalled that Mike outpaced them all, admitting, "We couldn't keep up."[12] Owen later became a fireman at Engine Company 53, Ladder Company 43 in Manhattan, and he credited Mike's workouts in helping him meet the firefighter's physical requirements. Owen was on duty on September 11, 2001, and would lose an uncle, a lieutenant with the Fire Department close to retirement, at the World Trade Center that day. Mike would wear into battle in Afghanistan the sleeve emblem of his buddy's fire company.

Mike entered Bisset's program in January 1999. In his first physical test, he completed the swim in 9 minutes and the run in 9 minutes and 22 seconds, and he completed within the allotted time 90 push-ups, 58 sit-ups, and 18 pull-ups. Mike had exceeded the navy's requirements and fallen short on only the sit-up requirement of the SEAL RDAC. In the SEAL world, it's an all-or-nothing situation. Mike kept at it, pushing himself ever harder. In his final strength test on September 11, 1999, he was able to do 102 push-ups, 87 sit-ups, and 22 pull-ups, swim the distance in 7 minutes and 47 seconds, and run the 1.5 miles in combat boots in 8 minutes and 55 seconds. In his evaluation, Bisset wrote, "This is an intensely motivated individual who has the focus, determination and perseverance to carry him through the rigors of Basic Underwater Demoliton/SEAL (BUD/S) training. . . . I would be most eager to have this individual serve in my wardroom."[13]

Later that month, Mike Murphy enlisted in the Navy's Officer Candidate School at Pensacola, Florida. In December, he completed the course and was commissioned an ensign. His commissioning was a bittersweet moment because it was also in December that "Pop," his beloved grandfather, passed away. Emmerich was there at the funeral and

Lieutenant Michael P. Murphy's official photograph. The decorations on his left breast include the SEAL badge (top); the National Defense Service Medal, the Navy Rifle Marksmanship Medal with expert device, the Navy Pistol Marksmanship Medal with expert device (middle, from left to right); and the Navy and Marine Corps Parachutist badge (bottom).
Photo: *U.S. Navy*

recalled, "I'd never seen Mike cry, and he just stood there crying with his hand on the casket."[14]

Meanwhile, Mike's relationship with Heather had grown from casual friendship to passionate commitment. A few weeks after his grandfather's funeral, Mike said that he wanted her to come with him to California when he attended the BUD/S school. Heather was torn. She had fallen in love with him, but she had just been accepted in the graduate program for school counseling at Long Island University. Her focus right then was on getting her master's degree, not on becoming a military wife. It was an emotional impasse, with neither wanting to give up their dreams or to end their relationship. In January 2001, with Heather in his thoughts and heart, but not at his side, Mike left for the Naval Special Warfare Training Center in Coronado, California, near San Diego, where he became a member of class 236.

THE BUD/S PROGRAM AND EARLY DEPLOYMENT

The six-month BUD/S program is perhaps the most intense, physically demanding experience any member of the U.S. military can have (women are excluded because of the high physical standards and because a federal law restricts their roles as special operations warriors). The process begins with a five-week indoctrination and pretraining program designed to weed out the least-qualified candidates. The attrition rate at this entry level is high. For example, in one class of 1,510 sailors, only thirty-four passed the preliminary tests and appeared for actual training. BUD/S training is broken into three phases. One web site about the SEALs (www.navyseals.com) warns candidates that, "The first phase is the toughest. It consists of eight weeks of Basic Conditioning that peaks with a grueling segment called 'Hell Week' at the midway point where you'll be tested to your limits. Hell Week is a test of physical endurance, mental tenacity and true teamwork where two-thirds or more of your class may call it quits."[15]

To help him get through the grueling training, Mike telephoned his father and asked for a photograph from home—it was a shot of Daniel Murphy recovering from his wounds in Vietnam. Mike looked at that photo often. He survived Hell Week, and in July 2002 was awarded his trident symbol. The navy lieutenant was now a SEAL.

His first posting was with SEAL Delivery Vehicle Team One (SDVT-1), so named because it primarily conducts missions from a special operations submarine based in Pearl Harbor, called a SEAL delivery vehicle. In October 2002, Murphy went to Jordan and participated as a liaison in Exercise Early Victor 2002. This was a Special Operations Command Central (SOCCENT) exercise involving 1,400 special operations forces training with Jordanian, British, Omani, and Kuwaiti troops.

In 1997, the Department of Defense had divided the globe into administrative regions known as unified commands. One of those regions is U.S. Central Command, responsible for the Middle East, Southwest Asia, and the African nations bordering the Red Sea as well as Ethiopia and Somalia. SOCCENT is a subordinate command unit within U.S. Central Command and is responsible for planning special operations missions. Following the exercise in autumn 2002, Mike Murphy was assigned to SOCCENT in Florida. He was deployed in Qatar as one of 250 SEALs assigned to support Operation Iraqi Freedom in 2003.

Murphy's role in Operation Iraqi Freedom remains classified, but SEALs were responsible for a variety of missions, including assisting in the rescue of Army Private Jessica Lynch, the seizure of several strategic oil platforms and the al Faw oil refinery and port facilities, and the capture of the Mukarayin Dam, located fifty-seven miles north of Baghdad. Murphy's next deployment was to Djibouti to assist in SDV mission planning.

Murphy, meanwhile, had remained in touch with Heather Duggan, exchanging e-mails that further cemented the bond between them. Heather later said, "I truly think Mike and I both knew we were a couple as soon as the first e-mail correspondence began."[16]

Following his tour of duty in Southwest Asia, Murphy returned to the SEAL team's home base in Hawaii. In April 2003, he bought Heather a plane ticket to Hawaii. Heather recalled, "As soon as I walked toward him at the airport, I knew that I was going to have a hard time leaving. So I called my mom a few days later and said I was moving to Hawaii."[17] Eight months later, during Christmas vacation back on Long Island, Murphy took Heather to see the Christmas tree at Rockefeller Center in New York City. There, surrounded by holiday cheer and crowds of happy tourists, Murphy dropped to one knee, presented Heather with a ring, and proposed. They soon picked a date for their wedding: November 19, 2005. But that April, Lieutenant Murphy was ordered to Afghanistan in support of Operation Enduring Freedom—Afghanistan.

LAND OF THE "PEOPLE OF THE HORSE"

Since the time of Alexander the Great, Afghanistan has been a land at the crossroads of Eurasian conquest and commerce. About the size of Texas, Afghanistan is a landlocked country bordered on the west by Iran and on the other three sides by fellow "stans." The suffix *stan* is derived from the Farsi word meaning "country," "nation," or "land." Historians believe that the word *Afghan* is taken from the Sanskrit word *Ashvaka*, which means "people of the horse." Thus, Afghanistan can be interpreted as "land of the people of the horse." It shares its northern border with Turkmenistan, Uzbekistan, and Tajikistan, and its western and southern border with Pakistan. The dominant geographic features in Afghanistan are its mountain ranges, most notably the Hindu Kush (which crudely translates as "pass of India"). Only 12 percent of its land is arable.

Afghanistan is less a nation than it is a loose confederation of tribes and nationalities that on occasion, and not always willingly, is ruled by a central government. Modern Afghanistan was founded in 1747, when Ahmad Shah Durrani, a member of the country's largest ethnic group, the Pashtun (about 42 percent), moved his seat of power from the Pashtun-controlled region of Kandahar north to Kabul, located on the commercially vital Trans–Hindu Kush caravan trade route. Ahmad Shah Durrani is to the Afghans what George Washington is to the United States, and he achieved a rare distinction in the history of Afghanistan in establishing for a period strong central government rule over most (though not all) of the country.

During the nineteenth and early twentieth centuries, Afghanistan, then a monarchy, was one of the pawns in what British intelligence officer Arthur Conolly called in 1840 "the Great Game"[18] and what the Russians called "the Tournament of Shadows."[19] Both terms referred to the chesslike jockeying for hegemony in Central Asia between those two empires. Britain had better luck holding off the Russians than it did in subduing the Afghans, whose guerilla tactics and intimate knowledge of the mountainous terrain enabled them to annihilate more than one British army sent against them.

ENTER THE RUSSIANS

In 1919, Britain signed the Treaty of Rawalpindi, officially granting independence to Afghanistan. That same year, as the British were on their way out, the two-year-old Soviet Union, the communist revolutionary successor to imperial Russia, began moving in. The Soviet leader Vladimir Lenin's offer to establish a diplomatic relationship with Afghanistan was accepted. This was followed by economic assistance and trade treaties that established a close but not controlling bond. That began to change in 1955, when a new treaty was signed that extended the existing pact of neutrality and nonaggression. This new treaty expanded Soviet economic, infrastructure, and military assistance.

In 1973, Mohammad Sarder Daoud led a coup that overthrew the indifferent and corrupt rule of his cousin, King Zahir Shah. Daoud promptly declared Afghanistan a republic, with himself as president. Because the Soviet-backed People's Democratic Party of Afghanistan (PDPA) had been instrumental in Daoud's coup, they expected to become major players in the new government. Instead, Daoud turned on them and tried to eradicate the party. Daoud then embarked on a sweeping program of social and political change that, instead of advancing the country, plunged Afghanistan into chaos. The PDPA was able to reorganize, and in 1978 seized power and killed Daoud and most of his family. The leader of the new communist government, Nur Muhammad Taraqi, embarked on another set of changes designed to alter the social fabric of the nation. They included the replacement of laws founded on Islamic tradition with those based on Marxism: men had to shave their beards, and the education system was made coeducational. The tribes living in the remote mountainous regions ignored the whipsawing changes to their traditional way of life as much as they could, but resentment was building.

RISE OF THE MUJAHIDEEN

On June 22, 1978, the first shots of rebellion were fired in a conflict that became the ten-year Soviet-Afghan War. The citizens of Nangalam, a village located on the western end of the Pesh River Valley in Kunar Province, fired upon government officials who were attempting to enforce the new secular laws. The government responded with overwhelming force, sending in tanks, artillery, infantry, and aircraft that proceeded to level the village. All but two citizens managed to safely flee into the hills. The troops found a widow with her young child. The two were doused with gasoline and burned alive, and the charred corpses discarded on one of the village's main intersections. News of the atrocity spread swiftly. The communist government quickly found itself locked in a war of rebellion with those who saw themselves as the warriors of Islam—the mujahideen, "those who struggle." Soviet aid to the Taraqi government dramatically increased, but things continued to spiral out of control. In December 1979, the Soviet government made the fateful decision to send in troops. The decade-long Soviet-Afghan War had officially begun.

Meanwhile, in the United States, at the urging of National Security Advisor Zbigniew Brzezinski, President Jimmy Carter authorized Operation Cyclone, on July 3, 1979, which was so covert that initially not even Congressional leaders were aware of it. This was the now infamous program to supply the mujahideen with cash and American weapons that Congressman Charlie Wilson helped keep fully funded and thriving.

For ten years, weapons and supplies were funneled to the mujahideen by the CIA, working through Pakistan's controversial intelligence organization, the ISI (Inter-Services Intelligence). During that period, the Afghan-Pakistan border became an arms bazaar, where local Afghans and foreign mercenaries fighting the Soviet army received a cornucopia of small arms, RPGs, machine guns, mortars, rockets, Stinger shoulder-fired air-defense missiles, and other easily transportable weapons. An accounting for what was delivered and to whom was virtually nonextant. To this date, no one knows for sure exactly how much was distributed, actually used, or squirreled away. The only organization that might know is the ISI, and that organization, with a long history of playing both sides against each other (including its own government), isn't talking.

One fact that is known is that a number of foreigners who joined the mujahideen did so not out of a sense of Islamic solidarity but out of a burning hatred of the Soviet Union, the United States, and other Western nations, and they saw this as a way of obtaining much-needed weapons for their own uses later. The most important person in that group was the son of a wealthy Saudi businessman, whose success against the Soviets was only a prelude to his war against the West. Osama bin Laden would prove that the United States was not beyond the reach of dedicated terrorists on September 11, 2001. Operation Cyclone, begun by President Carter and expanded in the Reagan administration to trap the Soviet Union in a Vietnam-like war, was successful. But it was a pyrrhic victory.

RISE AND FALL OF THE TALIBAN

The defeat and departure of the Soviet Union in 1989 left an already weakened Afghanistan shattered. Into the political void swept the Pashtun-based Taliban, led by Mullah Mohammed Omar. Promising to root out corruption and establish order and stability, the Taliban was initially welcomed by an Afghan population weary of war and chaos. But once control had been consolidated, the Taliban imposed the strictest interpretation of Islamic Sharia law ever seen, which brutally repressed any dissent and all but returned the nation to the lifestyle of the eleventh century. It also turned the country into a base of operations for Osama bin Laden's terrorist organization, al Qaida.

Taliban rule over Afghanistan, though strong, was not absolute. Individual warlords who had fought as mujahideen against the Soviets retained their power bases and substantial stockpiles of weapons. In 1996, some of these warlords, feeling directly threatened, led a civil war against the Taliban. This war culminated in 2001, following the terrorist attacks of September 11, with Operation Enduring Freedom, the American-led invasion that overthrew the Taliban.

In 2002, Hamid Karzai became the interim president of Afghanistan, and in 2004, a new constitution was ratified. Legislative elections for the new National Assembly were scheduled for September 18, 2005. But the country was still in a fragile state, with pro-Taliban and al Qaida cells operating freely in a number of regions. One of the most notorious was Kunar Province, in northeast Afghanistan along the Pakistan border. In that area was an up-and-coming insurgent, the leader of a Taliban splinter group called the Bara bin Malek Front, whose name was Ahmad Shah Dara-I-Nur. Shah, who wanted to become a major player in the terrorist movement, regularly traveled across the border to sanctuaries in Pakistan to get supplies and new recruits and to promote himself. He made sure at least two of his men had video cameras to record operations. He would then pass the recordings to As-Sahab, al Qaida's media production house, which would then post them on the Internet or distribute additional copies through dead-drop couriers.

OPERATION RED WINGS

American forces in Afghanistan knew that terrorists were planning to do everything they could to sabotage the elections, from trying to stop people from voting to assassinating the newly elected officials. To interdict Shah's attempts in the area, Marine Major Tom Wood, the operations officer of the marine battalion based in the region, created a plan that was a joint Marine Corps and special operations mission, code-named Operation Red Wings. (Later accounts, publications, and web sites would incorrectly refer to the mission as Redwing or Red Wing.)

Though Shah and his cadre were the targets, their capture or deaths was just the first, short-term goal of Red Wings. A second part addressed the long-term goal the marines had for the region, the improvement of the lives of the villagers. To accomplish both goals, Major Wood broke Red Wings down into five phases: the first two were to be led by special operations, the other three handled by the marines. The first phase involved reconnaissance and surveillance by a SEAL team to identify and confirm the location of Shah and his men. The second phase called for two SEAL teams to be inserted into the area: one to kill or capture Shah and his cohorts, and a second to establish a security cordon to prevent counterattacks.

GETTING READY

Major Wood presented his plan to his SEAL counterpart, Lieutenant Commander Erik Kristensen, who would exercise command over the first two stages. Kristensen changed some of the details. Instead of having his teams enter the suspected area on foot, as Wood proposed, he planned to use the time-tested special operations tactic of a night helicopter insertion by fast rope—troops would rappel down swinging rope lines as quickly as possible. As the noise of the helicopter would inevitably alert anyone nearby, the tactic included a two-part diversion designed to get Shah and his supporters to lower their guard by getting them used to the helicopters' presence. The first was a series of "dummy drops" conducted during the night leading up to the actual drop itself. Then, on the evening of the real drop, a second helicopter would accompany the one with the SEAL insertion team, and, shortly before and after the drop, it would conduct a series of touch-and-go fake landings on a number of locations in the immediate area to confuse any listeners.

The rugged terrain posed serious communications problems. The deep, rocky valleys created numerous line-of-sight blackout areas affecting radio transmissions and reception.

An undated photo of Lieutenant Michael Murphy somewhere in Afghanistan.
Photo: *U.S. Navy*

The only radio known to have totally overcome this problem was the powerful (20 watt) PRC-117. But the PRC-117 was big (3 inches high, 10.5 inches wide, and 9.5 inches deep) and heavy—almost 10 pounds without its rechargeable lithium battery. The decision was made to go with the smaller PRC-148 MBITR ("em-biter") containing a computer chip that allowed it to make a secure link with a communications satellite.

Kristensen chose Lieutenant Michael P. Murphy to lead the team that would attempt to engage Shah with sniper fire. Unfortunately, the rocky and forbidding terrain and lack of locations with sufficient ground cover for camouflage meant that Kristensen would have to deploy just four men, the smallest possible team. The three SEALs along with Murphy were Navy Hospital Corpsman Second Class Marcus Luttrell, Petty Officer Second Class Matthew G. Axelson, and Petty Officer Second Class Danny P. Dietz. Luttrell and Axelson would be the snipers/shooters, and Murphy and Dietz would serve as spotters. The mission was to last no more than four days.

Meanwhile, Major Wood's brilliant intelligence officer, Captain Scott Westerfield, had succeeded in compiling a rather complete dossier on Shah and his operation. Westerfield identified four likely locations where Shah and his men could be expected to appear on or around June 28. Two were on the east side of the mountain Sawtalo Sar, and two others were on the west. Meetings were held to review the Predator unmanned aerial vehicle images of the area and identify observation and ambush sites, helicopter insertion sites, and landing zones. The decision was made to insert the team about a mile south of the nearest observation and ambush site, near the summit of Sawtalo Sar, the idea being that it's easier to travel downhill. The team would then advance as fast as possible with the goal of reaching the first observation and ambush site around dawn. They would be traveling light, carrying only about forty-five pounds of gear each. Ominously, all four men had a premonition about the mission. As they made their final preparations, each added extra magazines to their load, just in case.

INTO THE ENEMY'S BACKYARD

On the night of June 27, 2005, Lieutenant Mike Murphy and his men boarded the MH-47 Chinook that would ferry them to their mountaintop landing zone. The helicopter then took off from Bagram Air Base into the cold night sky and headed to their destination. Forty-five minutes later the Chinook hovered twenty feet above their landing site. The four SEALs quickly rappelled to the ground on the fast rope. Within seconds, the Chinook was gone, and the SEALs were on their own.

It was supposed to be a covert drop, with the only indication of their arrival being the sound of the helicopter's rotors. But a mistake had been made. The helicopter's crew chief, accustomed to direct-action raids where speed, not secrecy, is paramount, had accordingly detached the fast rope, allowing the olive-drab line to fall to the ground. In plain view of anyone who might come along during the day was a thirty-foot-long piece of evidence that Americans were there. Groping over the rugged terrain in the gloom, Murphy and Axelson grabbed tree branches and other vegetation to cover it. Luttrell, meanwhile, got on his radio and contacted the AC-130 gunship riding shotgun overhead:

"Sniper Two One, this is Glimmer Three—preparing to move."[20] After getting confirmation, and with the partially coiled rope now hidden as best they could, the team shouldered their rucksacks and began their trek to their observation and ambush site.

It was monsoon season in India, which meant that Afghanistan was subject to unpredictable thunderstorms and thick fog. One storm burst over the SEAL team shortly after they landed. The cold, wind, rain, and steep terrain overgrown in places with thick vegetation made the trek a test of endurance and skill. They managed to reach the nearest of the two designated observation and ambush sites near dawn. Though the location offered a clear view of the valley and village below them, it did not provide adequate shelter, and the SEALs were vulnerable to being discovered by a passing local such as a goatherd (what's known as being "soft compromised").

Shortly after they took up position, a thick fog bank moved in between the SEALs and the village below. They realized that if fog appeared once, it would probably appear again. They would have to move. Murphy took Axelson with him and began searching for a nearby site that wouldn't be affected by the weather and that would, he hoped, offer them some protection from detection. After about an hour, he returned and told Dietz and Luttrell they had found one about a thousand yards away.

The new location proved to be better for observation and sniping—they had a clear and unobstructed view of the entire village. If Shah were there, they'd spot him in an instant. Unfortunately, the new site was even more exposed than the first, with only one convenient path in and out. If they were spotted and that path cut off, they'd have to either shoot their way out or attempt to escape down the dangerously steep mountain slope.

FATAL DISCOVERY

The SEALs got into position and began their observation. The morning passed quietly. Then, at about noon, Luttrell heard the sound of approaching footsteps. Minutes later three goatherds and about a hundred goats appeared. The SEALs quickly surrounded and detained them. Danny Dietz, responsible for communicating with headquarters, got on his radio and sent back a faint, scratchy message that sent a chill down the backs of the men at headquarters, "We've been soft compromised."[21] The operation had just gone wrong—to what extent remained to be determined.

The SEALs began discussing their options. None of the alternatives facing them were attractive. The three Afghans, one a boy, were clearly goatherds—they did not have firearms, their only "weapon" an ax for chopping wood. Though the Afghans were able to tell the SEALs that they were not Taliban, that didn't mean they weren't sympathizers or that they wouldn't tell the Taliban or Shah's men of the SEALs' location if they were set free. Worse, Dietz was having communications problems. He wasn't sure his first message had been received. What he did know was that he would not be getting any answer back. The team was in a radio blackout area. After a short debate in which votes were taken, according to Marcus Luttrell, Lieutenant Murphy confirmed their decision: "We gotta let 'em go."[22] The Afghans and their goats were allowed to leave.

Five minutes after the goatherds had disappeared down the

trail, the SEALs had shouldered their gear and were double-timing in the opposite direction. Even though they planned to continue their mission (aborting the mission had not been discussed), they knew they couldn't stay where they were. They retraced their route to their original location and once again took up position there.

As the minutes ticked by, it appeared that perhaps the herders had not told the insurgents about them. But, about two hours after they had released the Afghans, the SEALs started hearing the noise of movement above and to the left of their position. A large insurgent force that they initially estimated to be at least eighty men, armed with AK-47 assault rifles and RPG launchers, was approaching their position.

Evidence from the ensuing engagement, plus a video of the attack—one of two made by Shah—indicates the Afghan force may have been smaller than the SEALs estimated. Murphy's Medal of Honor citation puts the number between thirty and forty. Regardless, the fact was that Shah was intimately familiar with the terrain and knew how to use it to best advantage. And he did, attacking from above with his men spread out. Most devastating of all, unlike the SEALs, Shah possessed good communications. He had a commercial two-way radio that somehow was not affected by the blackout that nullified the SEALs' radios, and he expertly used it to position his men where they would be the most effective. But if the SEALs could manage to buy some time, with their superior training they stood a good chance of turning the tables on Shah and his men. And, therefore, time was the one thing Shah was determined not to give them.

Lieutenant Murphy immediately ordered Dietz to again try to raise headquarters in Bagram, this time for help. And, once again, because of the terrain and atmospheric conditions, Dietz could transmit but not receive messages; at Bagram, the words that everyone there hoped they wouldn't hear came over the loudspeaker: *"Contact!* We're *hard* compromised!"[23] A rescue mission was needed immediately, and preparations were made to launch it.

Meanwhile, the others quietly took aim as the insurgents spread out to the left and right in a classic flanking maneuver. When the lead fighters were about twenty yards from their position, the SEALs opened fire. As hell erupted around them, Dietz delivered more unwelcome news. Once again, he told them he couldn't establish contact with headquarters. Strictly speaking, that wasn't the case. Dietz *had* been able to reach headquarters, he just didn't know it.

With their escape route blocked by a superior force in a superior position, and with fighters about to surround them, Lieutenant Murphy ordered his men to retreat down the mountain. After slipping, sliding, and rolling helter-skelter down the rocky slope, with bullets constantly whizzing about them, Luttrell and Murphy landed hard on a piece of flat ground some distance below their outpost. Luttrell would later discover he had cracked some vertebrae. Murphy was wounded—shot in the abdomen. Axelson and Dietz soon joined them. Dietz was wounded, too: his right thumb had been shot off.

Unfortunately, Luttrell, their corpsman, had lost his medical supplies during the descent. There was nothing he could do to help either Murphy or Dietz. Worse, the gunfire from the insurgents had not let up. Their only hope for survival was to keep traveling down the steep slope toward the village far below. If the SEALs could get inside one of the huts, they'd have a better chance of holding out against the enemy.

Once again, as the Afghans closed, Lieutenant Murphy ordered the SEALs to jump. They next landed on a small escarpment about thirty feet below. The insurgents, meanwhile, maintained a steady rate of heavy fire at the retreating SEALs. Dietz was hit twice more. Though he was severely wounded, they had to keep going. Axelson and Luttrell took the lead in the descent and, after they reached the next position, provided cover fire for Murphy and Dietz.

The running firefight continued, with the SEALs having to also engage insurgents who had managed to get into position ahead of them. This time, though, there were only three SEALs able to fight. Dietz was dead, and the others were forced to leave their comrade's body behind. Somehow, Murphy, Axelson, and Luttrell managed to run the gauntlet of RPGs and bullets as they continued their descent. But there were too many enemy fighters and too many bullets. Axelson was hit, in the chest and head.

A CALL FOR HELP

After the three had reached their latest defensive position, Lieutenant Murphy knew he had to make his call now, or it would be too late. He took out his Iridium satellite phone and tried to call. The signal was blocked by the rocks above him. The only way he'd be able to connect with the communication satellites was to move out in the open. Moments later, and in clear view of the enemy, Lieutenant Michael P. Murphy moved out from cover and hit the speed-dial button on the phone.

Lieutenant Michael Murphy at a base camp in Afghanistan. On his right sleeve is the patch of his friend Owen O'Callaghan's New York Fire Department company.
Photo: *U.S. Navy*

This time, he got through.

Ignoring the AK-47 bullets ricocheting off the hard ground around him, Murphy said, "My men are taking heavy fire... we're getting picked apart. My guys are dying out here ... we need help."[24]

Just then, an AK-47 round struck him in the back and burst through his chest. The impact knocked Murphy forward and caused him to drop his rifle and phone. Somehow, he managed to reach down and pick both up. After listening on the phone for another moment, he replied, "Roger that, sir. Thank you."[25] Then he hung up and staggered back to his fellow SEALs.

Rescue was finally on the way.

The three surviving men were SEALs, but they were not supermen. Lieutenant Murphy managed to reach a defensive position on a section of the slope above Marcus Luttrell and Matthew Axelson before he was finally gunned down. Seconds later, the concussion from an RPG explosion knocked Luttrell down the slope, an event that ultimately helped save his life and made him the only survivor of the ordeal. Luttrell's last sight of Axelson was of him using his sidearm; Axelson had three magazines left for his pistol. When a search party found his body days later, only one magazine remained unused. But as badly as the mission was turning out, what was about to happen would mark June 28, 2005, as one of the worst in U.S. special operations history.

As the SEAL team was being cut down, the attempted rescue had ended in disaster. A quick reaction force of two MH-47D Chinooks, four MH-60 Blackhawks, and two AH-64D Apache

Longbow helicopters was dispatched from Bagram to try and extract the surviving SEALs. As they flew into the target area, however, they ran into a trap and were subjected to a fusillade of RPG fire, just as had happened twelve years earlier during the infamous "Black Hawk down" firefight in Mogadishu, Somalia. One RPG flew into the open rear ramp door of one of the Chinooks, causing it to lose control and crash into a ravine. The helicopter was destroyed and all personnel aboard, including sixteen SEALs, were killed. Nineteen highly trained special operations warriors and a valuable MH-47 Chinook helicopter had been lost, and Operation Red Wings was a complete disaster.

Somehow, Marcus Luttrell survived. Though suffering numerous shrapnel wounds in addition to his other injuries, he managed to evade the enemy long enough to be discovered by a friendly villager who, following the tradition of *Pashtunwalli*—a generations-old blood code of hospitality—protected him from Shah and his men. Meanwhile, one of the largest U.S. search-and-rescue operations since Vietnam was trying to locate any survivors from the SEAL team, with three hundred personnel committed to the effort. Members of the army's Seventy-fifth Ranger Regiment finally rescued Luttrell on July 2, five days after Murphy and his team had dropped onto the side of the mountain. A village elder had brought a note from Luttrell to a nearby marine encampment, describing his location and condition.

MEMORIALS AND HONORS
The special operations community has a reputation for remembering its own. One year after the "Battle of Murphy's Ridge," as it came to be known, Rear Admiral Joe Maguire

presided over a memorial ceremony at the headquarters of the Naval Special Warfare Command in Coronado, in which memorial trees and plaques were dedicated to the three SEALs who died on Sawtalo Sar.

The team would receive additional honors. Axelson, Dietz, and Luttrell were awarded the Navy Cross. On October 11,

The cover of the program booklet for Lieutenant Michael P. Murphy's Medal of Honor ceremony at the Hall of Heroes in the Pentagon.
Photo: *U.S. Navy*

2007, the White House announced that Lieutenant Michael Patrick Murphy would be the fourth SEAL in history to receive the Medal of Honor. On October 22, 2007, family, friends, and fellow special operations professionals gathered in Washington, D.C., to celebrate the memory and deeds of Lieutenant Michael P. Murphy—the first Medal of Honor winner for actions during combat in Afghanistan. Later that same day, the celebration of Mike Murphy and his life continued at the navy memorial a few blocks from the White House, where his navy and special operations peers gathered in a quiet ceremony to share stories and memories of the young man from New York who had given so much in service to his country. The following year, on May 7, 2008, Secretary of the Navy Donald C. Winter announced that DDG-112, an *Arleigh Burke*-class destroyer, would be christened the *Michael P. Murphy*.

THE FALL OF SHAH

Ahmad Shah had two men recording the battle on June 28. He prepared a propaganda video that contained scenes of the ambush, its aftermath, and some additional footage, a total of eleven minutes and twenty-three seconds. Posted on Google, it was still available for viewing on August 7, 2009, under the heading "Operation Red Wing Ambush Propaganda Video." Part of it shows some of his men stripping clothing, watches, and other gear off the bodies of Dietz and Murphy. The New York Fire Department Engine Company 53, Ladder Company 43 shoulder patch that Murphy wore is clearly visible.

This victory boosted Shah's reputation among his peers, and he reportedly received a letter of praise from Osama bin

Laden. But he did not live much longer. On April 17, 2008, Shah was killed by Pakistani border police, on the Pakistan side of the Afghan-Pakistani border, when he failed to stop at a police checkpoint...thus becoming the final casualty of Operation Red Wings.

NOTES

1. Honnick, Paul D., "SDV Team One Salutes Fallen Heroes," July 10, 2007, http://www.navy.mil/search/display.asp?story_id = 30489 (accessed August 5, 2009).
2. O'Shaughnessy, Patrice, "How a Loving Son from New York Lived and Died for Us All," *New York Daily News*, April 15, 2007.
3. "Navy Lieutenant Michael P. Murphy," *Fallen Heroes of Operation Enduring Freedom*, ed. Tim Rivera, http://www.fallenheroesmemorial.com/oef/profiles/murphymichaelp.html (accessed August 5, 2009).
4. Evans, Martin C., "Born to Serve: Chapter Two; Growing Up in Patchogue," *New York Newsday*, May 6, 2007, http://www.newsday.com/news/local/Suffolk/ny-enseal2,0,2123939,print.story (accessed October 12, 2007).
5. O'Shaughnessy, Patrice, "Loving Son."
6. "Navy Lieutenant Michael P. Murphy."
7. "Navy Lieutenant Michael P. Murphy."
8. Evans, Martin C., "Born to Serve: Chapter Four: A Father's Experience," *New York Newsday*, May 6, 2007, http://www.newsday.com/news/local/Suffolk/ny-enseal4,0,2910363,print.story (accessed October 12, 2007).
9. Evans, "Born to Serve: Chapter Four."
10. Smith, W. Thomas Jr., "'College-Prep' for SEALs?" http://www.military.com/opinion/0,15202,87214,00.html (accessed August 4, 2009).
11. Ibid.
12. O'Shaughnessy, "Loving Son."
13. Evans, Martin C., "Born to Serve: Chapter Five; Rigorous Training," http://www.newsday.com/news/local/Suffolk/ny-enseal5,0,3303580,print.story (accessed October 12, 2007).
14. O'Shaughnessy, "Loving Son."

15. "BUD/S (Basic Underwater Demolition/SEAL) Training," *Navyseals.com*, http://www.navyseals.com/node/108 (accessed February 2010).
16. Evans, Martin C., "Born to Serve: Chapter Six: Earning the Trident," *Newsday.com*, May 6, 2007, http://www.newsday.com/news/ local/Suffolk/ny-enseal6,0,3696797,print.story (accessed October 12, 2007).
17. Ibid.
18. Yapp, Malcolm, "Legend of the Great Game," *2000 Lectures by the British Academy*, (Oxford: Oxford University Press, 2001), 181.
19. Anonymous, "The Great Game Goes On," *Postscripts*, http://notorcblogspot.com/2006/05/great-game-goes-on.html (accessed August 6, 2009).
20. Luttrell, Marcus, with Patrick Robinson, *Lone Survivor: The Eyewitness Account of Operation Redwing and the Lost Heroes of Seal Team 10*, (New York: Little, Brown, and Co., 2007), 191.
21. Darack, Ed, *Victory Point: Operations Red Wings and Whalers; The Marine Corps' Battle for Freedom in Afghanistan* (New York: BerkleyCaliber, 2009), 129.
22. Luttrell with Robinson, *Lone Survivor*, 207.
23. Darack, *Victory Point*, 129–130.
24. Luttrell with Robinson, *Lone Survivor, 237*.
25. Ibid, 237.

BIBLIOGRAPHY

BOOKS

Couch, Dick. *Down Range: Navy SEALS in the War on Terrorism*. New York: Three Rivers Press, 2005.

Darack, Ed. *Victory Point: Operations Red Wings and Whalers; The Marine Corps' Battle for Freedom in Afghanistan*. New York: BerkleyCaliber, 2009.

Graw, Lester W., and Michael A. Gress, ed. *The Russian General Staff: The Soviet-Afghan War: How a Superpower Fought and Lost*. Lawrence, KS: University of Kansas Press, 2002.

Lorimer, John Gordon. *Grammar and Vocabulary of Waziri Pashto*. Calcutta, India: Office of the Superintendent of Government Printing, 1902.

Luttrell, Marcus, with Patrick Robinson. *Lone Survivor: The Eyewitness Account of Operation Redwings and the Lost Heroes of SEAL Team 10.* New York: Little, Brown and Co., 2007.

MAGAZINES

Zimmerman, Dwight Jon. "Above and Beyond the Call of Duty on Murphy's Ridge: Lieutenant Michael P. Murphy and Operation Redwing." *Year in Special Operations 2008.* Tampa, FL: Faircount Media Group, 2008.

NEWSPAPERS

Hernandez, Raymond. "A Protector as a Child, Honored as a Hero." *New York Times,* October 22, 2007.

O'Shaughnessy, Patrice. "How a Loving Son from New York Lived and Died for Us All." *New York Daily News,* April 15, 2007.

———. "Navy SEAL Was an Officer and a Gentleman Right to the End." *New York Daily News,* April 16, 2007.

INTERNET

Beller, Peter C. "Navy Mission of Officer Was Secret to Parents." *FreeRepublic.com,* July 8, 2005. http://www.freerepublic.com/focus/f-news/1439409/posts (accessed July 16, 2007).

Evans, Martin C. "Born To Serve: Chapter Eight; Military Life." *Newsday.com,* May 6, 2007. http://www.newsday.com/news/local/Suffolk/ny-enseal8,0,4483231,print.story (accessed October 12, 2007).

———. "Born to Serve: Chapter Five; Rigorous Training." *Newsday.com,* May 6, 2007. http://www.newsday.com/news/local/Suffolk/ny-enseal5,0,3303580,print.story (accessed October 12, 2007).

———. "Born to Serve: Chapter Four; Two Relationships." *Newsday.com,* May 6, 2007. http://www.newsday.com/news/local/Suffolk/ny-enseal4,0,2910363,print.story (accessed October 12, 2007).

————. "Born To Serve: Chapter Nine; The Tragic End." *Newsday.com*, May 6, 2007. http://www.newsday.com/news/local/suffolk/ny-enseal9,0,4876448,print.story (accessed October 12, 2007).

————."Born to Serve: Chapter One; On the Mountain." *Newsday.com*, May 6, 2007. http://www.newsday.com/news/local/Suffolk/ny-enseal1,0,1730712,print.story (accessed October 12, 2007).

————. "Born To Serve: Chapter Seven; Getting Serious." *Newsday.com*, May 6, 2007. http://www.newsday.com/news/local/Suffolk/ny-enseal7,0,4090014,print.story (accessed October 12, 2007).

————. "Born To Serve: Chapter Six; Earning the Trident." *Newsday.com*, May 6, 2007. http://www.newsday.com/news/local/Suffolk/ny-enseal6,0,3696797,print.story (accessed October 12, 2007).

————. "Born to Serve: Chapter Three; Two Relationships." *Newsday.com*, May 6, 2007. http://www.newsday.com/news/local/Suffolk/ny-enseal3,0,2517146,print.story (accessed October 12, 2007).

————. "Born to Serve: Chapter Two; Growing Up in Patchogue." *Newsday.com*, May 6, 2007. http://www.newsday.com/news/local/Suffolk/ny-enseal2,0,2123929,print.story (accessed October 12, 2007).

Henican, Ellis. "Michael Murphy Put His Heart into the Fight." *Newsday.com*, October 12, 2007. http://www.newsday.com/news/local/longislandlife/ny-nyhen125409882oct12,0,892455,print.column (accessed October 12, 2007).

Honnick, Paul D. "SDV Team One Salutes Fallen Heroes." July 10, 2007. http://www.navy.mil/search/display.asp?story_id=30489 (accessed August 5, 2009).

"Letter Shares Fate of Destroyed SEAL Team in Afghanistan." *Military.com*, August 23, 2005. http://www.military.com/NewContent/0,13190,Defense-watch_082305_Letter,00.html (accessed August 1, 2009).

Roggio, Bill. "Bara bin Malek Front Commander Killed in Pakistani Shootout." http://tankerbabelc985.vox.com/library/post/mullah-ahmad-shah-killed-by-pakistani-police-while-attempting-to-runa-policy-check-point.html (accessed July 2, 2009).

Rupert, James. "The Shepherd Who Saved the SEAL." *Newsday.com*, May 6, 2007. http://www.newsday.com/news/local/suffolk/ny-enherd,0,6989701,print.story (accessed October 12, 2007).

Smith, W. Thomas Jr. "'College-Prep' for SEALs?" *Military.com*. http://www.military.com/opinion/0,15202,87214,00.html (accessed August 4, 2009).

"Tribute: 11 Navy SEALs Fallen in Afghanistan 8/28/05." *Militaryphotos.net*. http://www.militaryphotos.net/forums/ showthread.php?t =71680 (accessed August 1, 2009).

5

★ ★ ★ ★ ★ ★

The Many Forms
of Valor

Though the Medal of Honor is known as a decoration recognizing combat valor, up until World War II it was also
possible for an individual in the military to receive one for
extraordinary valor performed in noncombat situations and
during peacetime. A total of 193 Medals of Honor were
awarded for noncombat valor. The largest group of recipients was in the navy, where 185 were awarded.

Of that navy group, most recognized men who risked their
lives to save a fellow sailor from drowning or who saved the
ship they were on. Typical of such actions were those of Fireman First Class Thomas Cavanaugh and Apprentice David
M. Buchanan. On December 12, 1898, the boiler on Cavanaugh's ship, the USS *Potomac*, malfunctioned, causing a
dramatic rise in steam pressure that threatened to explode
the boiler. Cavanaugh's citation recounted, "Volunteering to

enter the fireroom, which was filled with steam, Cavanaugh, after repeated attempts, succeeded in reaching the auxiliary valve and opening it, thereby relieving the vessel from further danger."[1]

Buchanan's citation reads, "On board the USS *Saratoga* off Battery, New York Harbor, 15 July 1879. On the morning of this date, Robert Lee Robey, apprentice, fell overboard from the after part of the ship into the tide which was running strong ebb at the time and, not being an expert swimmer, was in danger of drowning. Instantly springing over the rail after him, Buchanan never hesitated for an instant to remove even a portion of his clothing. Both men were picked up by the ship's boat following this act of heroism."[2]

The most famous men to receive noncombat Medals of Honor were the aviator Charles Lindbergh and the polar explorer Commander Richard Evelyn Byrd Jr. Both Lindbergh and Byrd received their Medals of Honor by acts of Congress—a rarity—and were awarded them on the same day, December 14, 1927. Lindbergh, who later became a colonel in the army air corps reserve, received his in recognition of being the first to make a solo flight across the Atlantic Ocean. His citation stated, "For displaying heroic courage and skill as a navigator, at the risk of his life, by his nonstop flight in his airplane, the *Spirit of St. Louis*, from New York City to Paris, France 20–21 May 1927, by which Capt. Lindbergh not only achieved the greatest individual triumph of any American citizen but demonstrated that travel across the ocean by aircraft was possible."[3]

Byrd, who rose to the rank of rear admiral, received his Medal of Honor for being the first to fly over the North Pole, with pilot Floyd Bennett, on May 9, 1926—an event challenged at the time by others and ultimately disproved in 1996 when Byrd's diary was made available to the public. The account of that day reveals that his navigational fixes were altered, showing that, while he got close, he did not reach the North Pole. His citation reads, "For distinguishing himself conspicuously by courage and intrepidity at the risk of his life, in demonstrating that it is possible for aircraft to travel in continuous flight from a now inhabited portion of the earth over the North Pole and return."[4]

THE TIFFANY CROSS MEDAL OF HONOR

It was because the Medal of Honor could be awarded for both noncombat and combat actions that the navy, at the end of World War I, commissioned the jewelry designer Tiffany & Company of New York to create a Medal of Honor design specifically for "combat valor" recipients. The original five-pointed star design would henceforth be awarded for noncombat valor. The result was the Tiffany Cross, one of the few design missteps in the firm's history.

Authorized by Congress on February 4, 1919, the Tiffany Cross had at its top a metal bar with the word Valour, spelled in the British manner. Suspended from it was a blue silk ribbon with thirteen stars. The medal was a Maltese cross with anchors on each arm, and in the center was an American eagle surrounded by the words "United States of America." The eagle and legend were encircled by a wreath.

The design proved unpopular. The most common complaint was that it reminded people of Germany's own medal for valor, the Iron Cross. It even more resembles a minor

The Tiffany Cross Medal of Honor. The eight points of the Maltese Cross design represent the eight virtues of a knight. The cross itself represents the four compass directions and the sun. Photo: *U.S. Navy*

The Austro-Hungarian Karl-Troops Cross, a dark gray medal suspended from a red ribbon containing white streaks, was created in 1916 and presented to soldiers who had served twelve months of active duty and participated in at least one battle. Its Maltese Cross–style medal and wreath design is strikingly similar to the later designed Tiffany Cross Medal of Honor. Photo: *Collection of Dwight Jon Zimmerman*

World War I medal awarded by the Austro-Hungarian Empire, the Karl-Troops Cross (*Karl-Truppenkreuz*). Another contributing factor to its unpopularity may have been the spelling of the word *Valour*. Just for reasons of cultural history, both lexicographic and military, it was an odd choice, one never explained. On top of that, during the interwar years the U.S. Navy had a love-hate relationship with the Royal Navy. Perhaps this was an expression of nautical diplomacy by someone in the Navy Department? If so, it didn't work.

In 1942, when noncombat criteria for the Medal of Honor was abolished, the navy reverted back to its original five-point-star design. Because no records were kept regarding which navy Medal of Honor design was awarded, the exact number of Tiffany Cross recipients is unknown. Of all Medal of Honor designs, the air force Medal of Honor has the technical distinction of being the most rare. Authorized in 1965, only thirteen have been awarded, all for acts occurring during the Vietnam War. Yet because the navy's Tiffany Cross Medal of Honor was abolished after only twenty-three years of use, and was awarded possibly to as few as seventeen men (a high estimate places it in the low thirties), it is regarded as the rarest of the group. As such, in the illegal collector's market it is the most valuable.

BENDING THE RULES:
THE CASE OF GENERAL DOUGLAS MACARTHUR
On at least one occasion, political expediency has trumped regulations, as was the case in the Medal of Honor awarded to General Douglas MacArthur. The first six months of World War II following the Japanese attack of Pearl Harbor

on December 7, 1941, was among the blackest of periods in American military history. In the Atlantic Ocean, German submarines were sinking merchant ships with impunity. Japanese forces in the Pacific and Asia were racking up one conquest after another, and there was nothing the ill-prepared United States could do to stop either. The most tragic situation was in the Philippine Islands, which at the time was a United States protectorate. General Douglas Mac-Arthur was the commander of American and Philippine troops on the islands. Because the disaster at Pearl Harbor had crippled the navy's Pacific fleet, the Philippines was an isolated outpost that could not be resupplied or reinforced. MacArthur had to fight with what he had for as long as he could, buying as much time as possible for the desperately rearming United States before ultimately surrendering.

Army Chief of Staff General George Marshall was no fan of MacArthur's—and MacArthur, whose military genius was rivaled only by his enormous ego, rarely held in check his contempt for Marshall. Though Marshall did have a vindictive streak, he was also pragmatic, and (however much he publicly denied it) an astute politician. Marshall recognized MacArthur's military genius and value to the morale of the nation and was willing to set aside animus for the greater good of the country. If that meant awarding MacArthur the Medal of Honor, then so be it. At the time, plans were being prepared to order MacArthur to leave the Philippines for Australia, where he could command the counteroffensive. (MacArthur would depart from the Philippines in March, after having been ordered to do so by President Franklin Roosevelt; the last American and Philippine troops finally surrendered in May 1942.) Awarding MacArthur the Medal of Honor would offset any Japanese propaganda that accused Mac-Arthur of cowardly deserting his post.

On January 30, 1942, at the end of the first month of the Japanese siege of MacArthur's troops on the Bataan peninsula, Marshall cabled Major General Richard K. Sutherland, MacArthur's chief of staff at the army's headquarters on the Philippine island of Corregidor, instructing him to "transmit at proper time your recommendations and supporting statement with appropriate description of any act believed sufficient to warrant [MacArthur the Medal of Honor]."[5]

There things stood for about a month. Then, on February 26, Congressman James E. Van Zandt of Pennsylvania, a Republican (MacArthur was held in high regard in Republican circles), introduced House Resolution 6685, authorizing President Roosevelt to present the Medal of Honor to MacArthur. In an internal memo, Marshall told Secretary of War Henry Stimson that he "felt that the honor would mean more if it developed from War Department rather than Congressional recognition."[6] What Marshall left unsaid, but which Stimson no doubt understood, was that it better reflected on Roosevelt's administration if the War Department did the deed. And Republicans in Congress could hardly grouse about being trumped, because Stimson was a respected Republican in Roosevelt's bipartisan cabinet.

About three weeks later, Sutherland cabled a suggestion that MacArthur's award "be based upon his utter contempt of danger under terrific aerial bombardments" and for his "magnificent leadership and vision."[7] Sutherland also recommended that the citation be written in Washington, because such a lengthy coded message coming from Corregidor risked compromising the only secure code they had.

Marshall personally wrote MacArthur's Medal of Honor citation and forwarded it to Stimson, with a cover letter that observed, "...while there is no specific act of General Mac-Arthur's to justify the award of the Medal of Honor under a literal interpretation of the statutes, I feel that the services that he has rendered merit some recognition far above that of any other decoration which we now confer." Marshall used as his precedent the awarding of the Medal of Honor by Congress to Charles Lindbergh for his 1927 solo crossing of the Atlantic Ocean. (Perhaps reflecting the strong interservice rivalry that existed then, he did not include Byrd, a Navy man, in his argument.) Marshall concluded, "I submit this recommendation to you not only because I feel that General MacArthur is deserving of the honor but also because I am certain that this action will meet with popular approval, both within and without the armed forces, and will have a constructive morale value."[8]

Within two weeks, in a ceremony in Canberra, Australia, General Douglas MacArthur received the Medal of Honor, making him and his father, Lieutenant General Arthur MacArthur, the first of only two father-son pairs to receive the decoration, the elder MacArthur having received his for action in the Civil War.

Years later, they were joined by Major General Theodore Roosevelt Jr. and his father, President Theodore Roosevelt, both of whom received theirs posthumously: the son for leading troops on Utah Beach during D-day, June 6, 1944, and the father for his actions on San Juan Hill during the 1898 Spanish-American War.

It could be argued that, however unintended, MacArthur's 1942 Medal of Honor corrected an earlier snub. In 1914, the

This official photograph of General David H. Petraeus contains a typical example of a senior officer's Pyramid of Valor decorations. The left breast contains his individual medals. The three bottom rows contain NATO, United Nations, and foreign civil and military decorations. Above them are his U.S. campaign decorations. The uppermost rows contain his individual achievement medals. These include the Bronze Star with V device (indicating it is for a combat-related action), the Legion of Merit with three Oak Leaf Clusters (indicating three additional awards), and the Distinguished Service Order with one Oak Leaf Cluster. The badges immediately surrounding these medals include the Combat Action Badge (top), the Master Parachutist Badge (lower left), and the Air Assault Badge (lower right).
Photo: *Department of Defense*

then captain Douglas MacArthur led what would today be considered a special operations mission during the Veracruz Expedition, the temporary seizure of Mexico's primary gulf port in order to thwart German exploitation in the country. For his part in that action, MacArthur's commander recommended him for the Medal of Honor, which was endorsed by Army Chief of Staff Leonard Wood. But the review board ultimately rejected the recommendation.

VALOR DELAYED

While heroism itself has always been class- and color-blind, the individuals responsible for officially honoring it have not always been as egalitarian. Racist attitudes and policies combined to deprive recognition by means of the Medal of Honor of the heroic deeds of men from minorities who served the nation in times of war. There were, however, exceptions. Probably the most conspicuous was the case of Robert Augustus Sweeney of the U.S. Navy, an African American and one of the nineteen double Medal of Honor recipients. He received both during peacetime in the early 1880s in two separate incidents involving the rescues of drowning sailors.

At the end of the Civil War, the Union army contained about 179,000 African American troops, organized into segregated units commanded by white officers. These "colored units," as they were known, accounted for roughly 10 percent of the army.[9] (The army remained segregated until 1948, when President Harry Truman integrated the military by executive order.) The navy had about 19,000 African Americans. Prejudice confined most colored units to garrison or other noncombat, menial duties. The most famous colored unit was the Fifty-fourth Massachusetts Regiment (subject of the movie *Glory*). Of the 1,522 Medals of Honor distributed during the Civil War, twenty-five[10] went to African Americans, six to Jewish Americans,[11] and two to Hispanic Americans.[12]

Of the 426 Medals of Honor awarded during the Indian Wars, African-American troops received 18, with 14 of them going to the "Buffalo Soldiers"[13]—members of the first all–African-American regiments in the U.S. Army established by Congress after the Civil War. In addition, fifteen Medals of Honor went to Native Americans[14] who served as cavalry scouts, and two went to Jewish American soldiers.[15]

During the Spanish-American War, 110 Medals of Honor were awarded,[16] with six going to African Americans.[17]

In World War I, the United States fielded about 2 million troops in France.[18] Approximately 350,000, or about 17.5 percent of the total, were African Americans.[19] Once again, the segregated units were for the most part confined to support roles away from the front lines, though this time African Americans filled the junior-officer ranks. When a German offensive threatened to rupture the French lines, some black regiments were temporarily attached to the French army to stop the German advance. One such unit was the 369th Infantry Regiment, the "Harlem Hellfighters." This unit fought with such distinction during that period that the entire unit was awarded the Croix de Guerre and 171 members received France's highest award, the Legion of Honor.[20]

When World War I ended, the United States awarded a

total of 118 Medals of Honor:[21] five went to Jewish Americans,[22] one to an Hispanic American,[23] and none were awarded to African Americans.[24]

During World War II, approximately 13 million men and women served in the military.[25] African Americans were the largest minority, with approximately one million.[26] By the end of the war, 432 Medals of Honor had been awarded.[27] Of that total, thirty-eight went to Hispanic Americans,[28] ten to Native Americans,[29] three to Jewish Americans,[30] two to Asian Pacific Americans,[31] and *none* to African Americans.[32]

Because of the statute of limitations regarding presentations, it appeared that a review to correct inequities was impossible. Then, in 1987, Congressmen Joe DioGuardi and Mickey Leland, while conducting research on another matter, discovered a case file dated 1918 containing the Medal of Honor recommendation for Corporal Freddie Stowers, an African American. A native of Anderson County, South Carolina, Stowers served in Company C of the 371st Infantry Regiment. On September 28, 1918, his company was one of the lead units in an attack in the Champagne Marne sector of northern France. The company soon suffered 50 percent casualties. Corporal Stowers rallied his squad and pressed the attack against a German machine-gun nest, which they destroyed. He then led an attack against the enemy's second trench line even while mortally wounded.

DioGuardi and Leland brought the file to the army's attention. It was determined that the file had been misplaced, and the case was officially revived. In a White House ceremony presided over by President George H. W. Bush on April 4, 1991—attended by Stowers's two sisters and his great-grandnephew, who had served in the first Gulf War as a staff sergeant in the 101st Airborne—Corporal Freddie Stowers posthumously received his Medal of Honor.

Two years later, the army asked Shaw University, the nation's oldest black college, to research and prepare a study "to determine if there was a racial disparity in the way Medal of Honor recipients were selected"[33] during World War II. When the university's team finished its research, it determined that a disparity existed in ten cases where soldiers had received the Distinguished Service Cross, and it recommended that the army award those ten individuals with the Medal of Honor. The army reviewed the files and recommended that seven of the ten receive the award. Congress passed the necessary legislation lifting the statutory limit, and on January 13, 1997, President Clinton officially presented the recipients their awards. Of the seven, only one, Vernon J. Baker, was alive to receive the decoration.

In 1996, Congress directed the army to conduct a similar review, this time focusing on Asian-Pacific Americans who received the Distinguished Service Cross in World War II, "to determine whether any such award should be upgraded to the Medal of Honor."[34] This time a team from the Department of Defense's Defense Language Institute, an educational and research institution, conducted a review. It completed its research in 1998, finding that twenty-two individuals should receive the Medal of Honor.

On June 21, 2000, President Clinton presented the medals to the recipients or their families. Thirteen Medals of Honor were awarded to men of the "Purple Heart Battalion," the 442nd Infantry Regiment, a storied Japanese-American unit that fought in Italy, southern France, and Germany. One of those thirteen at the White House that day was Senator Daniel Inouye of Hawaii, who lost the use of his right arm during the action for which he finally received the Medal of Honor.

In 2001, Congress ordered that the army conduct a similar review for Jewish American and Hispanic American servicemen. As a result, in 2005, the Holocaust survivor and Korean War veteran Tibor Rubin received his Medal of Honor from President George W. Bush.

VALOR UNRECOGNIZED:
JOE FOSS AND POST-9/11 AIRPORT SECURITY

For at least half of the twentieth century, Medal of Honor recipients were widely recognized and treated as celebrities by the general population. The Medal of Honor recipient Army Sergeant Alvin York's exploits in World War I were turned into a 1941 movie starring Gary Cooper. During and following World War II, recipients reached their peak of acclaim, becoming as famous as movie stars. In fact, the Medal of Honor recipient Captain Audie Murphy, the most-decorated serviceman in World War II, actually became a successful movie star after the war. How much things have changed since then—both toward the recipients and the medal itself—was revealed in Phoenix, Arizona, on January 11, 2002.

Captain Joe Foss became the Marine Corps's leading flying ace in World War II with 26 airborne victories against enemy aircraft. Foss received his Medal of Honor from President Roosevelt in a White House ceremony on May 18, 1943. He later served as a colonel in the Korean War, was elected governor of his home state of South Dakota, served as the first president of the American Football League, and later was a president of the National Rifle Association (NRA). He was also a member of the Air National Guard, eventually retiring with the rank of brigadier general.

In retirement, Foss settled in Arizona. In 2002, Foss was planning to visit the United States Military Academy at West Point, where he had been invited to deliver a lecture. But at the America West Airline terminal at Phoenix Sky Harbor International Airport, on January 11, 2002, the eighty-six-year-old man was asked to step to one side for additional inspection by security personnel. The screeners had seen some "suspicious objects" in his jacket as it was going through the security X-ray machine.

Among the items the screeners found was a dummy-bullet key chain, with a hole drilled in the base of the cartridge to render it nonfunctional—a gift from actor Charlton Heston, who was then the president of the NRA. Foss was also carrying a combination penknife/file with the Medal of Honor insignia and a five-pointed object that, to the airport security personnel, resembled the Japanese throwing-star weapon known as a *shuriken*. Foss tried to explain to the security personnel that the object they were turning over and over and passing back and forth to each other was his *Medal of Honor*.

Foss found himself shunted from one group of security personnel to another. Three times he had to take off his cowboy hat, his bolo tie, his belt with its "Dakota Gun Collectors" buckle, and his boots. When he asked what would happen to his key chain, penknife/file, and Medal of Honor, the three items that the security personnel intended to keep, he was told that they would be "destroyed."[35] For forty-five minutes, Brigadier General Foss was detained and interrogated as a possible terrorist suspect, and he wound up missing his flight. Finally, he was allowed to board a later flight, after the security personnel agreed to let him mail to himself his key chain and penknife/file. Somehow, he succeeded in convincing them to allow him to carry his Medal of Honor on board.

News of this interrogation of a Medal of Honor war hero created a storm of controversy, the media using it as an example of the overreactive abuse of passengers by airport security personnel. In interviews, Foss said, "I wasn't upset for me. I was upset for the Medal of Honor, that [the security people] just didn't know what it even was. It represents all of the guys who lost their lives—the guys who never came back; everyone who put their lives on the line for their country. You're supposed to know what the Medal of Honor is."[36]

BUYING AND SELLING VALOR

There are war stories, and then there are war lies. Over time, memories fade. And as the years increase, it's common for tales of an individual's wartime exploits to become greater as well. This "burnishing of one's legacy" is one of the reasons historians place more veracity on oral histories and interviews taken soon after an event, when memories are fresh and fact-checking is easier. But telling thrilling tales to grandchildren is one thing. Lying about one's military record and wearing the panoply to support it, for financial or other gain, is fraud.

It was against this possibility of fraud regarding possession of the Medal of Military Merit that General George Washington established the *Book of Merit* in which "the name and regiment of the person with the action so certified are to be entered...which will be kept at the orderly office." In addition, if anyone falsely claimed to have been awarded the decoration, that person "shall be severely punished."[37] Congress, on the other hand, did not include any penalty for fraudulent claims or displays when it passed the original legislation creating the Medal of Honor.

The Medal of Honor Legion was successful in finally tightening the qualifications for recipients and striking from the honor roll those who improperly received them. When the army's Medal of Honor was totally redesigned in 1903, a patent was issued. When it expired in the 1920s, Congress passed legislation making illegal the production, distribution, or wearing of the Medal of Honor (except, of course, for actual recipients). For years, the maximum fine for unauthorized sale or possession of a Medal of Honor was $250—provided that the seller, buyer, or wearer was caught, an extremely rare occurrence. Since dealers in collectibles could sell a Medal of Honor for $500 or more, this fine was regarded as simply a cost of doing business.

A common misconception is that the United States's military medals, like the country's coins and currency, are manufactured by the U.S. Mint. The U.S. Army Institute of Heraldry is the government agency responsible for the design of medals, crests, flags, and other official symbols for the military and government agencies. But the manufacture of medals themselves is awarded to private firms through low-bid contract competitions. That includes the Medal of Honor.

For many years, the company that made the Medal of Honor was His Lordship Products, Inc., later named H.L.I. Lordship Industries. Founded in 1948 and originally based in New York City (it later moved to Hauppauge, Long Island), it began operations by making high-quality nautical-themed jewelry and mementos, eventually branching into branded commemorative products and such knickknacks as key chains with company logos.

In 1959, the company received its first military contract, producing the cap badge for the navy's WAVES (Women Accepted for Volunteer Emergency Service). Within a few short years it was awarded contracts to produce commemorative items such as the PT-109 tie clasps handed out by President John F. Kennedy, as well as medals for the military such as the Legion of Merit, the Air Force Cross, the Purple Heart, the Commendation Medal and Distinguished Service Medal for each military branch, the Republic of Vietnam Service Medal, and the Medal of Honor.

The terms of the Medal of Honor contract called for "100 percent inspection, no defects."[38] As a result, as much as 25 percent of the production run was rejected for flaws. Regarding the production cost of the medal itself, in a 1969 article that originally appeared in *Stars and Stripes*, William McAllister, a vice president of the company, said, "We make certain we never make a penny on them. The cost is figured as finely as we can get it, and that is the full amount of our bid. You just couldn't possibly want to make money on something like the Medal of Honor, and I'm sure that's the way most people would feel about it." McAllister went on to say that periodically he would receive letters from servicemen or former servicemen requesting to buy replacement Medals of Honor for those they claimed to have been either lost or misplaced. McAllister stated that he would write back, informing them that they needed to contact government authorities. The article concludes with his declaring, "The brass medal, worth only a few cents, isn't for sale at any price."

That was in 1969.

In October 1996, H.L.I. Lordship Industries entered a guilty plea "to multiple federal charges including the unauthorized production and sale [at $75 each] of 350 Medals of Honor"[39] that were sold to individuals and memorabilia dealers. These were not shoddy black-market knockoffs. These counterfeit Medals of Honor were made from U.S. government dies and materials used to make the official Medals of Honor—the equivalent of someone having the U.S. Mint's own printing plates, ink, and paper with which to make counterfeit currency. In addition to being fined $80,000, the company had to forfeit the money it had received from the illegal sale and was barred from receiving any government contracts for fifteen years.

FBI Special Agent Tom Cottone was the one who did the sleuthing and exposed H.L.I. Lordship Industries. Over the years, Special Agent Cottone made it a personal mission to ferret out the illegal trafficking and display of the Medal of Honor and other decorations. Cottone suspected that H.L.I. actually sold more than a thousand illegal Medals of Honor in the memorabilia market, but the statute of limitations only enabled him to charge the company for the 350 sales. Of the dozens of cases he successfully closed, he later observed, "Every [Medal of Honor] I've taken off the neck of these imposters has come from that company."[40]

Arguably the most sensational fraud Cottone exposed was the Illinois district court judge Michael O'Brien, who illegally possessed not one but *two* Medals of Honor. Before 1919, it was possible for an individual to receive more than one, and as has previously been noted, nineteen men have done so. But legislation passed after World War I has since made the awarding of the Medal of Honor a one-time thing. Judge O'Brien had the medals displayed in his chambers. The backs of the medals were inscribed with the recipient's name and date of the action for which the decoration was awarded. In the judge's case, the date revealed on one medal was July 22, 1958. The only military operation during that time was Operation Blue Bat, the landing of the U.S. Marine Corps during the Lebanon crisis. There is no record of any Medals of Honor awarded during that campaign.

O'Brien's brazen deception as a medal recipient led to his leading local parades, giving speeches, and being regarded as a local celebrity. Had he confined his activities to just his community, chances are his fraud would not have been discovered. But in 1995, he chose to apply to the Illinois Department of Motor Vehicles for a special Medal of Honor license plate. Harold Fritz, an actual Medal of Honor recipient, was alerted by a friend who worked at the DMV. Fritz called the FBI. Facing federal charges, O'Brien chose to resign to avoid prosecution.

Cottone has uncovered Medal of Honor frauds at each of four Medal of Honor recipient gatherings he has attended. But perhaps the most bizarre exposé he participated in occurred during a ceremony in which he was being honored. In October 2002, Cottone was one of four people being recognized by the Marine Corps with the highest tribute they can accord someone not of the service, that of "honorary marine." One of the other individuals was Navy Captain Roger Dean Edwards, an ordained Episcopal priest. Cottone was being recognized for his efforts in exposing medal fraud, Captain Edwards for his lifesaving work in assignments with the Marine Corps. Even among the distinguished assemblage that included the then Marine Corps commandant general James L. Jones, Edwards stood out. His full dress uniform contained almost two dozen ribbons, including the Navy Cross, Distinguished Flying Cross, Silver Star with Oak Leaf Cluster, Legion of Merit, Bronze Star with Oak Leaf Cluster, the Purple Heart with two Oak Leaf Clusters, and the Defense Meritorious Service Medal, among other decorations.

Cottone became suspicious after he read Edwards's biography, which was printed in the ceremony's program. Something about the captain's career and the wealth of decorations on his chest seemed too good to be true. Cottone later pulled Edwards's file and discovered that it was. In 2004, Edwards was court-martialed on multiple counts. He pleaded guilty to wearing twelve unauthorized decorations. His thirty-six-year career, in which he had made an important contribution to lifesaving medical technologies in Operation Iraqi Freedom, was in ruins.

STOLEN VALOR ACT OF 2005

On August 5, 1958, President Dwight Eisenhower signed the charter establishing the nonprofit organization the Congressional Medal of Honor Society. Based in Mt. Pleasant, South

Carolina, its purpose is to protect and preserve the dignity of the Medal of Honor, to assist needy recipients, and to protect recipients from exploitation. It is the historical repository for the Medal of Honor and contains a list of every Medal of Honor recipient as well as biographies of each individual.

Another vigilant organization is HomeofHeroes.com. Based in Pueblo, Colorado, and operated by C. Douglas Sterner, a two-tour Vietnam War veteran, and Pamela Sterner, it was launched on July 26, 1998. It has been recognized by both the Congressional Medal of Honor Society and the FBI as a primary database resource in the identification and tracking down of medal frauds.

It was Sterner's senior college thesis paper on medal frauds and the loopholes in federal laws regarding military awards that was the catalyst for what came to be known as the Stolen Valor Act of 2005. Introduced in the House of Representatives by Congressman John T. Salazar of Colorado on July 19, 2005, and in the Senate by Senator Kent Conrad of North Dakota on November 10, 2005, the act was signed into law on December 20, 2006. The purpose of the legislation is to tighten the existing law and increase the penalties for the unauthorized wear, manufacture, sale, or claim—written or verbal—of *any* military decorations and medals. The maximum prison sentence was raised and is now one year, and fines range from a few hundred dollars to hundreds of thousands. Since then, more than two-dozen individuals have been prosecuted under the new law.

NOTES

1. Home of Heroes, "Cavanaugh, Thomas, Medal of Honor Citation," *HomeofHeroes.com*,

http://www.homeofheroes.com/moh/citations_/Cavanaugh_
thomas.html (accessed August 14, 2009).

2. Home of Heroes, "Buchanan, David M., Medal of Honor Citation,"
   HomeofHeroes.com,
   http://www.homeofheroes.com/moh/citations_peace/Buchanan_
   david.html (accessed August 14, 2009).
3. Home of Heroes, "Lindbergh, Charles A., Medal of Honor Citation,"
   HomeofHeroes.com,
   http://www.homeofheroes.com/moh/citations_peace/Lindbergh_
   charles.html (accessed August 14, 2009).
4. Home of Heroes, "Byrd, Richard Evelyn, Jr., Medal of Honor
   Citation," *HomeofHeroes.com*,
   http://www.homeofheroes.com/moh/citations_peace/byrd.html
   (accessed August 13, 2009).
5. Bland, Larry I., *The Papers of George Catlett Marshall*, (Baltimore:
   Johns Hopkins University Press, 1991), 3:148.
6. Ibid, 3:148.
7 Ibid, 3:148.
8. Ibid, 3:148.
9. "Teaching with Documents: The Fight for Equal Rights: Black
   Soldiers in the Civil War."
   http://www.archives.gov/education/lessons/blacks-civil-war/
   (accessed August 16, 2009).
10. Wikipedia, "List of African American Medal of Honor Recipients,"
    Wikipedia.com
    http://en.wikipedia.org/wiki/List_of_African_American_Medal_of
    _Honor_recipients (accessed August 16, 2009).
11. Wikipedia, "List of Jewish Medal of Honor Recipients,"
    Wikipedia.com, http://en.wikipedia.org/wiki/List_of_Jewish_Medal
    _of_Honor_recipients (accessed August 16, 2009).
12. Wikipedia, "List of Hispanic Medal of Honor Recipients,"
    Wikipedia.com
    http://en.wikipedia.org/wiki/List_of_Hispanic_Medal_of_Honor_
    recipients (accessed August 16, 2009).
13. Wikipedia, "List of African American Medal of Honor Recipients."
14. Wikipedia, "List of Native American Medal of Honor Recipients,"
    Wikipedia.com,
    http://en.wikipedia.org/wiki/List_of_Native_American_Medal_of
    _Honor_recipients (accessed August 11, 2009).

15. Wikipedia, "List of Jewish Medal of Honor Recipients."
16. Home of Heroes, "Medal of Honor Statistics," *HomeofHeroes.com*, http://www.homeofheroes.com/moh/history/history_statistics.html (accessed August 16, 2009).
17. Wikipedia, "List of African American Medal of Honor Recipients."
18. Johnson, Thomas H., ed., *The Oxford Companion to American History*, (New York: Oxford University Press, 1966), 874.
19 "African American Odyssey: World War I and Postwar Society (Part 1)," Library of Congress, http://memory.loc.gov/ammem/aaohtml/exhibit/aopart7.html (accessed August 16, 2009).
20. *"La Guerre 1914–1918-Halluin (87) Les Soldats Afro-Américains Honorés*," http://brandodean.over-blog.org/article-24738556.html (accessed August 16, 2009).
21. Home of Heroes, "Medal of Honor Statistics."
22. Wikipedia, "List of Jewish Medal of Honor Recipients."
23. Wikipedia, "List of Hispanic Medal of Honor Recipients."
24. Wikipedia, "List of African American Medal of Honor Recipients."
25. Dear, I.C.B. and M.R.D. Foot, ed., *The Oxford Companion to World War II*, (New York: Oxford University Press, 1995), 1192, 1198
26. Ibid, 6.
27. Home of Heroes, "Medal of Honor Statistics."
28. Wikipedia, "List of Hispanic Medal of Honor Recipients."
29. Wikipedia, "List of Native American Medal of Honor Recipients."
30. Wikipedia, "List of Jewish Medal of Honor Recipients."
31. Wikipedia, "List of Asian American Medal of Honor Recipients," *Wikipedia.com*, http://en.wikipedia.org/wiki/List_of_Asian_American_Medal_of_Honor_recipients (accessed March 28, 2010).
32. Wikipedia, "List of African American Medal of Honor Recipients."
33. U.S. Army Center of Military History, "African American World War II Medal of Honor Recipients," http://www.history.army.mil/html/moh/mohb.html (accessed August 11, 2009).
34. U.S. Army Center of Military History, "Asian Pacific American World War II Medal of Honor Recipients," http://www.history.army.mil/moh/ap-moh1.html (accessed August 11, 2009).

35. McCafferty, Dan, "Decorated WWII Veteran Detained, Searched at Airport," *CNN.com*, February 27, 2002, http:archives.cnn.com/2002/US/02/27/war.hero.cnna/ (accessed August 14, 2009).
36. Mikkelson, Barbara, "Medal Detector," *Snopes.com*, 2002, http://www.snopes.com/military/medal.asp (accessed August 14, 2009).
37. Sterner, Pamela M., "Closing the Loopholes in Title 18 Regarding Military Awards," 2004, http://www.homeofheroes.com/temporary_files/moh_legislation.html (accessed July 9, 2009).
38. The information about His Lordship Products originally appeared in an article in the January 19, 1969 European edition of *Stars and Stripes*, an independent newspaper distributed to the U.S. military community. It was available on the Congressional Medal of Honor Society website as late as September 5, 2007. Though available as late as August 18, 2009 on the *Stars and Stripes* website (www.stripes.com/article.asp?section=126&article=23361&archive=true), the article has since been deleted from the Congressional Medal of Honor Society website.
39. Sterner, "Closing the Loopholes."
40. Bailey, Laura, "Foundation Member is a Medal Cop, One-Man Fraud Squad," *Marine Corps Times*, undated, http://www.homeofheroes.com/herobill/News/cottone.htm (accessed August 18, 2009).

BIBLIOGRAPHY

BOOKS

Astor, Gerald. *The Right to Fight: A History of African Americans in the Military*. Cambridge, MA: Da Capo Press, 2001.

Bland, Larry I. *The Papers of George Catlett Marshall* Vol. 3. Baltimore: Johns Hopkins University Press, 1991.

Byrd, Richard Evelyn. *Discovery: The Story of the Second Byrd Antarctic Expedition*. New York: Putnam, 1935.

Dear, I.C.B. and M.R.D. Foot, ed. *The Oxford Companion to World War II*. New York: Oxford University Press, 1995.

Johnson, Thomas H., ed. *The Oxford Companion to American History*. New York: Oxford University Press, 1966.

Perret, Geoffrey. *There's a War to Be Won: The United States Army in World War II.* New York: Ivy Books, 1997.

Zimmerman, Dwight Jon. *First Command: Paths to Leadership.* St. Petersburg, FL: Vandamere Press, 2005.

MONOGRAPHS

Sterner, Pamela M. "Closing the Loopholes in Title 18 Regarding Military Awards." 2004. http://www.homeofheroes.com/temporary_files/moh_legislation.html (accessed July 9, 2009).

INTERNET

Bailey, Laura. "Foundation Member is a Medal Cop, One-Man Fraud Squad." *Marine Corps Times*, undated. http://www.homeofheroes.com/herobill/News/cottone.htm (accessed August 18, 2009).

Center of Military History. "African American World War II Medal of Honor Recipients." http://www.history.army.mil/html/moh/mohb.html (accessed August 11, 2009).

———. "Asian Pacific American World War II Medal of Honor Recipients." http://www.history.army.mil/moh/ap-moh1.html (accessed August 11, 2009).

Cornell University Law School. "U.S. Code Collection. Title 10,3741. Medal of Honor: Award." http://www.law.cornell.edu/uscode/html/uscode10/usc_sec_10_00003741——000-notes.html (accessed August 11, 2009).

Eisman, Dale. "Medals of Dishonor." *Virginian-Pilot*, July 31, 2004. http://www.leatherneck.com/forums/archive/index.php/t-15980.html (accessed August 18, 2009).

George Bush Presidential Library and Museum. "Remarks at a Ceremony for the Posthumous Presentation of the Medal of Honor to Corporal Freddie Stowers." April 24, 1991. http://bushlibrary.tamu.edu/research/public_papers.php?id=2916&year=1991&month=4 (accessed August 16, 2009).

Hennessey, Walter. "Creating the Medal of Honor." *Stars and Stripes*, January 19, 1969.

http://www.stripes.co/article.asp?section=
126&article=23361&archive=true
(accessed August 18, 2009).
Home of Heroes. "Buchanan, David M., Medal of Honor
Citation." *HomeofHeroes.com*.
http://www.homeofheroes.com/moh/citations_peace/
Buchanan_david.html (accessed August 14, 2009).
————. "Byrd, Richard Evelyn, Jr., Medal of Honor Citation."
HomeofHeroes.com.
http://www.homeofheroes.com/moh/citations_peace/byrd.html
(accessed August 13, 2009).
————. "Cavanaugh, Thomas, Medal of Honor Citation."
HomeofHeroes.com.
http://www.homeofheroes.com/moh/citations_/Cavanaugh
_thomas.html (accessed August 14, 2009).
————. "Lindbergh, Charles A., Medal of Honor Citation."
HomeofHeroes.com.
http://www.homeofheroes.com/moh/citations_peace/
Lindbergh_charles.html (accessed August 13, 2009).
————. "Medal of Honor Statistics." *HomeofHeroes.com*.
http://www.homeofheroes.com/moh/history/history_
statistics.html (accessed August 16, 2009).
————. "Stowers, Freddie, Medal of Honor Citation."
HomeofHeroes.com.
http://www.homeofheroes.com/moh/citations_1918_wwi/
stowers_freddie.html (accessed August 16, 2009).
————. "Tiffany Cross Info Needed." Forum. *HomeofHeroes.com*.
http://www.homeofheroes.com/cgi-bin/yabb2/YaBB.pl?num
=1074649893 (accessed August 14, 2009).
Klingbeil, Abigail. "FBI Agent Nails Medal of Honor Imposters."
Saratogian, July 4, 1998.
http://www.homeofheroes.com/a_homepage/community/
imposters/cottone.html (accessed July 9, 2009).
*"La Guerre 1914-1918-Halluin (87) Les Soldats Afro-Américains
Honorés."*
http://brandodean.over-blog.org/article-24738556.html
(accessed August 16, 2009).
Library of Congress. "African American Odyssey: World War I

and Postwar Society (Part 1)."
http://memory.loc.gov/ammem/aaohtml/exhibit/aopart7.html
(accessed August 16, 2009).

MacFarquhar, Neil. "Memento Dealer Held in Sale of Fake
Medals." *New York Times*, November 10, 1995.
http://www.nytimes.com/1995/11/10/nyregion/memento_
dealer-held-in-sale-of-fake-medals.html?pagewanted=print
(accessed July 9, 2009).

McCafferty, Dan. "Decorated WWII Veteran Detained, Searched
at Airport." *CNN.com*. February 27, 2002.
http://archives.cnn.com/2002/US/02/27/war.hero.cnna/
(accessed August 14, 2009).

McRae, Bennie J. Jr. "African Americans in World War II."
http://www.lwfaam.net/ww2/ (accessed August 16, 2009).

Mersky, Peter B. "Time of the Aces: Marine Pilots in the
Solomons."
http://www.nps.gov/archive/wapa/indepth/extContent/
usmc/pcn-190-003122-00/sec5.htm
(accessed August 14, 2009).

Mikkelson, Barbara. "Medal Detector." *Snopes.com*, 2002.
http://www.snopes.com/military/medal.asp
(accessed August 14, 2009).

Salazar, John T. "Stolen Valor Act of 2005."
http://www.house.gov/Salazar/Stolen%20Vaolr.shtml
(accessed July 9, 2009).

Shakelford, Michael. *Medals of Austria-Hungary.*
http://www.gwpda.org/medals/austmedl/Austria.html
(accessed August 14, 2009).

Sterner, C. Douglas. "The Stolen Valor Act of 2005."
http://www.pownetwork.org/phonies/stolen_valor_media_
information_sheet.htm (accessed July 9, 2009).

"Teaching with Documents: The Fight for Equal Rights:
Black Soldiers in the Civil War."
http://www.archives.gov/education/lessons/blacks-civil-war/
(accessed August 16, 2009).

Wikipedia. "List of African American Medal of Honor
Recipients." *Wikipedia.com.*

http://en.wikipedia.org/wiki/List_of_African_Amerian_Medal _of_Honor_recipients (accessed August 16, 2009).
————. "List of Asian American Medal of Honor Recipients." *Wikipedia.com.* http://en.wikipedia.org/wiki/List_of_Asian_ American_Medal_of_Honor_recipients (accessed March 28, 2010).
————. "List of Hispanic Medal of Honor Recipients." *Wikipedia.com.* http://en.wikipedia.org/wiki/List_of_Hispanic_Medal_of_ Honor_recipients (accessed August 16, 2009).
————. "List of Jewish Medal of Honor Recipients." *Wikipedia.com.* http://en.wikipedia.org/wiki/List_of_Jewish_Medal_of_ Honor_recipients (accessed August 16, 2009).
————. "List of Native American Medal of Honor Recipients." *Wikipedia.com.* http://en.wikipedia.org/wiki/List_of_Native_American_Medal _of_Honor_recipients (accessed August 11, 2009).
————. "Stolen Valor Act of 2005." *Wikipedia.com.* http://en.wikipedia.org/wiki/Stolen_Valor_Act_of_2005 (accessed July 9, 2009).

6

★ ★ ★ ★ ★ ★

Michael Anthony Monsoor

───────────────── ★ ─────────────────

*For conspicuous gallantry and intrepidity at the risk of his life
above and beyond the call of duty as automatic weapons gunner for Naval Special Warfare Task Group Arabian Peninsula,
in support of Operation Iraqi Freedom on 29 September 2006.
As a member of a combined SEAL and Iraqi Army sniper
overwatch element, tasked with providing early warning and
stand-off protection from a rooftop in an insurgent held sector
of ar Ramadi, Iraq, Petty Officer Monsoor distinguished himself by his exceptional bravery in the face of grave danger. In
the early morning, insurgents prepared to execute a coordinated attack by reconnoitering the area around the element's
position. Element snipers thwarted the enemy's initial
attempt by eliminating two insurgents. The enemy continued
to assault the element, engaging them with a rocket-propelled
grenade and small arms fire. As enemy activity increased,*

Petty Officer Monsoor took position with his machine gun between two teammates on an outcropping of the roof. While the SEALs vigilantly watched for enemy activity, an insurgent threw a hand grenade from an unseen location, which bounced off Petty Officer Monsoor's chest and landed in front of him. Although only he could have escaped the blast, Petty Officer Monsoor chose instead to protect his teammates. Instantly and without regard for his own safety, he threw himself onto the grenade to absorb the force of the explosion with his body, saving the lives of his two teammates. By his undaunted courage, fighting spirit, and unwavering devotion to duty in the face of certain death, Petty Officer Monsoor gallantly gave his life for his country, thereby reflecting great credit upon himself and upholding the highest traditions of the United States Naval Service.

—Medal of Honor Citation, April 8, 2008

★

I truly thought he was the toughest member of my platoon.

Lieutenant Commander Seth Stone,

—Delta Platoon Commander[1]

A SEAL FROM SOUTHERN CALIFORNIA

On April 5, 1981, in Long Beach, California, Sally Monsoor gave birth to her and her husband George's third child, Michael Anthony. Shortly after his birth, the family moved to nearby Garden Grove, just south of Anaheim, in Orange County.

Known to his childhood friends and family as Mikey, Michael Anthony Monsoor attended Dr. Walter C. Ralston Intermediate School and, in 1999, graduated from Garden Grove High School.

Quiet, polite, and humble, Mike was neither an A student nor a gifted athlete. But with a steely resolve that impressed everyone, he was determined to persevere in everything he tried, including playing tight end and defensive end on the Garden Grove Argonauts football team. Kris Van Hook, the Garden Grove High School physical education department chairman, joined the school when Mike was still a sophomore. He remembered that, "[Michael] wasn't real big and not a real great athlete. He was just the kind of guy who worked really, really hard."[2]

Another of Monsoor's high school teachers, Ken Frank, who had him for world history in his junior year, remembered Mike as "a real pleasant kid who had a lot of energy" and was particularly interested in World War II, the Vietnam War, and the Marine Corps. This was hardly surprising, since Mike was born into a proud Marine Corps family. His father and his older brother, James, had served in the Marine Corps, and his grandfather, George, had served in the navy.

His sister, Sara, who became a pediatric nurse, recalled that "Michael was a very loyal individual. He was also very particular about the people he hung out with or would let into his circle. But, once you were in, you were in."[3] This staunch loyalty was confirmed by one of his best friends, Patrick Barnes, who said, "[Mike] was selective about the friends he made. But when you became his friend, you became his brother."[4] Monsoor's penchant for hard work and undying loyalty to his friends and extended family would help make him a trusted and depended-upon noncommissioned officer in the navy—a career move he was destined to make.

While Mike had his serious side, he also knew how to have fun. Growing up in Southern California, he loved water sports of all kinds, riding motorcycles, and driving his Corvette. During the winter he could be seen snowboarding on the ski slopes. His favorite holiday was Halloween, and even as teens, he and his friends would go all out in dressing up in costume for the evening.

Occasionally, a name has meaning that defines the individual to whom it is given, and that was the case with Michael. A devoted Catholic of Christian Arab descent, his patron saint was Michael, *the guardian of warriors*. In addition, Monsoor in Farsi means, "blessed by God to be victorious"[5] or "defended, protected by God."[6]

With a proud family tradition of military service as his guide, Mike decided upon a career in the military. On March 21, 2001, he followed in his grandfather's footsteps and enlisted in the U.S. Navy.

He was sent to the navy's Recruit Training Command in Great Lakes, Illinois, north of Chicago. There he completed basic training and attended quartermaster A school, earning his quartermaster rating. After a short tour of duty at naval air station Sigonella, Italy, on the island of Sicily, Monsoor decided to try to qualify to become a SEAL. He entered Basic Underwater Demolition/SEAL (BUD/S) training in Coronado, California. Forced to withdraw when he suffered a broken heel, Monsoor was then posted to Europe where he stayed for two years. But his determination to become a

SEAL remained firm. At one point his mother visited him in Italy, and she saw that he was focused on "working out, swimming and running"[7] to make sure that he was fit enough to reenter the BUD/S program. Mike returned to Coronado in 2004 and graduated at the top of his class in March 2005. The next month he passed the tests that changed his rating from quartermaster to master-at-arms. This meant he had a military-police qualification regarding law enforcement, antiterrorism, force protection, and expeditionary warfare. He was assigned to SEAL Team 3 Delta Platoon, based in Coronado. In early 2006, he was notified that he and his platoon would be deployed to al Anbar Province, Iraq, that April. It was a posting he expected—and wanted. But before he debarked for his new post he gladly seized the chance to accompany his brother, Joe, on Joe's 1,700 mile, end-of-spring-break road trip from Garden Grove back to Minot State University, in North Dakota.

During the two-day trip, Mike talked to Joe about many things. One of them was the discipline it took during that first BUD/S course after he had broken his heel. Joe later said, "He still had to pass more physical tests. He was running hard in the sand, and the pain mounted, but he told himself, 'Don't pass out, I can't pass out.' But he couldn't continue." On the beach at the Coronado training center is a large ship's bell. Any time a SEAL candidate has reached his limit and can't continue, he approaches the bell and rings it, signifying that he's quitting the program. In an agonizing moment in which Mike faced the mounting pain of his injury and the realization of what it meant, Joe said, "He rang the bell." But true to his core beliefs, Monsoor knew he would try again and that he would ultimately succeed.

Petty Officer Second Class Michael Anthony
Monsoor on patrol in Iraq.
Photo: *U.S. Navy*

Now, Petty Officer Second Class Michael Anthony Monsoor was going to war as a SEAL heavy-weapons machine
gunner and communications operator, in a country that,
three years after Operation Iraqi Freedom, was in chaos and
wracked by civil war.

GOING TO HELL IN A HANDBASKET IN IRAQ

In June 2004, Major General James Mattis, commander of
the First Marine Division, which was responsible for security
in al Anbar Province, visited Ramadi. He told the Marine battalion stationed there, "Ramadi must hold, or the rest of the

province goes to hell."[8] In 2006, his prediction was coming true. The situation in Iraq, and in al Anbar Province in particular, was disastrous. The respected Marine Corps chief of intelligence in Iraq, Colonel Pete Devlin, filed a classified, internal Marine Corps intelligence report titled "State of the Insurgency in Iraq." It stated, in part, that there were *no functioning government institutions* in Anbar and that the power vacuum was being filled by insurgents from the terrorist group al Qaida in Iraq. In an ominous resonance with the Vietnam War, the five-page document, dated August 16, quotes an army officer as saying, "We haven't been defeated militarily but we have been defeated politically—and that's where wars are won and lost."[9] At that time, the most violent city in al Anbar Province was Ramadi, where, in the words of the embedded AP reporter Todd Pitman, the "sheer scale of violence . . . was astounding."[10]

The wide variety of reasons for the situation in Iraq were testimony to the extent and depth of the problems. Broadly, they could be grouped into eight major trends:

- Shia and Sunni sectarian fighting, led by the growth of some twenty-three militias around Baghdad, formed the foundation of the civil war.
- Baghdad and other major cities—such as Basra and Baquba—were almost completely divided into sectarian strongholds, as both Sunnis and Shia fled from neighborhoods in which they were a minority.
- The Sunni Arab insurgency remained focused in western al Anbar Province and benefited from the relocation of U.S. troops needed to quell sectarian violence in Baghdad.

- Attacks continued to be focused on civilians. In 2006, the two worst months for combined Iraqi civilian and security force casualties were August (233 security/police, 2,733 civilian, for an average of about 95 a day) and September (150 security/police, 3,389 civilian, for an average of about 118 a day).[11]
- The Shiite community was internally divided, increasingly along militia-support lines.
- U.S. military attention focused on curbing the heightened concentration of violence in Baghdad, while violence outside of the capital continued to intensify, particularly in key areas such as Baquba, Basra, Mosul, and Fallujah.
- Kurdish unrest festered in the north.
- There was increasing diplomatic pressure from bordering nations—Saudi Arabia, Syria, Iran, and Turkey—concerned that the Iraqi civil war would spread into their territory.[12]

Efforts by the Iraqi government to deal with the violence were crippled by the deteriorating economic conditions and rampant governmental corruption. And although Iraq ranked in the top five of the world's oil reserves, its heavily damaged infrastructure had created a severe energy crisis within the country. Oil production remained below pre-invasion levels, and electricity in Baghdad averaged less than seven hours a day. High unemployment, high inflation, and a burgeoning black market added to the economic chaos.[13]

Then there was the "brain drain." Though insurgent attacks affected every level of Iraqi society, insurgents specifically targeted educators and health-care providers. According to statistics compiled by the Iraqi Ministry of Education, "over 300 teachers and employees in the Ministry were killed and 1,158 wounded in 2006. . . . The highest rate of assassinations of Iraq academics—44 percent—occurred in Baghdad; Anbar, Mosul, and Basra each accounted for 10 percent of the total number of assassinations. . . . Almost no Ramadi schools opened for the 2006 school year due to threats from al Qaeda."[14] The problem was acutely dire for health-care workers. Both Sunni and Shiite doctors were targeted. As disastrous as it was that 455 doctors had been killed between the years 2003 and 2006, compounding it was the fact that more than seven thousand health-care workers had fled the country during the same period.[15]

In March 2006, Congress appointed the Iraq Study Group, a ten-person bipartisan panel, led by the former secretary of state James Baker III and the former representative Lee Hamilton. Its findings were released in December of that year. One of the most troubling problems it identified was the extent of corruption in the Iraqi government. One Iraqi official, speaking anonymously, estimated that corruption cost Iraq between five and seven billion dollars a year.[16] Instead of spending oil revenues to rebuild damaged or wrecked infrastructure, the money was funneled to private bank accounts, relatives of tribesmen, or, most troubling of all, to insurgent organizations intent on destabilizing the government.

The battle for money and its distribution that was being fought in Baghdad had far-reaching consequences for the U.S. military's attempt to restore order and to train and rebuild the Iraqi security forces in the provinces, particularly al Anbar Province.

American military attempts to recruit Iraqis were hamstrung by the government's inability to pay wages to police forces in al Anbar Province. U.S. Marine Brigadier General Robert Neller, deputy commander of U.S. troops in al Anbar, said that Sunni police officers told him they had not been paid in months, and for that reason, "People in Anbar think the [Shiite] government in Baghdad doesn't want them to succeed."[17] And even when they were paid, the salaries were so low and inflation so high that the money was virtually valueless.

Financially abandoned by their government, these and other security forces in the outer provinces supported their families the only way they could—by selling on the black market the weapons given to them by American troops. At least fourteen thousand weapons, most of them Glock pistols, found ready buyers. One black-market dealer said, "Almost all of [our] weapons come from the Iraqi police and army. They are our best suppliers. . . . In the south, if the Americans give the Iraqis weapons, the next day you can buy them here. The Iraqi army, the Iraqi police—they all sell them right away."[18]

Still, amid the chaos and doom, there were moments of humor, however dark or wry. For instance, a marine intelligence officer based in the provincial capital of Fallujah briefed a marine unit about to go on patrol, instructing them to be on the lookout for an insurgent believed to be living in the area they would enter. The description of the insurgent included the fact that he was a midget. A few hours later, the intelligence officer saw the patrol return with a truck-load of twenty-six flex-cuffed midgets. He discovered that "Fallujah was home to a small community of midgets, who banded together for support since they were considered as social outcasts." The patrol wanted to return to pick up the rest of the group, but the officer canceled the mission, "fig-uring [the insurgent] was long gone on his short legs after seeing his companions rounded up by the giant infidels."[19]

The same intelligence officer also noted something he couldn't help but admire: a broad daylight robbery by insur-gents of the main bank in Ramadi, where the thieves walked off with almost seven million dollars. As they exited, they happily waved to the marine combat outpost located beside the bank, and the oblivious marines genially waved back.[20]

RESTORING CONTROL IN AL ANBAR PROVINCE

Anbar is a predominantly Sunni province of about 1.2 mil-lion people that stretches from Baghdad west to the borders of Syria, Jordan, and Saudi Arabia and accounts for 30 per-cent of Iraq's land mass. At the turn of the twenty-first cen-tury, its capital, Ramadi, had about 500,000 people (as with many statistics in Iraq during the period, this is a best esti-mate) and, together with the major city of Fallujah (200,000–430,000 people), was part of the insurrection stronghold called the Sunni Triangle. Fallujah had been the site for Operation Phantom Fury in November 2004. This was an attempt by American, Iraqi, and British forces to regain control of the city from insurgents before the January 2005 national elections. Also known as the second battle of Fallujah, the two-month operation ended in a Coalition success with about 1,350 insurgents killed or captured, at a cost of 95 U.S. troops killed and 560 wounded and 11 Iraqi soldiers killed and 43 wounded—and the city was restored to Iraqi government control. But the high number of civilian casualties, estimated at 6,000, and the damage and destruction of 60 of the city's 200 mosques and at least half of the city's other buildings made it a controversial, if not pyrrhic, victory.

In 2006, Ramadi became an important battleground for what the embedded reporter Michael Fumento described as "both a litmus test for the counterinsurgency effort in Iraq and a laboratory"[21] in a broader strategy to secure the area and allow local Iraqi authorities to regain control of the region. Colonel Sean MacFarland, commander of the First Brigade combat team, First Armored Division, was made overall commander of the operation to subdue Ramadi. Among his mandates was to partner with Iraqi army and police units and train and mentor them in the conduct of counterinsurgency operations. With the experience of Fallujah a fresh memory, MacFarland's instructions were broad: "Fix Ramadi, but don't destroy it. Don't do a Fallujah."[22]

THE BATTLE OF RAMADI

With Fallujah in government hands, the center of power for the insurgency had shifted to Ramadi. On June 17, Colonel MacFarland launched a combined force assault on the city to root out and destroy the insurgents. U.S. Army and Marine Corps troops, SEALs, and Iraqi soldiers fought in what came to be called the Battle of Ramadi.

The main assaults on the city came from the north and the west and consisted of mechanized troops supported by heli-

Petty Officer Second Class Michael Monsoor with two SEAL
teammates while on patrol in Ar Ramadi, Iraq, in 2006.
Photo: *U.S. Navy*

copters and AC 130 Specter gunships. After scoring some initial successes, MacFarland's troops got bogged down in heavy
street fighting, and for several weeks the situation was so fluid
that it appeared MacFarland's effort was going to end in failure. Meanwhile, local resentment against al Qaida was building. Civilians hated the destruction of their homes and

businesses, the disruption of their lives, and the wide variety of terrorist killings, particularly the beheading of children. Then, the insurgents overplayed their hand by assassinating a local sheik, Abu Ali Jassim, on August 21. Jassim had encouraged members of his tribe to support the Coalition and join the Iraqi police force. Instead of leaving Jassim's body for burial, the insurrectionists took it and hid it in a field in violation of Islamic law. Within hours, the population in many neighborhoods turned against the insurrectionists. A group of forty sheiks from twenty tribes organized a movement called the *Sahwa Al Anbar* ("Anbar Awakening") that led to attacks on the insurgents by the local population in the suburbs. A new stage in the Battle of Ramadi had begun.

THE GRAVEYARD OF THE AMERICANS
Because his available force was relatively small, MacFarland chose an incremental block-by-block approach to eliminate insurgents and win over the local sheiks and residents. Targeting the places where enemy activity was strongest, he set up outposts designed to protect and secure the areas in which his troops had fought and to more quickly respond to any neighborhood flare-ups of fighting. The larger outposts were forward operation bases (FOBs); the smaller ones were combat operation posts (COPs).

In April 2006, Mike Monsoor's nineteen-man SEAL platoon was deployed to Ramadi and assigned to Task Unit Bravo, part of the U.S. Army's First Battalion, 506 Infantry Regiment (1-506) in FOB Camp Corregidor. The unit was assigned the Mulaab area, one of the most dangerous neighborhoods in Ramadi. Graffiti on building walls boasted that it was "the graveyard of the Americans."[23] The unit was tasked with a broad range of missions—among them patrols, raids, and providing sniper cover for search-and-seizure operations.

As the heavy-weapons machine gunner, carrying an Mk 48, Monsoor's position was immediately behind the point man when his team patrolled. This enabled him to provide heavy suppression fire to protect his platoon from a frontal enemy attack. Because he was also the team's communicator, on fifteen of the missions he carried a double load of ammunition *and* communication gear, collectively weighing over one hundred pounds. Yet even when temperatures topped 130 degrees Fahrenheit, Monsoor never complained.

Of all the missions he was on, only one out of four did *not* result in an enemy attack. Thirty-five of the missions erupted in firefights so fierce the streets were described as being "paved with fire." One such time occurred during a patrol on May 9. A teammate, caught in the middle of the street during a firefight, went down with a bullet wound to his leg. With another SEAL member providing cover, Monsoor, firing his Mk 48, dashed out into the street to rescue his teammate. Continuing to fire his machine gun with one hand while pulling the wounded SEAL with the other, and with insurgent bullets kicking up dust and concrete all around them, Monsoor managed to drag his teammate to safety without either of them being hit. For his courage under fire in this action, Mike Monsoor was awarded the Silver Star.

When he wasn't on the streets of Ramadi, Monsoor was above them—stationed in rooftop sniper posts. There, acting in his role as a communications specialist, he spotted enemy positions and called in supporting fire. Once again, he was awarded for his actions. Monsoor's contribution earned him the Bronze Star with V device (Valor), signifying he had earned it in combat.

With the situation tipping in favor of the Coalition forces, Colonel MacFarland decided the time was right for the next step. Codenamed Operation Kentucky Jumper, it was a clearance-and-isolation operation in southern Ramadi, using integrated American and Iraqi forces. The operation was scheduled to commence on September 29, 2006.

As he had always done before each previous mission, Monsoor attended mass before this one. Father Paul Halladay, the chaplain stationed in Ramadi at the time, conducted the service, which was on the feast day of Saint Michael, the protector of warriors.

Monsoor's assignment was to serve as the machine gunner for a combined-force team containing four SEALs and eight Iraqi Army soldiers. The team was tasked with a supporting role as a sniper-overwatch element guarding the battalion's western flank during ground operations. The morning of the twenty-ninth was clear, with good visibility. The combined SEAL and Iraqi team quickly found a rooftop location that gave them a good field of view for spotting and picking off any insurgent counterattacking force that might approach from the west.

Using tactical periscopes to scan for enemy activity, they soon spotted a group of four insurgents, armed with AK-47 assault rifles, conducting reconnaissance for follow-on attacks of the ground force. The snipers promptly engaged the enemy, killing one and wounding another. Not long after, a mutually supporting SEAL–Iraqi Army team killed another enemy fighter. After these two actions, area residents who supported the insurgents began blocking off the streets around Monsoor's team with rocks. The purpose was twofold, to warn away civilians and to alert insurgents that sniper teams were operating in the area. In addition, someone in a nearby mosque with a loudspeaker called upon insurgents to join together in an attack on the Coalition troops.

The first attack on their position began in the early afternoon. Suddenly, a vehicle loaded with insurgents firing automatic weapons charged the building. The SEALs promptly returned fire. One of the attackers shot a rocket-propelled grenade that hit the building. Though the SEALs and Iraqi soldiers knew the insurgents would follow up with additional attacks, the team stayed with the mission and refused to evacuate.

After reassessing the situation, the officer in charge, a SEAL lieutenant, identified the insurgents' most likely avenue of attack and positioned Monsoor with his heavy machine gun on the roof outcrop that overlooked it. Monsoor's location was near the rooftop's exit and between two SEAL snipers. This hide site allowed the three SEALs maximum coverage of the area.

Monsoor was using a tactical periscope when an insurgent managed to hurl a hand grenade up onto the roof. The grenade hit Monsoor's chest armor and bounced onto the rooftop. Monsoor was just a couple of steps away from the exit. He could have leaped through it to safety. But there were three other SEALs and eight Iraqi soldiers nearby, and no time to throw the grenade over the side.

Mike Monsoor shouted "Grenade!"[24] and threw himself

on it. The grenade detonated as he was covering it with his body. Shrapnel from the explosion hit the two SEALs closest to him, wounding them. But Monsoor had absorbed most of the blast. A medevac was called, and within minutes it carried the three wounded away. Miraculously, Monsoor was still alive when he arrived at the field hospital. But his wounds were mortal, and Father Halladay gave Monsoor last rites.

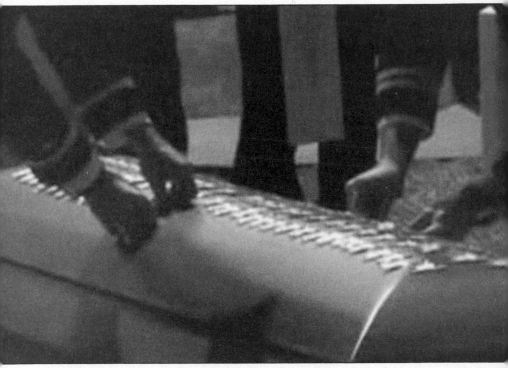

A screen-grab image taken from a YouTube video of Michael Monsoor's funeral, showing SEALs adding their badges to the lid of his coffin.
Source: *YouTube*

Thirty minutes after he had acted to save the lives of those with him, twenty-five-year-old Petty Officer Michael Monsoor was dead.

The lieutenant who was the officer in charge on the rooftop remembered that Monsoor "never took his eye off the grenade. His only movement was down toward it. He undoubtedly saved mine and the other SEALs' lives, and we owe him."[25]

Out of respect for the SEAL who had fought with them, members of the 1-506th held a special memorial service in his name. The Iraqi Army scouts whom Petty Officer Monsoor had helped train lowered their flag in memorial, and then, out of respect, sent it to his parents. Hard fighting for them all would continue into January 2007, but by the summer of that year, insurgent attacks in Ramadi had been eliminated.

Michael's body was taken to California, and he was buried at Fort Rosecrans National Cemetery in San Diego. As his coffin was being carried from the hearse to the grave site, the pallbearers walked between two rows of SEALs. When Monsoor's coffin passed, each SEAL placed his gold Trident badge on the coffin and pounded it into the wooden lid, embedding it there. By the time the casket arrived at the grave site, observers said the lid appeared to be covered in gold inlay.

HONORS

On April 8, 2008, in a ceremony at the White House presided over by President George W. Bush, Petty Officer Michael Monsoor's Medal of Honor was presented to his

The back of Petty Officer Second Class Michael Monsoor's Medal of Honor, showing its inscription.
Photo: *U.S. Navy*

parents. He became the third serviceman in the Iraq War, and the second from the navy, to receive the country's highest medal for valor. Also on that day, California Congresswoman Zoe Lofgren read into the *Congressional Record* the account of Monsoor's life and his self-sacrifice.

On October 29, 2008, Secretary of the Navy Donald C. Winter announced that DDG-1001, the second ship in the *Zumwalt* class of destroyers, would be christened *Michael Monsoor*. Four days earlier, on October 25, Michael Monsoor, SEAL Lieutenant Michael Murphy, and Marine Corporal Jason Dunham were honored with plaques in a rededication ceremony of the Semper Fi Marine Monument in San Clemente, California. It was the first time in the park's three-year history that both navy and marine personnel were honored together. Sara Monsoor attended the ceremony. In an interview with CNN that was later broadcast, she said, "I think that it is wonderful that they want to add him to this park with the marines. . . . My hope is that when people come here, these plaques inspire them to find out their stories and really inspire them to live their lives like these men did.

"I would like Mike to be remembered for his loyalty; he was a very respectful individual. . . . He was the type of person, when he set his mind to something, it was going to happen."[26]

NOTES

1. Krawzak, Paul M., "Family of Navy SEAL Michael Anthony Monsoor Will Accept Medal of Honor for Selfless Act of Heroism in Iraq," *SignonSanDiego.com*, April 8, 2008, http://www.signonsandiego.com/news/military/20080408-9999-1n8monsoor.html (accessed August 8, 2009).
2. Ibid.
3. Sara Monsoor, interview by CNN, *CNN.com*, http://www.youtube.com/watch?v = NOMLNiow4tg&feature =related (accessed August 9, 2009).
4. Bharath, Deepa, "Local Navy Seal, Michael Monsoor, Killed in Iraq," *Orange County Register*, October 4, 2006, http://la.indymedia.org/news/2006/10/181370_comment.php (accessed August 8, 2009).
5. Wikipedia, "Mansur," *Wikipedia.com*, http://en.wikipedia.org/wiki/Mansur (accessed August 9, 2009).
6. *Babynology*, http://www.babynology.com/meaning-mansoor-m32.html (accessed August 9, 2009).

7. Reyes, David, "Military Deaths," *Los Angeles Times*, October 8, 2006, http://articles.latimes.com/2006/oct/08/local/me-monsoor8 (accessed August 8, 2009).

8. Tyson, Ann Scott, "A Deadly Clash at Donkey Island," *Washington Post*, August 19, 2007, http://www.washingtonpost.com/wp-dyn/content/article/2007/08/18/AR2007081801270_pf.html (accessed August 9, 2009).

9. Ricks, Thomas E., "Situation Called Dire in West Iraq," *Washington Post*, September 11, 2006, http://www.washingtonpost.com/wp-dyn/content/article/2006/09/10/AR2006091001204.html (accessed March 8, 2009).

10. Fumento, Michael, "The New Band of Brothers: With the 1st Battalion, 506th Infantry Regiment, 101st Airborne Division in Ramadi," *Weekly Standard*, June 19, 2006, http://www.fumento.com/military/ramadi.html (accessed August 7, 2009).

11. Cordesman, Anthony H. with Emma Davies. *Iraq's Sectarian and Ethnic Violence and the Evolving Insurgency: Developments through mid-December 2006*, (Washington, D.C.: Center for Strategic and International Studies, 2006), 69.

12. Ibid, 3–4.

13. Ibid, 4.

14. Ibid, 40.

15. Ibid, 42.

16. Ibid, 30.

17. Ibid, 30.

18. Ibid, 39.

19. Donaldson, Will, "Email from Iraq," http://www.hqmc.net/index2.php?option=com_content&task=view&id=284&pop=1&page=0&ltemid=30 (accessed August 9, 2009).

20. Ibid.

21. Fumento, Michael, "Return to Ramadi," *Weekly Standard*, November 27, 2006, http://www.fumento.com/military/ramadireturn.html (accessed March 8, 2009).

22. Michaels, Jim, "An Army Colonel's Gamble Pays Off in Iraq," *USA Today*, April 30, 2007,

http://www.usatoday.com/news/world/iraq/2007-04-30-ramadi-colonel_N.htm (accessed August 10, 2009).

23. Fumento, Michael, "A Debt That Can Never Be Repaid: Michael Monsoor is Awarded the Medal of Honor," *Weekly Standard*, April 21, 2008, http://www.fumento.com/military/monsoormedal.html (accessed August 7, 2009).
24. Wikipedia, "Michael A. Monsoor," *Wikipedia.com*, http://en.wikipedia.org/wiki/Michael_A._Monsoor (accessed August 8, 2009).
25. Fumento, "Return to Ramadi."
26. Monsoor, interview.

BIBLIOGRAPHY

BOOKS

Ricks, Thomas E. *Fiasco: The American Military Adventure in Iraq*. New York: Penguin, 2006.

MAGAZINES

Odierno, Raymond T. "The Surge in Iraq: One Year Later." *Heritage Lectures*. March 13, 2008.
Zimmerman, Dwight Jon. "Petty Officer Michael A. Monsoor and Operation Kentucky Jumper." *Year in Special Operations 2009*. Tampa: Faircount Media Group, 2009.

MONOGRAPHS

Cordesman, Anthony H., with Emma Davies. *Iraq's Sectarian and Ethnic Violence and the Evolving Insurgency: Developments through mid-December 2006*. Washington, D.C.: Center for Strategic and International Studies, December 14, 2006.

INTERNET

Babynology. http://www.babynology.com/meaning-mansoor-m32.html (accessed August 9, 2009).
Bharath, Deepa. "Local Navy SEAL, Michael Monsoor, Killed in Iraq." *Orange County Register*, October 4, 2006.

http://la.indymedia.org/news/2006/10/181370_comment.php (accessed August 8, 2009).

"Bush Awards Medal of Honor to Navy SEAL." *MSNBC.com.* http://www.msnbc.msn.com/id/24017137 (accessed March 8, 2009).

Cavas, Christopher P., and Phillip Ewing. "DDG 1001 Named for MoH Recipient Monsoor." *Landstuhl Hospital Care Project,* October 31, 2008. http://www.landstuhlhospitalcareproject.org/Honorees/ Michael%20A.%20Monsoor/Michael%20A.%20Monsoor.htm (accessed August 8, 2009).

Congressional Record. http://gpoaccess.gov/crecord/digest/2008/ d08au081.pdf (accessed March 8, 2009).

Donaldson, Will. "Email from Iraq." http://www.hqmc.net/index2.php?option=com_content&task =view&id=284&pop=1&page=0&Itemid=30 (accessed August 9, 2009).

Downey, Elizabeth. "A Fitting Tribute to a Slain Navy SEAL Gains Attention." *FOXNews.com.* http://www.foxnews.com/story/0,2933,376243,00.html (accessed March 8, 2009).

The Feast of St. Michael's. http://www.feastofstmichael.com (accessed August 10, 2009).

Fumento, Michael. "A Debt That Can Never Be Repaid: Michael Monsoor Is Awarded the Medal of Honor." *Weekly Standard,* April 21, 2008. http://www.fumento.com/military/monsoormedal.html (accessed August 7, 2009).

———. "Memories of a Hero: Posthumous Recipient of Nation's Highest Honor." *New York Post,* April 9, 2008. http://www.fumento.com/military/monsoor.html (accessed March 8, 2009).

———. "The New Band of Brothers: With the 1st Battalion, 506th Infantry Regiment, 101st Airborne Division in Ramadi." *Weekly Standard,* June 19, 2006. http://www.fumento.com/military/ramadi.html (accessed August 7, 2009).

———. "Return to Ramadi." *Weekly Standard,* November 27, 2006.

http://www.fumento.com/military/ramadireturn.html (accessed March 8, 2009).

Krawzak, Paul M. "Supreme Sacrifice: Family of Navy SEAL Michael Anthony Monsoor Will Accept Medal of Honor for Selfless Act of Heroism in Iraq." *SignonSanDiego.com*, April 8, 2008. http://www.signonsandiego.com/news/military/20080404-9999-1n8monsoor.html (accessed March 8, 2009).

Laxo, Dominique M., "Medal of Honor Recipients Honored at San Clemente Park." *U.S. Navy*, October 29, 2008. http://www.navy.mil/search/display.asp?story_id=40571 (accessed February 1, 2009).

Marek, Ed. "Three Navy SEALs, Three Heroes Among Many." *Talking Proud!* April 13, 2008. http://www.talkingproud.us/Military040808A.html (accessed March 8, 2009).

McCloskey, Judy. "Michael Anthony Monsoor." *CatholicMil.org*. http://www.catholicmil.org/index.php?option=com_content&view=article&id=606:miachel-anthony-monsoor&catid=1:latest&Itemid=131, (accessed March 7, 2009).

McKeeby, David. "Iraqis Taking Their City Back from Terrorists, Says U.S. Colonel." *America.gov*. http://www.america.gov/st/washfile-english/2006/July/20060714173321idybeekcm0.9509851.html (accessed March 8, 2009).

"Michael A. Monsoor." *NavySEALS.com*. http://www.navyseals.com/Michael-monsoor (accessed August 8, 2009).

CNN interview of Sara Monsoor. Monsoor, Sara. Interview by CNN. http://www.youtube.com/watch?v=NOMLNiow4tg&feature=related (accessed August 9, 2009).

Perry, Tony. "Sailor Killed in Iraq Awarded Medal of Honor." *Los Angeles Times*, April 1, 2008. http://articles.latimes.com/2008/apr/01/local/me-moh1 (accessed March 8, 2009).

Reyes, David. "Military Deaths." *Los Angeles Times*, October 8, 2006. http://articles.latimes.com/2006/cot/08/local/me-monsoor8 (accessed August 8, 2009).

Ricks, Thomas E. "Situation Called Dire in West Iraq."
Washington Post, September 11, 2006. http://www.washing-
tonpost.com/wp-dyn/content/
article/2006/09/10/AR2006091001204.html
(accessed March 8, 2009).
Schlussel, Debbie. "Michael Monsoor: Un-Hyphenated (Arab)
American Hero."
http://www.debbieschlussel.com/archives/003630print.html
(accessed March 8, 2009).
"Supreme Sacrifice." *OCregister.com*, October 14, 2006.
http://www.ocregister.com/ocregister/homepage/abox/
article_1312785.php# (accessed August 8, 2009).
Tyson, Ann Scott. "A Deadly Clash at Donkey Island."
Washington Post, August 19, 2007.
http://www.washingtonpost.com/wp-dyn/content/
article/2007/08/18/AR2007081801270_pf.html
(accessed August 9, 2009).
U.S. Department of Defense. "DoD News Briefing with Colonel
Sean B. MarcFarland from Iraq." September 29, 2006.
http://www.defenselink.mil/utility/printitem.aspx?print=
http://www.defenselink.mil/transcripts/transcript.aspx?
transcriptid=3738 (accessed March 8, 2009).
———. "SECNAV Names New *Zumwalt*-Class Destroyer USS
Michael Monsoor." October 30, 2009.
http://www.navy.mil/search/display.asp?story_id=40604
(accessed February 1, 2009).
Wikipedia. "Mansur." *Wikipedia.com*.
http://en.wikipedia.org/wiki/Mansur
(accessed August 9, 2009).
———. "Michael A. Monsoor." *Wikipedia.com*.
http://en.wikipedia.org/wiki/Michael_A._Monsoor
(accessed August 8, 2009).

7

✮ ✮ ✮ ✮ ✮ ✮

Ross A. McGinnis

---✮---

For conspicuous gallantry and intrepidity at the risk of his life above and beyond the call of duty: Private First Class Ross A. McGinnis distinguished himself by acts of gallantry and intrepidity above and beyond the call of duty while serving as an M2 .50-caliber Machine Gunner, 1st Platoon, C Company, 1st Battalion, 26th Infantry Regiment, in connection with combat operations against an armed enemy in Adhamiyah, Northeast Baghdad, Iraq, on 4 December 2006.

That afternoon his platoon was conducting combat control operations in an effort to reduce and control sectarian violence in the area. While Private McGinnis was manning the M2 .50-caliber Machine Gun, a fragmentation grenade thrown by an insurgent fell through the gunner's hatch into the vehicle. Reacting quickly, he yelled "grenade," allowing all four members of his crew to prepare for the grenade's blast.

Then, rather than leaping from the gunner's hatch to safety, Private McGinnis made the courageous decision to protect his crew. In a selfless act of bravery, in which he was mortally wounded, Private McGinnis covered the live grenade, pinning it between his body and the vehicle and absorbing most of the explosion.

Private McGinnis' gallant action directly saved four men from certain serious injury or death. Private First Class McGinnis' extraordinary heroism and selflessness at the cost of his own life, above and beyond the call of duty, are in keeping with the highest traditions of the military service and reflect great credit upon himself, his unit, and the United States Army.

—Medal of Honor Citation, June 2, 2008

————————————★————————————

You know, I never really pictured what a Medal of Honor winner is supposed to look like. I would think of someone like a John Wayne character from the movies. Where the guy is macho and tough, and fears nothing. But that is not anywhere close to what my son Ross was like.

—Tom McGinnis,
father of Specialist Ross Andrew McGinnis[1]

Tom McGinnis's observation about his son is telling. What *does* a Medal of Honor hero look like? Is there something in the way they look at people or comb their hair that offers an insight into their future acts of bravery and initiative on foreign battlefields? Does their limited life history—Medal of Honor recipients are usually young when they are recognized—give any indication of the future "above and beyond the call of duty" acts they will carry out? Some might say yes when looking at recipients like Sergeant First Class Paul Ray Smith and Lieutenant Michael P. Murphy. Both had family histories of military service, which perhaps gave an indication of their potential for future valor and dedication to their fellow servicemen.

The same, however, cannot be said to be true of Private First Class Ross Andrew McGinnis (posthumously promoted to specialist), who gave his life to save four fellow soldiers from certain death in the form of an enemy hand grenade. Had someone known Ross McGinnis before his short army career (just under eighteen months—he enlisted on his seventeenth birthday), they might well have missed the signs of someone who was to become an extraordinary soldier. Instead of having a long lifetime to amass a list of respected deeds and accomplishments, Ross McGinnis packed everything into just nineteen and a half years, culminating his short life with the ultimate act of valor and self-sacrifice.

There are no templates for heroes. It is therefore not surprising that someone as close as his own father might have missed knowing how Ross would respond one bad day in a suburb of Baghdad.

EARLY LIFE

Ross Andrew McGinnis was born to parents Tom and Romayne on June 14, 1987, in Meadville, Pennsylvania. He was the youngest of three children, and the only boy in the

Ross and his father Tom in the McGinnis kitchen, shortly before leaving to participate in a Cub Scout bakeoff. The large number of silver arrowheads (the Cub Scout equivalent of Boy Scout merit badges) indicate Ross was active in the Cub Scout program.
Photo: *U.S. Army*

family. When Ross was three, the McGinnises moved to the small town of Knox (population approximately 1,100), about one hundred miles north of Pittsburgh. He grew up as part of a normal, small-town American family.

Two sides of Ross's personality emerged in childhood: one good, the other less so. On the good side, family, friends, teachers, and ultimately his fellow soldiers remember him as being an amazingly happy and positive young man. Even in baby photos, there is an amazing smile that only became more pronounced as he grew up. Ross always could leave a room laughing by cracking a joke or telling a story.

His boyhood was filled with the sort of fun typical of small-town, rural life. He enjoyed hunting; was a member of the Boy Scouts; and, though he was at best average, he loved playing baseball, basketball, and other sports. And in what is a sort of "right of passage" for many teenagers, when he was old enough, Ross worked part-time at a local McDonald's.

Ross had a strong sense of personal loyalty and devotion to family, friends, and coworkers, even to the point of letting his own well-being suffer. His mother Romayne recalled: "I just think it was something that he definitely looked out for his friends. Ross went the extra mile for his friends, no matter whether they were high school . . . they were Boy Scouts . . . they were at McDonald's . . . Ross stood by his friends. . . ."[2]

He also deeply loved his mom and dad. It is hard to exaggerate the impact that the Internet has had in helping deployed troops stay in touch with loved ones and friends back home. Ross was among the many who created his own

MySpace page. Before his deployment to Iraq in 2006, Ross wrote of his parents: "My Mother and Father, they created me, and have been the best parents ever. They have been there for me through the thick and thin, through tough times when there was no light at the end of the tunnel, and I love them greatly for it."[3]

Ross had never been a strong student, and in fact he didn't like school. When looking at photos of Ross both at school and from the army, his mother was struck by a singular fact: in almost every service photo of Ross he was smiling—and even when he wasn't, it looked as if he enjoyed being where he was. But there was not a single school photo in which Ross smiled or appeared to be happy.

Teachers remembered Ross McGinnis as a so-so student who nevertheless had some special qualities. One teacher recalled McGinnis as an "all or nothing student," while others, like Bill Irwin, who taught classes on government at Keystone Junior-Senior High School, have said, "Tests . . . that wasn't his gig. But if he could talk about it . . . debate about it . . . that was Ross!" His French teacher, Franki Sheatz, remembered, "He never did any more or any less than the other kids in class . . . but he was charming, in his own little way."[4]

And then there was Ross's bad side—a "party animal" wild streak that got him into trouble. At age fourteen he was experimenting with marijuana, which led to an arrest for possession and a year's probation. But whatever his shortcomings, Ross had long harbored a quiet ambition, since early childhood, to become a U.S. Army soldier. Like Jason Dunham, who shared his birthday with that of the Marine

Corps, Ross McGinnis also shared his birthday with a military branch: June 14 is the "birthday" of the U.S. Army.

His mother recalled a preschool incident where Ross was coloring a picture and she asked to see it. Ross showed her that he had drawn a soldier and said that he wanted to be one someday. The idea clearly stuck with him. In 2004, on his seventeenth birthday—the earliest date he was legally able to do so—Ross McGinnis went down to the Military Entrance Processing Station (MEPS) in Pittsburgh, Pennsylvania, and signed up to become a soldier. While at the MEPS, he chose to enter the army under the delayed entry program, which allowed him to get the training program he desired.[*]

TRANSFORMATION

In the fall of 2005, after having graduated from Keystone Junior-Senior High School, Ross left his home in Pennsylvania for the hills and forests of Fort Benning, Georgia. Home of the U.S. Army's Infantry Center, Fort Benning has long been the place where American soldiers have gotten their first taste of life in the U.S. military. For many, it is the beginning of a short means to another end: either a journey designed to pay for college or an exit from the world they have lived in up to that point. For Ross McGinnis, however, basic training, followed by his advanced individual training, was a truly transformational experience. Instructors recalled a young man who took instantly to the hands-on training, discipline, and structure of army life. Ross also began show-

---

[*]Additional information about MEPS can be found online at:
  http://usmilitary.about./com/od/joiningthemilitary/a/mepsglance.htm.

ing leadership skills, helping fellow recruits through the basic and advanced training courses. Somewhere in his fourteen weeks at Fort Benning, a new and different Ross McGinnis emerged, one that would both surprise and amaze those who had known him back in Pennsylvania.

Eighteen-year-old Ross McGinnis with his mother Romayne at the Advanced Individual Training graduation ceremony at Fort Benning, Georgia, in 2005.
Photo: *U.S. Army*

When he returned home on leave following basic, it was as if a newly minted man had replaced the sometimes erratic boy who had left Knox a few months earlier. His mother remembered: "I actually felt relieved. Ross had some problems through high school, and I knew with the Army he would get the discipline he needed."[5]

His father was also impressed, remembering, "He hadn't grown any physically, but had definitely grown in other ways. He was more organized, more disciplined, and not the same 'party animal' he was when he left [for basic training]. When he came home on leave and was around civilians, he felt uneasy because other people seemed to be sloppy and lazy as compared to what it was like in the military. So he definitely was different and thought differently after he had gone through the training."[6]

Pictures from that time show a freshly minted soldier wearing a uniform ready to pass inspection from a drill sergeant, looking lean and together, standing tall, smiling, ready for his first assignment. Perhaps highlighting the changes was something few would have expected of Ross. Surprisingly—considering his less than happy experience at Keystone Junior-Senior High School—he returned to his alma mater to address the students about the army and his experiences thus far. Libby Hansford of the Keystone SMILES Program, a nonprofit service-learning organization in western Pennsylvania that combines education with community service, remembered his visit, saying, "It actually stunned the students. They were like, 'Wow! This is Ross, but this is a different person.' Walking tall with his uniform, it really got them to think that they could do it. Because Ross is . . . 'one of the guys' like you and me. Just a regular guy; yet they could see that transformation. They could see that he was making decisions for leadership and to better himself."[7]

INTO SERVICE

His home leave over, Private Ross McGinnis deployed in October 2005 to Schweinfurt, Germany. His first assignment was with First Platoon, C (Charlie–"Rocks") Company, First Battalion, Twenty-sixth Infantry Regiment, Second "Dagger" Brigade combat team of the First Infantry Division. Known as The Big Red One, the First Infantry Division was organized in World War I and is the oldest continuous service unit in the army. In becoming part of the army's most distinguished infantry formation, McGinnis joined the ranks of soldiers who had fought in the Argonne Forrest in World War I, Omaha Beach in World War II, Vietnam, and Iraq and Kuwait in Desert Storm. The record and history of his unit was not lost on Ross McGinnis. The newly promoted Private First Class (Pfc.) took to his new posting and began to make friends rapidly.

Both on post and in the neighboring town of Schweinfurt, Ross's charm, humor, and infectious smile made him a favorite wherever he went. But it was his other qualities—his loyalty to friends and fellow soldiers, along with his newly discovered personal vector in the Army—that made other soldiers want to work with him.

Ross's company commander, Major Michael Baka, recalled:

There were certain soldiers that did stand out, and Pfc. McGinnis was definitely one of those. He was only 18 years old when he arrived at the unit, very young, very eager. He had a comical personality, made a lot of jokes, and was very humorous amongst his platoon. He was one of a small number of soldiers who could keep up with me on a long run. I remember many Monday mornings in Germany where [McGinnis and I] would just get out and run five or six miles with my group keeping pace, and I remember being very impressed by that. He was very eager to learn.[8]

McGinnis was not just making positive impressions on post but in the surrounding community as well. It was in Germany that he met and fell in love with a pretty blond girl named Christina Wendel. In just a few months, the pair began to plan for a future life together, including a home and children. Of Christina, Ross wrote: "But most of all, my greatest Hero is the Love of my Life, Christina Wendel, there are no words to describe how I feel about her. She is my guardian angel, my best friend, and my lover. She is the strongest and most caring girl on the planet. I don't know what I would do without her. I Love you Schatzi, forever."[9]

By early 2006, all must have seemed right with the world for the young soldier who had found a focus in life, a true love, and direction in the U.S. Army. But while McGinnis had been becoming a soldier and building the foundation of a future for himself, the situation had become troubled in Iraq. Sectarian violence had dramatically ramped up in 2005. By 2006, a full-on civil war was ripping through parts of the country. The most dangerous of the insurgents was a newly formed terrorist branch of al Qaida, calling itself al Qaida in Iraq.

Regular rotations of U.S. Army brigade combat teams

(BCTs) were a part of occupation operations in Iraq, and McGinnis's Second BCT was scheduled to rotate there in the summer of 2006. There they would join up under the headquarters of the Second Infantry Division for operations in and around Baghdad. The deployment would be one of destiny for Pfc. Ross McGinnis.

2006 IN IRAQ: THE YEAR OF LIVING DANGEROUSLY
Through a combination of improved insurgent tactics by al Qaida in Iraq, growing secular violence within the country, and the shortsightedness of U.S. Secretary of Defense Donald Rumsfeld, 2006 was the year that America very nearly lost the war in Iraq. Rumsfeld had organized and overseen the original invasion plan of Iraq in 2003, which was developed on a limited force of manpower and with little in the way of postinvasion occupation planning, and he was unwilling to change strategy despite rapidly mounting evidence that Iraq was going to hell in a handbasket—and taking more and more American troops with it. In particular, Rumsfeld was completely opposed to adding any troops, a plan known as "the Surge option," to help put down the security threats. The result, in early 2006, was near anarchy in Iraq.

The al Qaida terrorist leader in Iraq, Abu Musab al-Zarqawi, was the greatest threat to stability, especially in western Iraq. His supreme achievement was the bombing of the al-Askari "Golden" Mosque in Samara in February 2006, one of the most important Shiite mosques in the world. Its destruction led to a massive wave of violence between Iraqi Sunnis and Shiites in which hundreds of civilian and militia fighters were killed. In June 2006, al-Zarqawi was killed by precision-guided bombs from a U.S. Air Force F-16 fighter jet. But his terrorist forces had created so much ongoing violence that only a vast influx of new U.S. troops appeared capable of dealing with the crisis.

As mentioned earlier, 2005 and 2006 were arguably the worst years of the Iraq War, with 846 and 822 U.S. personnel, respectively, being killed and thousands more wounded.[10] While these casualty counts never came close to those suffered at the height of the Vietnam War during the Tet Offensive in 1968, the effects on public opinion and politics back home were almost as negative. The November 2006 midterm elections were a disaster for the Republican Party, resulting in the loss of control of both houses of Congress.

The election results, combined with a scathing bipartisan report on the conduct of the war by the Iraq Study Group in December 2006, caused the Bush administration to completely change the course of the war in Iraq over the next year. Leadership changes, including the resignation of Secretary Rumsfeld, began within days of the 2006 election debacle. A new commanding general, David Petraeus, would bring a new strategy and over 21,000 fresh troops to Iraq by the middle of 2007.

While a positive influence in the long run, the effects of these changes were more than a year in the future when Pfc. Ross McGinnis and the troops of the Second BCT began to deploy in July 2006, arriving in Iraq on August 4.

INTO COMBAT

By August 2006, Pfc. Ross McGinnis and the troops of the Second Brigade combat team were being deployed around the suburb of Adhamiyah, northeast of downtown Baghdad.

A major center of secular violence at the time, Adhamiyah was home to over 300,000 well-educated Sunni Muslims, many of them senior members of the Ba'ath Party, which had run Iraq during the reign of Saddam Hussein. The period following the defeat of the Ba'ath government in 2003 was a tough one for the area because of the "de-Ba'athification" policies of the Coalition Provisional Authority. Unable to hold jobs and initially denied positions in the new government because of their past affiliations, most of the residents naturally became sympathetic to the Sunni insurgents and al Qaida in Iraq fighters. In addition, Adhamiyah sits near Sadr City, which, with a population of over a million, is one of the poorest Shiite neighborhoods and an area that became a flashpoint for all that was going wrong in Iraq.

By 2006, Adhamiyah was a dangerous place, with most of the Shiite population driven out following the violence after the "Golden" Mosque bombing in February. The previous September, more than nine hundred Shiite pilgrims had died crossing a packed bridge in Adhamiyah, drowning in the river below after jumping from the jammed span. It was into this crucible of Sunni resentment and violence in the late summer of 2006 that Ross McGinnis and his Second BCT were committed, along with several other similar units from the 101st Airborne Division and 172nd Stryker Brigade. In the "pre-Surge" days of late 2006, most of the U.S. actions involved "presence" activities, such as street patrols and "sweeps" to try and roust out and hunt down insurgent fighters. Unfortunately, the lack of any permanent U.S. forward basing in districts like Adhamiyah meant that these patrols and sweeps mostly became opportunities to be ambushed by improvised explosive devices (IEDs) and insurgents laying in wait among the narrow roads and packed buildings.

For Pfc. McGinnis and his fellow Second BCT troopers, this meant spending much of the time inside their secure compound at Forward Operating Base Apache, located between the Tigris River and Adhamiyah. Austere at first, FOB Apache was gradually improved with the addition of better food service, expanded Internet access, and better phone service. Regular patrols, raids, and sweeps into

Private First Class Ross McGinnis somewhere in Iraq.
Photo: *U.S. Army*

Adhamiyah meant ambushes were frequent, combat common, and casualties routinely incurred.

Two soldiers from McGinnis's Charlie Company were killed early in the deployment, badly shaking the unit. On October 17, a sniper killed Staff Sergeant Garth Sizemore while he was on patrol outside Apache. Five days later, Sergeant Willsun M. Mock and his interpreter were killed when an antiarmor landmine detonated beneath their vehicle. The men, both combat veterans with years of service in the army, were the fifth and sixth losses in Second BCT during the deployment. After the events of October, nobody in Charlie Company needed to be reminded that they were in a dangerous neighborhood.

Ross McGinnis was the youngest deployed soldier in Charlie Company. During patrols, he normally could be found riding aboard a Humvee, manning the M2 .50-caliber machine gun mounted on the roof of the vehicle. These machine-gun mounts had been improved since Sergeant Paul Ray Smith's action in 2003, with the addition of armor plates to help protect the gunner from ground-level fire. However, the mounts were still open topped and exposed, allowing insurgents on rooftops to shoot down into the vehicles and even drop grenades or small IEDs inside.

Despite the dangers and daily grind in Adhamiyah, Ross McGinnis kept his smile shining and his humor flowing to the other soldiers of Charlie Company. In a home video made early that fall, the young soldier could be seen making grim jokes with a wry smile, doing his best to keep things light:

"I'm Pfc. McGinnis . . . I'm the co-maker of this film. . . .

We've been in Iraq for about three good months right now . . . we've seen quite a bit of action already . . . we don't need to see much more. . . . But we got quite a bit of it on film . . . to make a pretty good film . . . for anybody watching this . . . this is our lives. . . ."[11]

Another soldier in his unit, Pfc. Brennan Beck, recalled that, "[Ross] would go into a room, and when he left, everyone was laughing. He did impersonations of others in the company. He was quick-witted; just hilarious. He loved making people laugh. He was a comedian through and through. He was not a garrison soldier. He hated it back in garrison. He loved it here in Iraq. He loved being a gunner. It was a thrill. He loved everything about it. He was one of our best soldiers. He did a great job."[12]

Through it all, Ross McGinnis stayed positive, kept in touch with his family and Christina, and became a combat soldier trusted and respected by his peers. By December, he had already been nominated for a Bronze Star and was a seasoned combat veteran. Everything he had been taught, everything he had learned, and all that he had become would dramatically culminate in a few short seconds on December 4, 2006.

DAY OF DESTINY

December 4, 2006, began with good news for Pfc. McGinnis— he was getting a promotion. His company commander, Major Baka, told the young private first class that paperwork was going to be filed making him a specialist (E-4). Then, as on so many other days in Iraq, Pfc. McGinnis found himself on an afternoon patrol—this time as part of a convoy of six First Platoon Humvees. Their mission was to scout the immediate area to find a suitable site to place a 250-kilowatt generator that would power almost a hundred homes in the neighborhood. McGinnis was sitting in the .50-caliber machine-gun mount of the last Humvee in line, facing backward. His job was to guard the rear of the convoy and take out any snipers or rocket-propelled-grenade gunners that might pop out of a door or suddenly appear on a rooftop. Also aboard his vehicle were four other soldiers: Sergeant Lyle Buehler (the driver), Staff Sergeant Ian Newland (the squad leader, sitting in the left rear passenger seat), Sergeant First Class Cedric Thomas (the platoon sergeant, sitting in the "shotgun" seat on the forward passenger side); and Pfc. Sean Lawson (the platoon medic, sitting behind Thomas).

The patrol began with the convoy exiting FOB Apache onto the main road toward Adhamiyah. Just a half a mile from the FOB, the convoy turned off the main road into a built-up area of Adhamiyah, cars and other vehicles jamming the narrow streets. Here the convoy got caught up in traffic and was forced to a halt.

That's when things went bad.

Without warning, a single rooftop insurgent tossed a hand grenade down toward the open hatch of McGinnis's .50-caliber gun mount. McGinnis saw the grenade and apparently tried to bat it out of the mount but missed. The grenade then fell through the hatch and into the interior of the vehicle, lodging at the front of the crew compartment. From above, McGinnis called down, "Grenade!" Thomas yelled back, "Where?" McGinnis replied, "It's in the truck!"

A long fuse for a grenade is seven seconds. The average

is four. McGinnis had to make a life-and-death decision in less than that.

From his position atop the Humvee, Ross McGinnis surely knew he could save himself simply by rolling out of the mount and dropping to the ground. This was in fact what he had been trained to do, and Major Baka in the convoy's fourth vehicle saw him momentarily stand up in the mount, apparently about to exit. But McGinnis, who could see the grenade from his vantage point, realized that none of the four men inside knew where the grenade had landed. He also knew that when the grenade went off in the confined space it would almost certainly kill all four soldiers with a blast of lethal fragments. There was no time for the four soldiers to get out. The doors were combat locked and hard to open.

It is almost impossible to imagine what must have gone through the mind of the teenage soldier during the moment he acted. No one would have blamed McGinnis for following training and leaping out to save his own life.

Instead, Private First Class Ross McGinnis dropped down from his machine-gun mount and, facing backward, pressed his back into the radio mount where the grenade was lodged. Thanks to his warning cry, the other four soldiers had a chance to cover their faces and turn away from where they now knew the blast would come.

The grenade exploded. The cabin filled with black smoke; Sergeant Thomas's door was ripped off its hinges; and the .50-caliber machine gun was thrown off of the roof mount.

Major Baka knew immediately what had happened. He later remembered, "This blast was very loud, and immediately following, there was gunfire. I saw two soldiers walking to another vehicle, wounded. . . . I knew right away a grenade made it into the gunner's hatch." Ordering his driver to turn their vehicle around and head for the damaged Humvee, Baka saw the surreal sight of his men reacting to the situation.

One of them was Thomas. The sergeant had been knocked unconscious for a few seconds by the blast. When he stepped out of the smoking vehicle, he saw the insurgent on the roof who had thrown the grenade. Thomas recalled, "I presumed he threw the grenade because of the way he was leaning over the side of the building to see the damage he had done." Despite lacerations on his neck, shoulder, and back, he said, "I started to engage [fire at] him [the insurgent]. I don't know if I wounded him or killed him. He disappeared."

Private First Class McGinnis had done what he could to absorb the blast with his body. The grenade had exploded into his back and side, just below his body armor. He was dead instantly. Though the other four soldiers survived, none of them escaped injury. Staff Sergeant Ian Newland suffered severe shrapnel wounds, requiring numerous surgeries and leaving over fifty pieces of the grenade inside his body. The driver, Sergeant Buehler, was hit by a piece of shrapnel on the right side of his head, while Pfc. Lawson, the platoon medic, was fortunate to suffer only a perforated eardrum and mild concussion. Lawson was able to start giving first aid to the others as the rest of the platoon came to help.

As things around the ambush site calmed down, the process of cleaning up and returning to the FOB began. Sergeant Newland was taken by medevac to the Landstuhl

Regional Medical Center in Germany to begin a long and painful path to recovery, rehabilitation, and eventually a medical discharge from the army. The convoy, including the damaged Humvee with McGinnis's body still inside, returned to FOB Apache, where the soldiers of Charlie Company were shocked at the loss of the young private.

Sergeant Thomas was back on patrol just a few days later. In describing the incident, he said, "It's tough. You deal with it the best you can. Your guys need you, your soldiers need you, and you just kind of bounce back from it, but it's something you'll never forget no matter how old you get. He's a hero to me, and I will never forget him, ever. He honestly saved my life. I think some people use 'saved my life' out of context, but he really saved four people's lives."

NOMINATION AND AWARD

Almost as soon as the convoy returned to FOB Apache and the reality of Ross McGinnis's death sank in, there were efforts by the stunned soldiers of Charlie Company to recognize the valor of their youngest member. Major Baka immediately recommended McGinnis for a Purple Heart and Silver Star, since he knew they could be endorsed and awarded in-theater in Iraq. Both were approved by December 11 and forwarded to his parents.

But already shaken by the selfless act he had witnessed just yards from his own vehicle, Major Baka was thinking about initiating a recommendation for a Medal of Honor award for Private First Class Ross McGinnis. As he later recalled, "I felt very strongly, it was very clear to me that his acts were completely selfless on his part, and without him doing that, I probably would have had four soldiers in that platoon killed or seriously wounded."

On December 8, 2006, Baka forwarded the recommendation package up the chain of command, in what resulted in one of the quickest Medal of Honor award cycles in modern history. The number of eyewitnesses, including the four surviving First Platoon soldiers, made it clear to the Army Awards Branch that Major Baka's recommendation was not only justified but probably imperative given the nature of McGinnis's sacrifice.

It was March 23, 2007, when Ross McGinnis, now posthumously promoted to specialist, was laid to rest on a beautiful sunny morning at Arlington Cemetery near Washington, D.C. Along with his family, two busloads of friends from Knox and dozens more in private vehicles made the all-night trip to Virginia to walk with Ross McGinnis to his final resting place. Three of the soldiers from the ill-fated Humvee were also in attendance to see off the young man who had saved their lives four months earlier. The ceremony was short, just twenty minutes in the cool spring air, before the urn holding his ashes was interred.

A little more than two months later, on June 2, 2007, Tom and Romayne McGinnis again journeyed to Washington, D.C., this time to a White House ceremony hosted by President George W. Bush, where they would accept for Ross the Medal of Honor for his actions in Iraq. President Bush summarized the young soldier's actions this way:

"No one outside this man's family can know the true weight of their loss. But in words spoken long ago, we are told how to measure the kind of devotion that Ross McGinnis showed on his last day: 'Greater love hath no man than this, that a man lay down his life for his friends.' "[13]

There were other ceremonies that week acknowledging Ross McGinnis's valor in Iraq, including the unveiling of a display in the Pentagon's Hall of Heroes. Through it all, Tom and Romayne McGinnis graced the proceedings with a quiet dignity.

On June 5, 2008, at Arlington National Cemetery, Virginia, a ceremony was held to unveil a new tombstone for Specialist Ross McGinnis, etched with his Medal of Honor. Photo: *U.S. Army*

REMEMBERING ROSS

Shortly after his death, Ross's parents issued the following statement about their son, revealing something of their feelings about him, his life, and what he had done during his short but eventful army career:

"Ross did not become our hero by dying to save his fellow Soldiers from a grenade. He was a hero to us long before he died, because he was willing to risk his life to protect the ideals of freedom and justice that America represents. He has been recommended for the Medal of Honor. . . . That is not why he gave his life. The lives of four men who were his Army brothers outweighed the value of his one life. It was just a matter of simple kindergarten arithmetic. Four means more than one. It didn't matter to Ross that he could have escaped the situation without a scratch. Nobody would have questioned such a reflex reaction. What mattered to him were the four men placed in his care on a moment's notice. One moment he was responsible for defending the rear of a convoy from enemy fire; the next moment he held the lives of four of his friends in his hands. The choice for Ross was simple, but simple does not mean easy. His straightforward answer to a simple but difficult choice should stand as a shining example for the rest of us. We all face simple choices, but how often do we choose to make a sacrifice to get the right answer! The right choice sometimes requires honor."[14]

From the men he saved, perhaps the most insightful comments were issued by Ian Newland, the most severely wounded of the four. Although he continues to recover following his discharge from the army, and needs a cane to

The display case containing Specialist McGinnis's Medal of Honor.
Photo: *U.S. Army*

walk at times, his is a special insight to the gift given him by Ross McGinnis:

> I remember it every day. . . . I see it every day. By all means I should have died that day. My kids would have been like so many others, growing up without their father who had died in Afghanistan and Iraq. My wife would have become a widow. There is not a single day or hour that goes by, when I do not take it all in. The smell of my daughter's hair, or the smile my son gives me anomalously out of nowhere. The soft touch of my wife's hand, just driving in the car . . . because of what Ross did. He gave me my wife and kids back. Someone gives you a life . . . lets you live . . .

gives you their life . . . can you thank them enough? Is
that possible? I think to thank him is to live my life to
the fullest.[15]

Since Ross McGinnis's death, many words have been
written, spoken, and recorded about this extraordinary
young man who found himself and lived a lifetime in so
short a span as a member of the U.S. Army. But perhaps the
best epitaph written for Specialist Ross Andrew McGinnis
was the one he himself wrote for his MySpace page, which
he updated three days before his death. In the "About Me"
space, he wrote:

My name is Ross McGinnis. I live 3 lives, in all 3 I am
the same person, but my 3 separate lives are not connected in any way. One of my lives is the one I had
growing up, I had my friends in high school and
around where I lived. And I had my family, my 2 older sisters and parents. I barely get to see this life any-
more. Another life of mine is my life in Germany. I
have another group of friends there, and this is where
I spent most of my life the past year. In this life is
where I met my true love, and my soul mate, Christina
Wendel. My 3rd life is my army life. Yet again another
large group of friends, who are more like a bunch of
brothers. The kind of brothers you can joke with and
cry with. The type you can make fun of all you want,
but as soon as someone else does, they are getting their
ass kicked. This is where I will be living my life for the
next year. Its not going to be an easy life here in Iraq,

I have already had a couple of life altering experiences. But they will not change me mentally, I won't let them. I just cannot wait for the day when I can connect all 3 lives into one. But that day will not be for a long time. I miss you Christina, Mom, Dad, Greg, Chris, Nick, Bryan, Brenner, Jens, Silvia, Dona, Randel. See you all when I come Home!!!

NOTES

1. U.S. Army, "Reflections on Pfc. Ross McGinnis," May 29, 2008, *YouTube.com*, http://www.youtube.com/watch?v=iEjELGU3bCU (accessed August 17, 2009).
2. U.S. Army, "Reflections."
3. McGinnis, Ross, "SkrawnyWhiteKid," *MySpace.com*, http://profile.myspace.com/skrawnywhitekid (accessed March 11, 2009).
4. U.S. Army, "Reflections."
5. U.S. Army, "Reflections."
6. U.S. Army, "Reflections."
7. U.S. Army, "MOH Teacher Reflection," June 2, 2008, *YouTube.com*, http://www.youtube.com/watch?v=nApoUcSBgkM&feature=channel (accessed August 17, 2009).
8. U.S. Army, "Reflections."
9. McGinnis, Ross, "SkrawnyWhiteKid."
10. "U.S. Casualties in Iraq," *GlobalSecurity.org*, http://www.globalsecurity.org/military/ops/iraq_casualties.htm (accessed March 29, 2010).
11. U.S. Army, "Medal of Honor—Pfc. Ross McGinnis: Staff Sergeant Ian Newland Interview," May 23, 2008. *YouTube.com*, http://www.youtube.com/watch?v=dOClztsqAbY (accessed August 17, 2009).
12. U.S. Army, "United States Army Europe Heroes: Medal of Honor: Spc. Ross McGinnis," http://www.hqusareur.army.mil/heroes/Spc_Ross_McGinnis_MOH.pdf (accessed August 18, 2009).

13. The White House, "President Bush Presents Medal of Honor to Private First Class Ross Andrew McGinnis," June 2, 2008, http://georgewbush-whitehouse.archives.gov/news/releases/2008/06/20080602-1.html (accessed August 18, 2009).
14. U.S. Army, "The Story of Spec. Ross A. McGinnis," *Medal of Honor: Operation Iraqi Freedom*, August 17, 2009, http://ww.army.mil/medalofhonor/mcginnis/profile/index.html (accessed February 27, 2010).
15. U.S. Army, "Medal of Honor—Pfc. Ross McGinnis: Staff Sergeant Ian Newland Interview."

BIBLIOGRAPHY

INTERNET

Associated Press. "Soldier Killed in Iraq to Get Medal of Honor." *MSNBC.com*, May 23, 2008. http://www.msnbc.msn.com/id/24794042 (accessed May 23, 2008).

"U.S. Casualties in Iraq." *GlobalSecurity.org*. http://www.globalsecurity.org/military/ops/iraq_casualties.htm (accessed March 29, 2010).

McGinnis, Ross. "SkrawnyWhiteKid." *MySpace.com*. http://profile.myspace.com/skrawnywhitekid (accessed March 11, 2009).

The White House. "President Bush Presents Medal of Honor to Private First Class Ross Andrew McGinnis." June 2, 2008. http://georgewbush-whitehouse.archives.gov/news/releases/2008/06/20080602-1.html (accessed August 18, 2009).

Wikipedia. "Knox, Pennsylvania." *Wikipedia.com*. http://en.wikipedia.org/wiki/Knox,_Pennsylvania (accessed August 10, 2009).

———. "Ross A. McGinnis." *Wikipedia.com*. http://en.wikipedia.org/wiki/Ross_A._McGinnis. (accessed March 11, 2009).

U.S. Army. "Medal of Honor—Pfc. Ross McGinnis: Staff Sergeant

Ian Newland Interview." *YouTube.com*, May 23, 2008.
http://www.youtube.com/watch?v=dOClztsqAbY
(accessed August 17, 2009).

———. "MOH Teacher Reflection." *YouTube.com*, June 2, 2008.
http://www.youtube.com/watch?v = nApoUcSBgk
M&feature = channel (accessed August 17, 2009).

———. "Reflections on Pfc. Ross McGinnis." *YouTube.com*, May
29, 2008. http://www.youtube.com/watch?v=iEjELGU3bCU
(accessed August 17, 2009).

———. "The Story of Spc. Ross A. McGinnis." *Medal of Honor:
Operation Iraqi Freedom*, August 17, 2009.
http://www.army.mil/medalofhonor/mcginnis/profile/index.html
(accessed February 27, 2010).

———. "United States Army Europe Heroes: Medal of Honor:
Spc. Ross McGinnis."
http://www.hqusareur.army.mil/heroes/Spc_Ross_
McGinnis_MOH.pdf (accessed August 18, 2009).

8

★ ★ ★ ★ ★ ★

Jared C. Monti

─────────────────── ★ ───────────────────

For conspicuous gallantry and intrepidity at the risk of his life above and beyond the call of duty: Staff Sergeant Jared C. Monti distinguished himself by acts of gallantry and intrepidity above and beyond the call of duty while serving as a team leader with Headquarters and Headquarters Troop, 3d Squadron, 71st Cavalry Regiment, 3d Brigade Combat Team, 10th Mountain Division, in connection with combat operations against an armed enemy in Nuristan Province, Afghanistan, on June 21, 2006.

While Staff Sergeant Monti was leading a mission aimed at gathering intelligence and directing fire against the enemy, his 16-man patrol was attacked by as many as 50 enemy fighters. On the verge of being overrun, Staff Sergeant Monti quickly directed his men to set up a defensive position behind a rock formation. He then called for indirect fire support, accurately targeting the rounds upon the enemy who had closed to within 50 meters of his position. While still directing fire, Staff Sergeant Monti personally engaged the enemy with his rifle and a grenade, successfully disrupting an attempt to flank his patrol. Staff Sergeant Monti then realized that one of his Soldiers was lying wounded in the open ground between the advancing enemy and the patrol's position.

With complete disregard for his own safety, Staff Sergeant Monti twice attempted to move from behind the cover of the rocks into the face of relentless enemy fire to rescue his fallen comrade. Determined not to leave his Soldier, Staff Sergeant Monti made a third attempt to cross open terrain through intense enemy fire. On this final attempt, he was mortally wounded, sacrificing his own life in an effort to save his fellow Soldier.

Staff Sergeant Monti's selfless acts of heroism inspired his patrol to fight off the larger enemy force. Staff Sergeant Monti's immeasurable courage and uncommon valor are in keeping with the highest traditions of military service and reflect great credit upon himself, Headquarters and Headquarters Troop, 3d Squadron, 71st Cavalry Regiment, 3d Brigade Combat Team, 10th Mountain Division, and the United States Army.

— Medal of Honor Citation, September 17, 2009

———————————————— ✮ ————————————————

THE SOLDIER'S CREED

I am an American Soldier.
I am a Warrior and a member of a team.
I will always place the mission first.
I will never accept defeat.

242

I will never quit.
I will never leave a fallen comrade.
I am disciplined, physically and mentally tough, trained
and proficient in my warrior tasks and drills.
I always maintain my arms, my equipment and myself.
I am an expert and I am a professional.
I stand ready to deploy, engage, and destroy the
enemies of the United States of America in close
combat.
I am a guardian of Freedom and the American way
of life.
I am an American Soldier.

Each of the men profiled in this book had a unique life story, as individual and varied as the men themselves. There is no fixed path on the road to an action that culminates in a Medal of Honor nomination. Sergeant Paul Ray Smith, scarred by his early battle experiences in Desert Storm in 1991, spent the next dozen years preparing himself and his men for the firefight near Baghdad International Airport during Operation Iraqi Freedom in 2003. Ross McGinnis, the class clown and town slacker, was transformed in a period of eighteen months into a self-sacrificing model soldier who knew that the needs of four fellow GIs superseded his own. For Jared Monti, however, the road to an exposed mountain battlefield in a dangerous province in Afghanistan—and the Medal of Honor nomination that followed—did not define him; it simply was how he got there.

GROWING UP
Jared C. Monti was born on September 20, 1975, in Abing-

don, Massachusetts, to Paul and Janet Monti. He grew up, along with his sister Nicole and brother Timothy, in nearby Raynham, where his father worked as a schoolteacher and his mother as a nurse.

From an early age, Jared Monti showed the qualities that would define his adult life. Among these was a wanderlust that his mother recalled first seeing when Jared was just four years old. Jared was playing in the yard when he tried to climb over the fence around their home and go exploring—only to get hung up by the hood of his sweatshirt. Rescued by a family member, he was undaunted and eagerly resumed exploring. Even migraine headaches, a chronic condition that plagued him throughout his life, did not stop him from climbing trees, scaling fences, and satisfying his need to see what surprises lay unseen down the road.

Young Jared was also known for his persistence. Cut three times from his high school basketball team, he kept trying out until finally, as a senior, he made the varsity team *and* became a leading scorer. He also became a championship wrestler, power lifter, and triathlete.

Early on, Jared knew he wanted to be in the military. Initially, his desire was to be a pilot. When he and his mother visited Jared's aunt in Virginia Beach, his mother would buy him U.S. Navy model planes at the nearby Norfolk Naval Air Station. He would then go out and collect photographs of the real planes. Jared's migraine condition, however, would keep him out of a cockpit. Nevertheless, determined to pursue a career in the military, Jared turned his attention to becoming a soldier.

At the age of seventeen, still a high school junior, Jared joined the Army National Guard under the delayed-entry program on March 11, 1993. While his friends from school were enjoying summer vacation that year, Monti was doing his basic training at Fort Leonard Wood, Missouri. When he returned for his senior year, Jared knew that it would be followed by a career in the army.

DONNING A UNIFORM

Shortly after graduation in the spring of 1994, Jared Monti entered active-duty service in the army and was sent to Fort Sill, Oklahoma, to finish his advanced individual training (AIT). There he was given instruction as a fire support specialist (13F), a recently created specialty in which an operator identifies targets and directs interdiction fire from artillery, rockets, and air strikes. Though somewhat under-appreciated at the time, firepower from precision strikes of this sort would become a key to America's strategy in the following decade in the conflicts in Iraq, Afghanistan, Somalia, and elsewhere.

Following his graduation from AIT, Monti was posted to serve with the First Battalion of the 506th Infantry Regiment (1-506 IN) at Camp Stanley in South Korea, where he helped monitor the demilitarized zone between North Korea and South Korea. Upon his return in 1995, he moved to Fort Bragg, North Carolina, and took the first of what, over the course of almost ten years, would be a series of continuing-education courses. Jared attended the Army Combat Life-savers course (1995), Basic Airborne School (1997), Primary Leadership Development course (1998), Basic Noncommissioned Officer (Sergeants) course (2001), Air Assault (Heli-borne Infantry) course (2002), and the Joint Firepower/Control course (2004). During this decade, Monti was given assignments that sent him back once again to South Korea. Eventually, he wound up with the army's Tenth Mountain Division, stationed at Fort Drum, New York.

Jared Monti had always been generous with friends and strangers, often giving what he had to those who had nothing. And his compassionate streak showed when, as a student in Massachusetts, young Jared would make a point of eating lunch with someone sitting alone. One winter, he cut down a spruce tree in his family's yard to give to a woman in the neighborhood who was a single parent, so that she and her kids would have a Christmas tree. He also spent his own money to buy ornaments and presents for them.

Once while at Fort Bragg, Jared saw the children of one of his fellow soldiers eating dinner on the floor of their home because they did not have a kitchen table. Without telling his roommate, Monti gave the family a newly purchased dining room set that had just been installed in his apartment. These were not random acts of kindness but rather expressions of Jared's outlook on life in the army and life in general.

INTO ACTION: BOSNIA AND AFGHANISTAN
American troops were rarely committed to combat during the years between the end of the Vietnam War and the end of the Cold War. But since 1989, they have been in almost continuous combat action, from minor engagements to full-scale war. This means that anyone who entered the military since the fall of the Berlin wall knew he had a good chance of seeing combat at some point during his military career. Jared Monti wound up seeing more than his share.

It began with a tour as part of the NATO peacekeeping

force in the Balkans in the 1990s. There he took his skills as soldier and leader into a danger zone, helping keep calm one of the most volatile regions in Europe.

In 2002, because of repeated stress injuries caused by his many parachute jumps, Monti was offered a medical disability discharge. When he learned that his unit would be deployed to Afghanistan in 2003, he refused the discharge. Monti, often called Grandpa by his men because at age twenty-eight he was almost ten years older than most of them, refused to let them go into combat without him. During that first deployment, Monti distinguished himself, earning the Bronze Star and the Army Commendation Medal for Valor.

In the fall of 2001, Afghanistan was where America struck back against al Qaida and its hosts, the ruling Taliban, in response to the terrorist attacks of September 11, 2001. Led by about four hundred special operations and CIA personnel members, the United States joined with the forces of the Afghan Northern Alliance in a stunning forty-nine-day campaign that culminated with the Taliban's surrender in December 2001. However, in 2002, the Bush administration began to treat Afghanistan as a "done deal," and the military began to focus its attention on Iraq. This negligence resulted in a slow-motion version of a train wreck for the Americans and their allies in the new Afghan government of the transition president Hamid Karzi.

In early 2002, the special operations units that had led the way in Afghanistan the previous autumn turned over occupation and security duties to large conventional force units, including the 101st Airborne (Air Assault) and Tenth Moun-

Jared Monti (left) and an unidentified soldier with a group of Afghan youths in an undated photo. The rank tab in the middle of his uniform indicates that at the time Monti was a staff sergeant.
Photo: *U.S. Army*

tain Divisions. These units ran a series of "sweep" operations into the mountains along the Afghan-Pakistan border, which caused the surviving Taliban-al Qaida units to scatter. But from that point forward, the Taliban grew stronger, and Afghanistan became progressively less vital to an American government more concerned with the growing insurgency in Iraq. By 2006, the ongoing occupation of Afghanistan was seen as a drain on the American effort in Iraq, and NATO allies were asked to contribute troops to the occupation and security efforts. Troops from Germany, Canada, Denmark, Australia, and the Netherlands, among others, began to take over in southern Afghanistan, allowing American and British troops to concentrate their efforts against the resurgent Taliban presence in the mountainous areas of the Afghan-Pakistan border region. But the American-NATO strategy at that time included interdiction sweeps that were too few and often ineffectual.

The basic problem was that while a sweep might move through an area successfully, the troops did not remain to occupy and pacify the locale. This meant that Taliban and al Qaida forces only had to "lay low"—blending into the indigenous population—and behave themselves while the troops roamed the area. It also meant that they could choose when and where to fight, using traditional guerilla tactics of hit-and-run ambush. But one hope held by the Taliban-al Qaida forces was that they could again pull off attacks similar to those during Operation Anaconda in 2002 and Operation Red Wings in 2005, where they were able to surround and attack isolated American units. Thus, the United States–NATO sweep operations of 2006 played into the insurgents' hands.

For Jared Monti and the Tenth Mountain Division, 2006 meant another rotation back to Afghanistan. Monti's unit, the Third Squadron of the Seventy-first Cavalry Regiment (Recon–3-71 CAV), Third Brigade combat team (Third BCT), Tenth Mountain Division, was assigned to the eastern provinces of Afghanistan. Now a staff sergeant, Monti had been assigned as a squad leader and was at the peak of his skills. Even though he suffered the chronic pain of migraines, Sergeant Monti succeeded in becoming beloved by the troops under his command and appreciated by the Afghan civilians he encountered. What nobody in his unit could have foreseen was that he was about to pass into legend.

THE BATTLE OF MOUNTAIN 2610*

In June 2006, the 3-71 CAV was assigned to conduct Operation Gowardesh Thrust, a squadron-sized** sweep in the Gremen Valley of Nuristan Province, Afghanistan. The operation was designed to disrupt Taliban-al Qaida operations in the Gremen Valley by limiting their movement and free use of the region near the border with Pakistan. The start of the operation involved using a sixteen-man patrol to infiltrate the area of operations in advance of the squadron's main drive up the valley. The patrol was composed of two squads, which featured a mix of snipers, forward observers, and scouts, moving north along a ridgeline overlooking the Gremen Valley. From their perch on the ridge, the 3-71 CAV soldiers could provide real-time observation and help direct artillery and air strikes against any enemy forces attempting to interdict the squadron's main effort.

Late on June 17, 2006, a convoy of trucks and Humvees moved the patrol to an allied mortar position south of the village of Baz-Gal, near the Gowardesh Bridge. Early the next day, the patrol moved out on foot from the mortar site into their patrol area on the ridge. For the next three days,

---

*In the military, topographical features, such as hills and mountains, are identified by their height, originally in feet but today recorded in meters. Thus "Mountain 2610" means that it is 2,610 meters above sea level. In instances where two or more features have the same height they are further identified by their compass location in relation to one another.
**A squadron in an American airmobile cavalry unit is the equivalent of an infantry battalion and contains about 1,000 troops.

the sixteen soldiers moved north up the ridgeline into progressively more rugged terrain. Because of the exhausting
nature of the trek, and with temperatures near 100 degrees
(Fahrenheit), the men moved mostly at night or in the cool
of mornings. During the days, they would stop and rest, taking the chance to observe activity in the valley below.

On June 20, 2006, the patrol's two squad leaders, Staff Sergeant Christopher M. Cunningham and Staff Sergeant Jared
Monti, halted the patrol on the ridgeline of Mountain 2610,
approximately three miles northwest of the village of
Gowardesh. With an elevation of more than 8,560 feet,
Mountain 2610 commanded an excellent view of several confirmed areas of interest,[*] including a number of insurgent
safe houses, and the summer residence of Hadji Usman, an
enemy commander, who was a confirmed and wanted insurgent target.

Working together, Cunningham and Monti decided to set
up their observation post on a flat area on top of a ridge,
approximately 165 feet long and 66 feet wide, with a trail
running along the northeastern side in front of a steep 80
degree slope extending down to the valley floor. On the
southern side of the position were some large rocks, a section of old stone wall, and a few small trees. The terrain
sloped gradually upward to the north, and on the northwest
side of the position was a line of dense vegetation composed
of trees and heavy brush among the smaller rocks. Between
the large rocks to the southeast and the tree line to the north

---

[*] An "area of interest" is a location that has been identified as having an
active enemy presence.

was a clearing approximately 130 to 165 feet long. The rocks and trees scattered around the perimeter of the position provided cover, concealment, and protection for the patrol as it began to observe the valley floor, more than three thousand feet below the ridgeline.

The sixteen soldiers spent the night of June 20 observing activity in the valley from their position on the ridgeline, but things were beginning to get a bit tense. By the morning of June 21, the patrol was dangerously low on both food and water, having consumed vast quantities of both during their hot and arduous climb up the mountain. After contacting 3-71 CAV headquarters by radio, an aerial resupply mission was scheduled for later that day. The resupply mission was originally coordinated to occur in conjunction with the 3-71 CAV Squadron's main drive, which was planned to include a heliborne, large air assault up into the Gremen Valley. The helicopter traffic associated with the squadron's air assault would have provided distraction for the resupply mission, reducing the risk that the delivery would compromise the patrol's position.

However, later that morning Sergeants Monti and Cunningham learned that the 3-71 CAV's push had been moved back to June 24, three days away. The delay extended the patrol's mission by several more days, making delivery of fresh supplies critical. The absence of other aerial traffic would increase the risk that the resupply mission would compromise the position of the patrol on the ridgeline. But because of the critical shortage of water, it was decided by the 3-71 CAV leadership that the resupply mission would go forward, despite the risk of its being observed.

The planned landing zone for the resupply mission was

located approximately five hundred feet from the patrol's position; Sergeants Cunningham and Monti brought the bulk of their soldiers to the landing zone to provide security and to move the supplies back to their position on the ridgeline. A smaller group remained back at the observation position to provide security there and to continue to survey the valley below. At approximately 1:30 P.M., a UH-60 Black Hawk delivered food and water to the landing zone, where the patrol's soldiers received the supplies and began transporting them back to the ridgeline position. Unfortunately, they had been seen.

Specialist Max Noble, the patrol's medic, was one of the soldiers who had been ordered to stay at the observation position while the rest of the patrol picked up the supplies at the landing zone. Noble was using a spotting scope to look down into the valley, and before the patrol's return he observed what appeared to be an Afghan male in the valley using binoculars to look over the patrol's position. Specialist Noble informed Sergeants Cunningham and Monti as soon as they returned, and all three then watched the man for several minutes before he picked up a bag and moved away. It was an ominous sign, and the two sergeants lost no time getting their men back into position and ready for what might turn into a fight.

As dusk approached, the patrol established a security perimeter around their position, and the sergeants assigned guard rotations between the men. The sixteen soldiers then divided up the supplies, cleaned their weapons and night-vision gear, and prepared for the night ahead. Sergeants Cunningham and Monti, along with Sergeant John R. Hawes, went behind one of the large rocks at the southeastern end of the position and began discussing courses of action in the likely event that their position had been observed and compromised. Privates First Class Brian J. Bradbury and Mark James, Private Sean J. Smith, Specialist Matthew P. Chambers, Specialist Shawn M. Heistand, and Specialist Franklin L. Woods were at the northwest end of the position, near the tree line. Sergeant Chris J. Grzecki, along with Specialists Noble and John H. Garner, were along the trail on the north edge of the position using spotting scopes to monitor the valley below. Everyone was awake and alert for trouble.

It found them soon enough.

At approximately, 6:45 P.M., Specialist Woods heard a sound of shuffling feet in the wood line immediately to the northwest of his position. Before he could alert the other soldiers, the patrol's position was hit by a heavy barrage of rocket-propelled grenades, medium machine-gun fire, and small-arms (AK-47s) fire. An enemy force of approximately fifty fighters was moving down the ridgeline under cover of trees from two supporting fire positions to the north and northwest. The soldiers of the American patrol could hear enemy fighters giving commands as they moved through the woods at the northwestern end of the patrol's position. The fight was on.

The six soldiers at the northwest end of the patrol's position immediately dove for cover when the enemy fighters fired. The attack came so quickly and with such ferocity that several of the soldiers at that end of the position were unable to move to unsling and aim their weapons. Others had weapons shot out of their hands by the intense fire from the tree line.

Specialist Heistand and Private First Class Bradbury were both near the wood line when the enemy opened fire. Heistand was armed with an M16 assault rifle, while Bradbury was an M249 squad automatic weapon gunner; both soldiers hit the ground and began to fire as soon as they could aim their weapons and squeeze the triggers. However, both soon realized that their fire was drawing the enemies' attention to their perilously exposed position near the wood line. Heistand immediately told Bradbury that they had to fall back to the southeast, where the large rocks would provide more cover for the pair. Specialist Heistand then jumped up and sprinted back toward the large rocks at the southern end of the position. Private First Class Bradbury was directly behind Specialist Heistand as they turned and began to run for the rocks. Unfortunately, Bradbury never made it back to the rocks. Hit by enemy fire, he fell to the ground within seconds of starting his dash for cover.

Private First Class James, Specialist Chambers, Specialist Woods, and Private Smith were also in the area near the wood line when the enemy attacked, and they, too, fell back toward the large rocks to the southeast. Chambers, Woods, and Smith successfully made it to cover without injury, but James was hit in the back and wrist by small-arms fire. Although wounded, James was able to crawl back toward the rest of the patrol on the southern end of the position. There, other members of the patrol grabbed James and pulled him to cover behind the rocks. Specialist Chambers, who had lost his weapon in the initial volley, then took James to a safer position back away from the rocks and began to administer first aid.

Sergeant Jared Monti at an outpost overlooking a valley in Iraq.
Photo: *U.S. Army*

From behind the rocks at the southern end of the patrol's position, Sergeants Monti, Cunningham, and Hawes also returned fire toward the tree line, attempting to cover for the patrol members falling back from the northeast. However, the intensity of the enemy small-arms fire, along with frequent volleys of RPGs, made it hazardous for the sergeants to rise from cover to accurately aim their return fire. The situation, already critical, now began to turn lethal for the soldiers of the American patrol.

Sergeant Patrick L. Lybert was in a prone position beside the remains of the small stone wall in front of the large rocks at the southeastern end of the patrol's position and was able to return fire with great effectiveness. However, although Lybert's position provided the best vantage to place precise fire onto the enemy fighters in the woods, it did not provide him full cover. Despite the risk, Lybert used carefully aimed shots and bursts from his weapon to delay the approaching enemy fighters, while the other soldiers of the American patrol improved their positions behind the rocks at the southern end.

As the patrol fell back behind the large rocks, Sergeants Cunningham and Monti took charge of the defense, quickly setting up a perimeter and posting their soldiers to guard possible gaps on their flanks. They directed the patrol's return fire and cautioned their soldiers to conserve ammunition. That done, Sergeant Monti grabbed his radio handset and cleared the squadron's network to begin a call for fire. He calmly informed 3-71 CAV's headquarters that the patrol was under heavy attack, was badly outnumbered, and was at risk of being overrun by enemy fighters. The situational formalities over with, Sergeant Jared Monti began the fight that would turn another U.S. Army sergeant into another American hero.

Despite the withering enemy fire, Monti provided accurate grid coordinates of the enemy's positions and likely avenues of approach as RPGs skipped off the rocks above his head. Because of the close proximity of the enemy fighters, Monti's call for fire was to have the incoming mortar and artillery rounds delivered "danger close" to his patrol's position. In addition, he ordered up airstrikes, but those would take a while to arrive. While Monti was calling in the fire support mission, Cunningham had moved along the rocks toward the eastern edge of the patrol's position to take charge of the defense at that end. Hawes remained on the western side of the position to defend that approach and to provide cover for Monti as he worked the radio calling for support fire. At that moment, the patrol lost its first soldier to enemy fire.

Sergeant Lybert was still out in front of the larger rocks, returning fire from behind the stone wall, when he was hit. At some point, members of the patrol saw Lybert's head fall forward and blood began to pour from his ear. Members of the patrol called out to Lybert, but he did not respond. Specialist Noble, the patrol's medic, was on the western side of the position near Sergeant Lybert but was unable to get to him because of the volume of enemy fire. However, Specialist Daniel B. Linnihan crawled out just far enough to grab Sergeant Lybert's weapon and drag it back behind the rocks for use by the remaining soldiers of the patrol.

About this time, the enemy fighters began to use supporting fire from the positions to the north and northwest to force the American soldiers to take complete cover and keep their heads down. As the Americans dug in deeper, the enemy force split into two groups to flank the patrol from the southeast and northwest. At the same time, a group of approximately fifteen enemy fighters moved forward through the wood line toward the patrol's western flank, while a smaller group maneuvered across the trail above the slope to attempt to flank the northeastern side of the position.

Observing the enemy movement, the American soldiers on either end of the position redirected their fire to protect their flanks. Patrol members with weapons traded off with unarmed members to ensure that the soldier in the best firing position had a weapon to defeat the flanking maneuvers. Private Smith was behind a large rock along the trail on the northeastern edge of the patrol's position, and from his position he managed to kill several enemy fighters attempting to move up the trail to flank the patrol. The Americans were holding their own, but they were still outnumbered and outgunned by the enemy force.

While continuing to communicate with the 3-71 CAV's headquarters, Sergeant Monti periodically had to drop his handset to personally engage the enemy with his M4 carbine. At one point, he noticed a group of enemy fighters closing in on the southwestern flank and pushed back their attack with several bursts from his M4. Then, as the enemy fighters closed within ten yards of the patrol's defensive perimeter, Monti threw a grenade into their path. Frustratingly, the weapon did not explode. But seeing an apparently live grenade in their path disrupted the enemy advance and caused them to scatter and fall back, denying them a firm and covered position on the patrol's flank. Sergeant Monti then went back to the radio and continued to call for fire. Finally, the initial rounds of American mortar fire began to fall on the advancing enemy force, quickly driving them back into a wood line north of the patrol's position. The mortar battery's commander requested Monti to adjust the incoming rounds, but the fire from the enemy position in the wood line was so intense that Monti was unable to even raise his head up to observe the origin point of the incoming rounds.

As the enemy fighters were forced back to the wood line, Sergeants Monti and Cunningham took an inventory of their soldiers and remaining weapons. They quickly realized that one of the soldiers from Monti's team, Private First Class Bradbury, was not accounted for. Monti called out to Bradbury several times but received no response. Finally, over the noise of the mortars and nearly constant small-arms fire, they heard Bradbury weakly reply that he was badly injured and unable to move. Bradbury lay in a shallow depression approximately sixty-five feet in front of the soldiers clustered at the southeast end of the position. The depression in the ridgeline prevented the patrol from actually seeing Bradbury, but it also protected him from enemy fire and observation. Unfortunately, there was no significant cover near the wounded soldier, and the enemy fighters in the wood line were as close to where Bradbury lay as Monti was.

For Staff Sergeant Jared Monti, it was the moment of truth in a life devoted to caring for and serving his friends, family members, fellow soldiers, and strangers in need. He quickly decided to act.

Monti recognized that Bradbury was exposed not only to fire from the enemy fighters but also to the incoming mortar fire. Calling out to the wounded soldier, Monti reassured him that he would be all right and that they were coming to get him. Sergeant Cunningham yelled across the rocks to Monti from his position that he would retrieve Bradbury. However, Monti insisted that Bradbury was *his* soldier, and that *he* would go and get him. Monti then handed the radio handset to Sergeant Grzecki and said, "You are now Chaos

Three-Five," Monti's radio call sign. Then, after tightening his chin strap, Staff Sergeant Jared Monti moved out from behind the protection of the rocks into the open area leading to Bradbury and directly into the withering enemy fire.

The wood line erupted in gunfire as dozens of enemy fighters focused their weapons on Staff Sergeant Monti, now running toward the wounded Bradbury. Other patrol members remembered hearing the distinct report of RPK machine guns as soon as Monti left the protection of the rocks. Moving low and fast, Monti approached to within just a few yards of Bradbury before heavy enemy fire forced him to move back; he dove behind the small stone wall where Sergeant Lybert's body lay. After taking a moment to verify that Sergeant Lybert was indeed dead, Monti rose from behind the stone wall and again moved out into a hail of enemy fire in his second attempt to save Bradbury. This time, the fire was even more intense and Monti only made it a few steps before a volley of small-arms fire, machine-gun bullets, and RPGs drove him back behind the cover of the stone wall again .

Unwilling to leave his soldier wounded and exposed, Staff Sergeant Monti decided to try and make a third attempt. This time, Monti yelled back to the patrol members behind the rocks that he needed more cover fire. He called back to Sergeant Hawes, who was armed with an M16 equipped with a grenade launcher, asking him to put rounds onto the enemy position while the other soldiers provided cover fire. Then, timing his movement to the sound of the exploding 40mm rounds and fire from the American combat rifles, Staff Sergeant Monti, for a third time, rose from his covered position and moved into the open, knowing full well he again would be the focus of the enemy fire. To the members of the American patrol, what happened next seemed to occur in slow motion.

Getting to his feet, Monti took several lunging steps through a withering fire toward his wounded soldier. At that moment an RPG was fired in his direction and exploded in his path. Unable to reach cover during the flight of the rocket, Monti fell, mortally wounded, only a few yards from Bradbury. Monti then attempted to crawl back toward the stone wall but was unable to move any real distance because of the severity of his wounds. The soldiers of the patrol called out to Monti, encouraging him to try to remain conscious. In return, Monti spoke briefly to the members of the patrol, telling them that he had made his peace with God. He recited the Lord's Prayer, and then asked Sergeant Cunningham to tell his parents that he loved them. Then, having given everything possible to save his soldiers and get them off of Mountain 2610 alive, Staff Sergeant Jared Monti died.

Concussions from nearby explosions increased as American mortar and artillery rounds now fell with accuracy onto the enemy positions. Allied air support was now on station as well, and the planes dropped a number of five-hundred-pound and two-thousand-pound bombs onto the enemy fighters with radioed directions from Sergeant Grzecki. As the supporting fire and air strikes began to take effect, the patrol members again fired their weapons against the enemy force, and the enemy fire began to slacken. As the fire from the tree line slowed, Sergeant Hawes crawled out from behind the rocks and made his way to Sergeant Lybert's body. Hawes took Lybert's remaining ammunition and handed it back to one of the soldiers behind the rocks. He then moved over to Monti's body, confirmed that he was dead, took his weapon and ammunition, and passed them back to the soldiers of the patrol. Cunningham and Smith then moved up along the trail to the east and made their way toward Bradbury. They found him approximately sixty feet in front of the rocks, and although seriously wounded, he was alive and able to communicate. Bradbury told them that there were approximately forty enemy fighters in the wooded area to the northwest; he had been able to hear them talking and giving commands during the engagement.

It was completely dark by the time Sergeant Cunningham brought the wounded Bradbury back behind the rocks so Specialist Noble could treat him. The patrol remained in their position for the rest of the night. The next morning, they moved up to the enemy position and found several blood trails and a bloody shoe, but no bodies. Later estimates by the intelligence folks at 3-71 CAV put the enemy fatalities at between fifteen and twenty.

The next morning, a medevac UH-60 Blackhawk helicopter came to pick up Bradbury, and what was already a tragedy turned into a disaster. As the litter carrying Bradbury and a medic was being hoisted up to the Blackhawk, the cable snapped, killing both men as they fell onto the ridgeline. Four men were dead, and all the surviving members of the patrol could do was gather their weapons and make their way off the mountain on foot. For them, Operation Gowardesh was over, and the results had been devastating.

REMEMBERING JARED

The witnesses to Staff Sergeant Monti's gallant attempts to rescue Bradbury made it clear that something more than a

Bronze Star was going to be needed to recognize what had happened up on Mountain 2610—that a Medal of Honor nomination was warranted. Thus began a three-year process in which every aspect of Sergeant First Class Jared Monti's actions (he received a posthumous promotion) were examined and assessed. As one senior administration official would say, "This kid was the ideal . . . a model of everything the Army wants their NCOs* to be."

Late in the summer of 2009, Janet Monti got the phone call at her home in Virginia Beach, inviting her and the entire Monti family to come to the White House to receive the posthumous award of Jared's Medal of Honor. Over 160 of Jared Monti's family, friends, and fellow soldiers gathered that week in Washington, D.C., as the American military said thank you for the actions and life of the seasoned veteran—yet still a young man—from New England. As he spoke in the White House on September 17, 2009, President Barack H. Obama, in his first Medal of Honor presentation, spoke of Jared Monti's life:

> Duty. Honor. Country. Service. Sacrifice. Heroism. These are words of weight. But as people—as a people and as a culture—we often invoke them lightly. We toss them around freely. But do we really grasp the meaning of these values? Do we truly understand the nature of these virtues? To serve, and to sacrifice. Jared Monti knew. The Monti family knows. And they know that the actions we honor today were not a passing

*Noncommissioned officers, here referring to sergeants.

An unidentified U.S. Navy lieutenant commander holds the display case containing Sergeant Jared Monti's Medal of Honor. The presentation ceremony was held in the East Room of the White House on September 17, 2009. On the left are Monti's parents, Janet and Paul Monti. On the right is President Barack Obama.
Photo: *U.S. Army*

moment of courage. They were the culmination of a life of character and commitment.

At Fort Sill, Oklahoma, the training center for fire-support coordinators was renamed in Jared Monti's honor. Back home in Massachusetts, a bridge over the river that Monti used to canoe on as a boy was renamed in his honor, and a foundation in his name has been established.

The most intimate remembrance of Monti, of course, comes from his mother, Janet, in a posting on the Internet:

This guy is my son, SFC Jared C. Monti. He died 6-21-06 trying to save the lives of 3 of his fellow soldiers. Brian Bradbury would have survived if the cable lifting him up to the helicopter didn't snap . . . he fell to his death. The helicopter pilot lost control due to that mishap & he crashed & died. Jared was shot twice while trying to save his comrades. Patrick was dead before he hit the ground. Jared was killed while trying to retrieve his body. The medic trying to save his life was also killed. He managed to save one soldier, his name is Derek. My son did what he does best looking out for his "boys" as he called them. He gave his life to save another and it's not the first time he risked his life saving his platoon. He received 2 Bronze Stars for both instances, the first one on his first tour in Afghanistan. I miss him more than words can express, will grieve his loss till the day I die but I have never been so proud.

That's who this guy was!

Janet Monti—Gold Star Mother

BIBLIOGRAPHY

"Sergeant First Class Jared C. Monti, *Medal of Honor: Operation Enduring Freedom.*" *U.S. Army.*
http://www.army.mil/medalofhonor/monti/index.html.
"Soldier's Creed." *U.S. Army.*
http://www.army.mil/soldierscreed/flash_version
(accessed September 26, 2009).

Epilogue

A nation that forgets its heroes is a nation destined to be forgotten.

—President Calvin Coolidge

Sergeant First Class Paul Ray Smith, Corporal Jason Dunham, Lieutenant Michael P. Murphy, Petty Officer Second Class Michael Anthony Monsoor, U.S. Army Specialist Ross A. McGinnis, and U.S. Army Staff Sergeant Jared C. Monti are among the more than five thousand servicemen and servicewomen who had been killed in the wars in Iraq and Afghanistan by 2009. Like the other war dead from those conflicts, their bodies arrived by airplane in flag-draped coffins at Dover Air Force Base, Delaware. All received the same respectful treatment: they were greeted in solemn ceremonies with honor guard by loved ones and/or officials before being transferred to their final resting places. This returning of war dead to American soil is a relatively recent tradition, dating back to the Korean War. Before that, almost all who died overseas were buried overseas—in some cases, in cemeteries constructed not far from the battlefields where they fell.

There are twenty-four permanent American burial grounds on foreign soil, containing the remains of 124,909 war dead. Among those are ninety-two Medal of Honor recipients, distinguished by the Medal of Honor etched on their headstones. Twenty of the cemeteries are located in Europe; eleven are in France. There is a government agency called the American Battle Monuments Commission that is responsible for the operation and maintenance of these sites. They are the final homes for men and women of high rank and low, distinguished or dishonored, as well as the remains of those whose names are unknown.

The World War II general George S. Patton Jr. lies in the Luxembourg American Cemetery and Memorial. The Normandy American Cemetery and Memorial, near Omaha Beach—used in the movie *Saving Private Ryan*—has another four-star general, Lesley J. McNair. Normandy is also the final home to two sons of an American president, the Medal of Honor recipient Brigadier General Theodore Roosevelt Jr. and his brother, Second Lieutenant Quentin Roosevelt. Quentin was killed in action in World War I and was originally buried near where his plane crashed. When Theodore Junior died a little over a month after the D-day landings in 1944, Quentin's body was exhumed and reinterred beside that of his older brother.

In the United States, responsibility for the care and maintenance of veterans' graves and cemeteries is held by a wide variety of private and government organizations and agencies. Arlington National Cemetery, for instance, is one of two administered by the U.S. Army. The National Parks Service is responsible for maintaining Revolutionary War and Civil War cemeteries. The rest are cared for by a combination of state, city, veterans', and nonprofit organizations. Every state, and the territory of Puerto Rico, has Medal of Honor recipients interred within its borders. Alaska, with two, has the fewest. Among the various cemeteries, Arlington itself has the most Medal of Honor recipients at 382.

Cypress Hills National Cemetery, in New York City, is the resting spot for 21,112 veterans and some of their spouses. It has the distinction of being the cemetery that has the second highest number of Medal of Honor recipients at twenty-four; three of these are double recipients.

MEMORIAL DAY, MAY 25, 2009

Cypress Hills National is one of a group of eighteen cemeteries that form the middle portion of the border between the boroughs of Brooklyn and Queens, in New York City.

The entrance of the eighteen-acre cemetery opens onto a flat plain that composes about half of the site before it rises in a steeply sloped hill less than a hundred feet high. Scattered among the government-issued white-marble headstones are a few placed by individuals or organizations. Additional memorial accents include a handful of special monuments, such as a stone French Cross for French sailors killed in New York harbor during World War I; the Second Division, American Expeditionary Forces Monument; and the British Navy Monument honoring a group of British sailors killed during the Revolutionary War. Trees mostly line the edges of the property and provide shade on the hill. The exception is the large one near the center of the level plain that commemorates the Medal of Honor recipients buried there.

In New York City, the Memorial Day weekend is the unofficial start of summer, with the weather typically providing a taste of the heat and humidity that will descend on the East Coast for the next several months. Those New Yorkers that can, head for beaches or summer homes. On May 25, 2009, at 9 A.M., bright sunshine signaled that this Memorial Day would be hot, and, thanks to the previous day's rain, humid. As the quiet morning began, the only visitors to Cypress Hills were some birds—mostly robins—and a few squirrels.

As in other military cemeteries, the colors green and white dominate. On this particular morning, both were vivid: the trees and grass, refreshed by the recent rain, and the sun-bleached marble headstones, whose regular shapes and even rows give military cemeteries their singular, poignant dignity. Because it was Memorial Day, with the exceptions of the graves of foreign troops and Confederate soldiers, small United States flags were in front of each headstone—placed there by Cub Scout packs and Boy Scout troops earlier in the weekend. But the previous day's rainstorm had toppled many of the flags.

By 10:00 A.M., three men were in the cemetery, one middle-aged, the other two more elderly. Though having shown up individually and at different times, they were there for the same purpose—to honor the dead and to reposition any flags that might have fallen. Quietly, with deliberation, and from different locations, they walked among the rows, bending down to replant a fallen flag where needed and moving on.

Nineteen of the twenty-four Medal of Honor recipients in Cypress Hills received their medals in conflicts great and famous (Civil War, Indian campaigns, World War I), as well as those small and forgotten (Korean campaign of 1871, Boxer rebellion, Haitian occupation). The other five individuals, including double recipient Louis Williams of the U.S. Navy, received theirs when the nation was at peace.

The most famous Medal of Honor recipient there, and the most famous of all veterans interred at Cypress Hills National Cemetery, is Marine Corps Sergeant Major Daniel J. Daly, one of only two marines to have been a double Medal of Honor recipient. Daly was awarded his first Medal of Honor in 1900 during the Boxer rebellion, in China, for having helped defend diplomats, their families, and other trapped foreigners from Chinese nationalist attacks. Sergeant Major Daly received his second medal in 1915 during the Haitian occupation, when he was instrumental in helping his thirty-five-man patrol defeat an ambush by more than four hundred Caco rebels. But the act that made Daly famous, and a Marine Corps legend, occurred in World War I. During the battle of Belleau Wood in 1918, his outnumbered unit was in danger of being overrun by a heavily armed German attack force. At the height of the battle, Daly led a successful counterattack with the now-famous rallying cry, "Come on, you sons of bitches! Do you want to live forever?"[1]

By noon, two more elderly men had arrived at Cypress Hills National. Like the others, they had come to honor the dead and to reposition fallen flags.

Since the beginning of organized warfare, countless speeches have been delivered in honor of fallen warriors and dead leaders. Marc Antony's eulogy for Julius Caesar, as written by William Shakespeare, is among the most famous of fictional speeches. Among the most eloquent of historical eulogies is President Abraham Lincoln's Gettysburg Address. Because his speech was so brief, only about three minutes long, and because it followed a two-hour peroration by another speaker, few among the thousands in the audience at Gettysburg heard Lincoln's now immortal words. Fortunately, copies of the speech were preserved and widely reprinted, ensuring it would not be forgotten.

Unfortunately, the same cannot be said for another moving eulogy to fallen troops—one delivered by Lieutenant General Lucian Truscott on Memorial Day 1945, at the then-new American cemetery near Anzio, Italy.

Truscott had entered the army in 1917. During World War II, his first assignment was to develop an American counterpart to the British commando units, and in that role, he was an observer on the Dieppe raid in 1942. He later participated in Operation Torch (the British and American invasion of North Africa in 1942) and fought in North Africa, Sicily, and Italy, ending the war as the commanding general of the Fifth Army.

On May 31, 1945, Lieutenant General Truscott was the main speaker at dedication ceremonies for the American military cemetery near Anzio, which was later named the Sicily-Rome American Cemetery and Memorial. The cemetery held approximately twenty thousand graves at that time, and the ceremony was attended by a number of distinguished guests, including several U.S. Senators. Also in the audience was the Pulitzer Prize–winning editorial cartoonist Bill Mauldin, creator of the much-beloved cartoon GIs, Willie and Joe. Mauldin's account is the most complete record of what happened after General Truscott reached the lectern.

He wrote that when it came time for the general to speak, "[H]e turned away from the visitors and addressed himself to the corpses he had commanded there. It was the most moving gesture I ever saw. It came from a hard-boiled old man who was incapable of planned dramatics. The general's remarks were brief and extemporaneous. He apologized to the dead men for their presence here. He said everybody tells leaders it is not their fault that men get killed in war, but that every leader knows in his heart this is not altogether true. He said he hoped anybody here through any mistake of his would forgive him, but he realized that was asking a hell of a lot under the circumstances. A senator's cigar went out; he bent over to relight it, then thought better of it. Truscott said he would not speak of the 'glorious' dead because he didn't see much glory in getting killed in your late teens or early twenties. He promised that if in the future he ran into anybody, especially old men, who thought death in battle was glorious, he would straighten them out. He said he thought it was the least he could do."[2]

EPILOGUE

In the early afternoon, under the bright, hot sun, another elderly man arrived at Cypress Hills National Cemetery on Memorial Day 2009. Dressed in a white short-sleeve shirt and tan slacks, like the handful of men before him, he began walking among the rows of headstones, pausing, here and there, to bend down and straighten a fallen American flag.

NOTES

1. "Sergeant Major Daniel J. Daly, USMC," *Marine Corps Legacy Museum*, http://www.mclm.com/tohonor/ddaly.html (accessed August 21, 2009).
2. D'Este, Carlo, *Fatal Decision: Anzio and the Battle for Rome*, (New York: HarperPerennial, 1992), 416.

Index

★ ★ ★ ★ ★ ★

INDEX

INDEX

INDEX

INDEX